19·95

CW00506735

⊦

𝒩

C252627

Thinking Machines

Thinking Machines

The Evolution of Artificial Intelligence

Vernon Pratt

Basil Blackwell

First published 1987

Basil Blackwell Ltd
108 Cowley Road, Oxford, OX4 1JF, UK

Basil Blackwell Inc.
432 Park Avenue South, Suite 1503
New York, NY 10016, USA

British Library Cataloguing in Publication Data

Pratt, Vernon
    Thinking machines: the evolution of
    artificial intelligence.
    1. Artificial intelligence
    I. Title
    006.3   Q335
    ISBN 0–631–14953–8

Library of Congress Cataloging in Publication Data

Pratt, Vernon, 1943–
    Thinking machines.

    Includes index.
    1. Artificial intelligence.   2. Machine learning.
    I. Title
    Q335.P7   1987   006.3   87–11647
    ISBN 0–631–14953–8

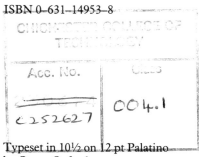
Typeset in 10½ on 12 pt Palatino
by Opus, Oxford
Printed in Great Britain by
Butler and Tanner Ltd, Frome

For P.
with love

Contents

Preface

I became interested in computers and what they could do out of a concern for the *threats* they appeared to represent: a threat to people's economic well-being through computers' potential to eliminate jobs, a threat to autonomy through their potential for surveillance and control, and a threat less defined than these but even more profound rising out of the alleged capacity of these machines to develop into *Homo sapiens* clones.

This book comes out of that concern, although it does not explore it as such. I have limited myself to attempting an account of how the more psychologically sophisticated powers of contemporary machines have come about, in the belief that this helps bring out the nature of what confronts us. I hope thus to contribute to the discussion we must have about how these machines can be of most use to us, and about how best to fight the forces already exploiting their potential to impoverish and constrain.

I cannot say this without confessing that in the course of learning about computers I have fallen under their spell. Although many of the tricks that have been worked with them so far will no doubt come to be seen, from a proper perspective, as the sort of playing about we generally engage in when we acquire a new gadget, the potential of computers for making an exceedingly creative contribution to the human condition is already clear. Faced with the ambivalence typical of invention we can only strive to do better than we always do.

For their help with this project of mine I have many people to think of. To Garth Wilkinson I owe a very special debt. He would have shared the authorship with me, had his other commitments permitted, and especially in its early days did much to stimulate and clarify.

Those I am privileged to live with, P. and T., have born the brunt, of course; and students, who have too often found me, as the Nigerians say, 'not on seat'. But colleagues have suffered stoically too: John Wakeford, who created the time; Bill Fuge, who in his absurdly generous way nurtured the spirit and sustained the will; Brian Wynne, who showed how it is done; and Duncan Laurence, arriving lately on the scene, tolerant and kindly. John Benson has illuminated my path on innumerable occasions, walking me so gently along the sunlit uplands of his understanding; so has John

O'Neill, a sympathetic guide to the craggy steeps he has made his own. Simon Brook of the Alvey group at Lancaster has been steadily encouraging.

Librarians are helpful, I suppose, by design; but those I have come across in connection with this work have exceeded that exacting specification. I think particularly of Mrs T.J. Goodman of the University Library at Lancaster, and the efficient and painstaking support she has consistently extended; and of Professor Dr Albert Heinekamp of the Leibniz archive in Hanover, who with great courtesy took time to show me the magnificent calculator under his care, and to draw certain manuscripts to my attention.

I have to thank, instead of a typist, the Tangerine Computer Systems Limited, now alas defunct, who in 1979 put a Rolls-Royce of a microcomputer kit onto the market: and Ralph Allen of Norfolk, for sustaining this glorious machine in recent years and for equipping it, incredibly, for actual use in the preparation of this book. Those who might have been asked to type it, however, have – this is the way it goes, of course – provided essential help in other ways, and I welcome the opportunity to acknowledge their unstinting and unreasonable support: Sarah Bracewell, Sue Armistead, Cathy Thomson, and Kathy Bateson.

Finally, because very important indeed, I think of David Martin of Blackwell: a model publisher, and so much more. Expert, encouraging, patient and a copious source of inspiration. He did nothing to dissuade me from this enterprise, and thus must carry a heavy responsibility for what follows.

Acknowledgements

We are grateful to the following for kind permission to reproduce material: John Murray Publishers Ltd for Fig. 10.4 redrawn from M. Daumas (ed), *A History of Technology and Invention*, vol. 3; McGraw-Hill Book Company for Figs 15.1 and 15.2 redrawn from E. A. Feigenbaum and J. Feldman (eds), *Computers and Thought*; Gordon and Breach, Science Publishers, for Fig. 8.1 and Table 2 reproduced from S. Fernbach and A. H. Taub (eds), *Computers and their role in the Physical Sciences*; Tavistock Publications Ltd for an extract from Michel Foucault, *The Order of Things*; The Harvester Press Ltd for Fig 9.1 redrawn from M. Gardner, *Logic, Machines and Diagrams*; Cambridge University Press for Figs 10.2 and 10.3 redrawn from D. R. Hartree, *Calculating Instruments and Machines*; Columbia University Press for Figs 3.7 and 3.8 redrawn from F. J. Murray, Mathematical Machines; Prentice-Hall, Inc. for Fig. 15.5 redrawn from A. Newell et al. (eds), *Information Processing Language-V Manual, 2/E*; Oxford University Press for an extract from G. H. R. Parkinson, *Leibniz: Logical Papers* (1965) and extracts and Fig. 12.1 from Alan Turing, 'Computing Machinery and Intelligence', *Mind*, vol LIX, no. 236 (1959); Springer-Verlag New York Inc. and the author for Figs 11.1 and 11.2 redrawn from Brian Randell (ed), *The Origins of Digital Computers*; for Figs 3.1 and 3.2 redrawn by permission of the publishers from *A History of Mechanical Inventions*, by A. P. Usher, Cambridge, Massachusetts: Harvard University Press; permission applied for from John Wiley and Sons for extract from E. C. Berkeley, *Giant Brains*.

Illustrations

The author and publisher are grateful to the following for permission to reproduce illustrations on these pages: AIP Niels Bohr Library, 166, 186 (right); Ann Ronan Picture Library 63, 116; Argent 3 (bottom); A T & T 153; Bild-Archiv der Österreichischen Nationalbibliothek, Vienna 181; Bodleian Library, Oxford 21; The British Library 28, 68, 78, 133, 134; Burden Neurological Institute 200; Cambridge University Library 87; Carnegie-Mellon University 213; Philippe Constantin 191; Crown copyright material, in the Public Record Office is reproduced by permission of the Controller of Her Majesty's Stationery Office (FO 850/234 no.6) 158; Department of Computer Science, University of Manchester 178; Department of Machine Intelligence, Edinburgh University 238; The Governing Body, Christ Church, Oxford 17 (bottom left); International Business Machines Corporation 144, 146; Los Alamos National Library 210; The Mansell Collection 13, 17 (top right), 58, 64, 66; Mary Evans Picture Library 42; The Master and Fellows of Trinity College, Cambridge 3 (top right), 96; The MIT Museum 140, 205; The Moore School of Electrical Engineering, University of Pennsylvania 164; National Maritime Museum, London 24; National Physical Laboratory 5 (bottom), 123; National Portrait Gallery 17 (top left and bottom right); Niedersächsische Landesbibliothek, Hannover 4, 54, 74, 86; Niedersächsische Staats-und Universitätsbibliothek, Gottingen 186 (left); The Raymond Mander and Joe Mitchenson Theatre Collection 179; The Royal Irish Academy 242; Smithsonian Institution 168; The Trustees of the Science Museum 3 (top left), 5 (top), 22, 40, 47, 50, 52, 83, 98, 99, 100, 106, 108, 110, 114, 126, 157, 160, 170, 193; Stanford Research Institute 236; The Trustees of the National Library of Scotland 84; University of Cambridge Computer Laboratory, Guttenberg Ltd., Manchester 142; Victoria and Albert Museum 118; Wellcome Institute Library, London 16.

Introduction

'Artificial intelligence' is a Modern idea: that is, the conditions for thinking about it were not realized before that great revolution in the Western conception of the world which occurred in the seventeenth century and which we associate with the rise of modern science. The reason has nothing to do with scientific and technical advance bringing feasibility to a hitherto fantastic project. It is the project itself, the very idea that thinking might go on inside a machine, that is born in the seventeenth century revolution.

It is true that today we have no very clear and detailed answer to the question of what 'thinking' is. But at a certain level of generality we have a conception of it. It is, we assume, a matter of manipulating representations. Sometimes it is argued that these representations are words – that thinking is manipulating words inside our heads. Sometimes it is argued that there are distinctive items such as 'ideas' or 'concepts' or 'propositions' which serve as the objects of thinking's manipulations. But behind these particular views is the shared assumption that in thinking we are dealing directly with representations and only indirectly with the realities the representations represent.

It is this assumption that makes the modern idea that computers might be got to think sound at least halfway intelligible. If thinking is manipulating representations, why should we not be able to let machine states 'stand for' things, and get processors to order and classify and transform these states? Such an idea of course leaves many obscurities. The picture of representations being manipulated draws heavily on the idea of someone or something looking at the representations and moving them about. But who or what are we to suppose does the looking? The seventeenth century philosopher John Locke, who did much to articulate the conception of thinking we live with today, spoke of 'the Mind' as fulfilling this role:[1] but what can correspond to this in the case of a machine? One of the points Locke was urging was that inasmuch as it is our 'Mind' that is perceiving representations, we must be aware of them. Can a machine be made 'aware'?

Enthusiasts live with these questions, or brazen them out, because they see the tremendous potential in the modern computer for the manipulation of representations and because they sense in the achievements made already the proof of the pudding – or at least a promising aroma.

In establishing a new conception of thinking, seventeenth century innovators did not complete the conceptual preparations for machine intelligence. A central issue of modern work is to establish the most appropriate way in which to represent knowledge in the machine if it is to be got to 'think' with power and efficiency, and, to begin with, approaches to this question were made rather on the wrong track. Until Kant, the assumption was that knowledge could be represented by constructing lists of the properties we know things to have. Only in the nineteenth century was the alternative conception of knowledge, as networks of propositions, gradually worked out, resulting first in the propositional logic, then in the predicate logic. Nevertheless, propositions and ideas are just different sorts of representation, and the fundamental reconceptualization was the seventeenth century one, when the representational view of thinking emerged. It is still with us, and buried so deeply among the other foundations of our modern picture of the world and our relation to it that it is quite a struggle to imagine that it could be otherwise.

We must offer some account, then, of the transformation that took place between the scholastic and the Modern conceptualizations of what we now cover with the term 'mind'. But there is more to the placement of AI (Artificial Intelligence) than outlining the conceptual preconditions for its emergence. There is also the question of what types of symbol manipulation came to be seen as significant. One of the factors bringing about the shift to the representational conception of thinking was the rise of mathematics, and understandably, therefore, it was the types of manipulation whose rules are the topic of this subject that first figured in mechanical symbol manipulators, notably the mechanical calculators that began to emerge in the seventeenth century. Later, the continuing study of validity in various patterns of reasoning revealed how other, non-mathematical symbol manipulations might be mechanized, first in the useless devices that allowed the mechanical modelling of the logic of terms, then in Babbage's plans for an algebra machine, and finally in the universal machines capable of modelling the predicate calculus.

So one dimension of the emergence of AI is the conceptual development that brought a representational model of thinking. Another is the progression in logic from the first sustained attempts at symbolization by Leibniz in the seventeenth century, through the thorough symbolization of the logic of terms by Boole in the nineteenth century, to the twentieth-century development of the predicate calculus by Frege, Russell and Whitehead. The third is the increasing sophistication of engineering: reaching from the wooden constructions of Schickard in the seventeenth century, through mechanical invention of the highest calibre by Babbage in the nineteenth century, to the harnessing of electricity and electronics in the modern computer.

But we must resist the idea that from the beginning of this period there was a *plan*, a shared ambition inspiring all those who in one way or another brought the modern computer and the 'artificial thought' it supports nearer to possibility. In that sense there is no 'story' of the emergence of artificial intelligence. Instead, what we see is a number of projects, each different, some successful and some abortive, whose relevance we can discern from

Gottfried Leibniz, Charles Babbage, and Alan Turing

our present perspective, because we can now see what had to happen, what conceptual foundations laid, before the intelligent computer could be designed and built and programmed.

Three Projects

Of the many, three projects in particular compel attention. Alan Turing's, proposed in 1936, is *our* project: to build a machine that will think. That of Gottfried Leibniz was to build a machine capable of carrying out whatever reasoning process we asked of it. And in between came the project of Charles Babbage, whose Analytical Engine would have been capable of algebra, and thus, he thought, of handling the unitary formal system in which alone the plurality of physical phenomena can be adequately described.

The significance of these projects is that they reveal the conceptualizations of mechanism, mathematics, reason and thought that are in general characteristic of their period. It is tempting, of course, to see them as milestones along the same road. While no-one envisaged a single goal towards which all of these enterprises were directed, their relationship is nevertheless intimate. Leibniz' general objective of building a reasoning machine is in some ways fulfilled by the post Turing 'expert system', in spite of the fact that Leibniz' approach to how it might be done has been rejected in its fundamentals. Likewise, the emergence of the modern high speed automatic calculator was hailed, sensibly in a sense, as Babbage's dream come true, in spite of the fact that our conception of symbol systems, and of

Leibniz' calculator

Babbage's Analytical Engine (the Mill)

Turing's Pilot ACE

algebra in particular, had undergone a sea–change in the interim. We can understand what Leibniz meant by 'reasoning' and what Babbage meant by 'algebra' as well as what Turing means by 'thinking'. Although our notions of these things are not quite what they were, we can recognize each thinker alike as addressing the problem of mechanizing in part or whole our mental processes.

Moreover, each thinker did rather more than articulate a project in the general field of the mechanization of thinking. Each actually planned and had executed a machine. Leibniz had his workman construct a desk calculator; Babbage supervised the construction of a 'difference engine', devised for the automatic production of mathematical tables; and Turing inspired the team that built one of the first modern computers, the Pilot ACE. In a sense, all these machines were calculators, and as such we can today rank them in order of power, speed and capacity, criteria which of course place them in chronological sequence. Thus these machines do indeed take on the guise of milestones, on the road to the Cray, perhaps, and to the supercomputers of tomorrow.

It turns out that the very machines that can calculate so powerfully can also with equivalent efficiency manipulate symbols in accordance with non-mathematical rules. This we now envisage as the capacity to represent processes of thought in general. But if we read that idea, that objective, back into either Leibniz or Babbage, we fall into anachronism.

Leibniz' project is where we begin. Like Babbage in the nineteenth century and von Neumann in the twentieth, Leibniz was as much concerned with the problems of the day as with progress in science, and indeed saw these two concerns as intimately connected. The importance of science lay partly in its potential to contribute to practical affairs. Mathematician and logician on the one hand, professional diplomat on the other, Leibniz saw the damage that disagreement and misunderstanding between people could do, and thought he saw how the scientific mastery of reason might help. It might, he thought, put paid to disagreement once and for all.

Reflection on the nature of logic had led him to (or at least sustained him in) the view that it was the inadequacy of language that was the source of such conflict. Its fault was that it failed to mirror accurately enough the structure of the world people were attempting to argue about, and the solution lay in linguistic reform. It was, he thought, necessary only to devise the appropriate form of symbol-system and disagreement would be a thing of the past, for then: 'if controversies were to arise, there would be no more need of disputation between two philosophers than between two accountants. For it would suffice to take their pencils in their hands, to sit down to their slates, and say to each other (with a friend to witness, if they liked): Let us calculate.'[2]

This, in essence, is Leibniz' project for the 'mechanization' of thought. He does not speak here of an actual machine, thought there are other passages where he indicates that he also had a machine in mind. As the proud inventor of an apparatus capable of arithmetic he was certainly qualified to have thought in those terms. In any case, the essential task for both these projects was the same: to revise our concepts so that they accurately reflected the structure of the world, and then to formulate rules of thumb which could be applied blindly or automatically to the premises of any reasoning process and yield the correct result. Whether such procedures were left to be carried out with pencil and paper or embodied in a piece of machinery was something (by the seventeenth century at least) of a detail. The invention of arithmetic machines had already shown that devices capable of following strict rules like those of addition could be built: all that had to be done, once our concepts had been put right, was to show that the rules of reasoning were equally strict, and to provide a clear articulation of them.

How exactly are these ideas of Leibniz' to be understood? Could they have been understood by a medieval thinker like St Thomas Aquinas? If not, what was it that made them thinkable by Leibniz' day? These are the questions that arise if we seek to understand the nature of our contemporary notions of getting a machine to think, because although our project is not Leibniz', both share, are made possible by, the same conceptual foundations.

In getting a grasp of what Leibniz was proposing, the emergence of arithmetical machines must be one focus of study, because this is intimately bound up with the emergence of conditions which made his ideas thinkable. So also must be developments in mathematics itself, which brought his proposal from the deepest recesses of hidden knowledge in the Middle Ages to the brilliant heart of the scientific revolution. Thirdly, we must consider logic, which is often thought of as the study of validity in reasoning, and how it came to present itself to Leibniz as something that could be quite quickly completed, and put to such devastating effect.

Notes

1 John Locke, *An Essay Concerning Human Understanding*, (1690), 1, 2, v.
2 Gottfried Leibniz, in C.I. Gerhardt (ed.), *Die Philosophischen Schriften von G.W. Leibniz* (Berlin, 1875–90), 7 vols, vii, p. 481.

Part I

Leibniz' Project

1   The Emergence of Representation

The pre-Modern conception of thought gave a central role to a concept that it is difficult to be clear about today, though it has left a legacy in our ordinary word 'in-form-ation': it is the concept of a form. There is nothing in our Modern way of thinking that corresponds to a 'form': but more than that, there is in the pre-Modern framework nothing quite corresponding to 'thinking'. Although there were conceptions of 'seeing', 'comtemplating', 'calculating', 'dreaming', 'remembering', 'tasting', and so on, these were not united under the umbrella notion of 'thinking'. The revolution involved, then, a rejigging of conceptions so thorough that it is not easy to find the words in which to discuss it. But 'seeing' is one of the things both Moderns and pre-Moderns are prepared to speak of, so we might explore a little using that term.

For the medieval Scholastic Thomas Aquinas, seeing was a matter of 'grasping' the form of a thing. What did this mean? Aristotle had done most to start the notion of a thing's 'form' off on its medieval course, and he invoked it first and foremost in connection with a question which had on the face of it little to do with seeing, nor even perhaps with thinking generally. His question was: what is it that makes a thing the kind of thing that it is?

We are surrounded by things of different kinds: houses, animals, tools, furniture and so on. What is it about a house that makes it a house rather than, say, a musical instrument? Aristotle quickly steers us away from any thought that the answer might have to do with the materials out of which the two kinds of things are made. Think, he suggests, of two kinds of thing that consist of exactly the same materials: a house, say, on the one hand, and that very same house demolished. You have the same materials, but a different kind of thing: a heap of rubble where before you had a house. One might put the point by saying that there is something more to a thing like a house than the materials that make it up; and that it is this 'something more' that makes of these materials not a heap of rubble – and not, say, a supplier's stock – but a house. Aristotle called 'it' the thing's form.[1]

Aristotle said more about his conception of a form, so that there is more to his approach than the mere labelling of a problem, and later writers (notably Aquinas, in fact) went further to develop the germinal idea into a comprehensive and coherent theory. As a germinal idea, though, it is rather like the suggestion that what makes a given assemblage of materials constitute a house is the *form of organization* to which the materials are subjected.

Even without further development, this picture of a thing as a parcel of matter falling under a form had two notable features. First, it gave a non-material dimension to things. A house was not just the wood and bricks and mortar that made it up. Nor was it, of course, these material components plus another, non-material, component, as though the form were some kind of spirit or soul or ghost pervading or inhabiting the matter – although many down the centuries have misused (or made use of) the Aristotelian conception in this way. It is just that for Aristotle a thing is made the kind of thing that it is by its form, and in specifying its form you have in some sense to go beyond the physical components of which the thing is made up.

Second, a thing's form gave it a dimension of generality. Once people began to think beyond their particular experiences to the generalities that their experiences could be thought of as instantiating – once they began to think of parallel lines, as well as parallel lines of mountains; of goodness, as well as this or that good person – they confronted the problem of what these general objects of knowledge were. Plato thought that as it is possible to think about 'things' that are 'general', there must exist general things for us to think about. The notion of a Form was first introduced in this context. Plato spoke of a whole realm of existence populated with Forms, understood as the 'generalities' required by our 'general' thoughts. While the concept of Aristotle's form was different, it too provided an approach to this problem. The Aristotelian form was not something that could exist on its own, even in a special realm. It was not separable from the thing it 'organized'. But by virtue of making that a thing of a particular kind, it conferred upon it an aspect of generality.[2]

It was this concept of form that the medievals, and indeed Aristotle himself, drew on for their understanding of some of the key things that we today refer to under the heading 'thinking'. *Seeing*, to take our particular example, was one of them.

What part might the notion of a form play in an account of perception? What we have to make sense of is the central role Aquinas gave to 'intelligibility'. Our intellect is the aspect or part of us which is responsible for perception, and it works, Aquinas apparently considered, by first rendering 'intelligible' the form of the thing seen, and then 'grasping' and retaining that form. We are terribly tempted to try and understand this as describing some kind of operation performed upon an object: my own words – 'works', 'grasping', 'retaining' – are themselves concessions to that temptation. It would be too crude to represent Aquinas as picturing the perceiver as breaking off the form of a thing and then swallowing it – too crude, and yet it is difficult to imagine that he could be meaning anything

The Wisdom of St Thomas Aquinas. Fresco by Andrea da Firenze in the Chapter House of Santa Maria Novella in Florence

totally different from this. Aquinas' own terms, 'abstraction' and 'reception', are less graphic in their impact than 'breaking off' and 'swallowing', but still it is hard for commentators with the Modern perspective to avoid drawing the conclusion that Aquinas thought of the form as in some way separate from the thing whose form it is.[3]

The root of our difficulty is, I think, our assumption that any account of perception must address itself to the problem of how contact can be made between the perceiver and the object perceived – contact across the gulf that separates the two. Our modern picture is that it is rays of light that cross the divide, registering on our retinas an image of the object out there. We may not reject out of hand the idea that Aquinas had a different theory, but we assume that he must be offering a different approach to the same problem. The fact is, though, that Aquinas saw no gap between perceiver and object that needed crossing, and no need to provide in his account of perception any kind of substitute for either 'light rays' or 'image'. I am not saying that he had an understanding of seeing that, when fully articulated, would imply that the notion of a gap was misplaced. It is just that if there was a gap, he did not see it: when he thought about perception the focus of his attention was wholly elsewhere. It is we Moderns that focus on the problem of achieving contact between perceiver and perceived. The problem Aquinas saw had rather to do with the fact that while the things we see are material, our own intellects are not. If he thought there was a gap to be bridged, it was this one; and it was to the bridging of this gap that the Aristotelian form seemed relevant. For insofar as a thing had a form, it had something about it that went beyond the material, so constituting a kind of common ground on which both immaterial intellect and otherwise material thing could stand.

What can we say of the relationship between the two once it has been shown that the common ground is there? It is not, according to Aquinas' perspective, a relationship as between manipulator and manipulated, doer and done to, subject and object. It is the relationship between an intellect and something that the intellect has understood.

Unhappily, we have of course to remember that 'understanding' was itself understood differently by Aquinas, so that we have no easy way of translating or even ourselves understanding what his outlook was. But we can appreciate at least that our relationship to a thing we understand – a sentence, say, or a theory – is quite different from the relationship we, from our own perspective, assume to exist between ourselves and an object we perceive. We do not assume that a sentence has to send out (or reflect) 'beams of meaning' for our minds to receive. Its meaning is rather something we think of ourselves as 'internalizing' or 'absorbing'. In some such way as this does the intellect, according to Aquinas, come to share in a thing's form.

The notion of a form played a similarly central role in other kinds of what we today subsume under 'thinking': imagining, planning, meditating, dreaming, and so on. It was also central to 'knowing'. Today, what is known, as far as science is concerned, are truths or propositions. But the Ancient conception was to think of 'knowing' as relating the knower to objects – Plato's Forms, for example, were for him the highest objects of knowledge. Aquinas, as a medieval, left this understanding of knowledge as it was, and it is still there in Francis Bacon, in the sixteenth and early seventeenth centuries, even as he strives to effect his revolution in knowledge.[4] The highest form of knowledge, Bacon records, is our knowledge of the forms. Moreover, because knowledge is, for this mighty tradition, a matter of grasping – sharing in – a thing's form, knowledge is a species of identity. A thing's form is what makes it the kind of thing that it is, so that in knowing it the knower must in some sense become the same sort of thing as the object known. To know a horse is in some sense to become a horse, or perhaps to become 'horsey', to know God is in some sense to become divine.[5] As Rorty makes clear, this pre-Modern conception of 'knowledge-as-identity-with-object'[6] is at least half-retained in the thesis of the indubitability of our sensory impressions held by the Modern John Locke.

The distinction then, within this tradition, between knowledge and seeing – since they both involve the grasping of forms – is a subtle one, and this is why commentators find it so difficult to work out whether when Aquinas talks about 'abstracting' forms he has his mind on perceiving things or extending our knowledge of them.[7] It is also why the fundamental 'metaphor' of knowledge as vision, launched by the Ancients and occupying people given to reflection ever since, is not so arbitrary – indeed not so metaphorical – after all.[8] To know is to understand, and so also is to see.

This 'hylomophic' framework, which, as I have been explaining, gave a central role to the notion of a form in its understanding of what we now regard as so many different aspects of mentality – seeing, remembering, imagining, dreaming, and so on – was a central objective of the conceptual revolutionaries of the seventeenth century. Francis Bacon was the earliest effective campaigner, though his assault was not direct. The thrust of his message was that life could be improved if only we tried to extend our knowledge of the world – a political call in essence. But he added to it his idea of how such new knowledge had best be acquired. The object of such effort, Bacon continued to assume, would be the grasping of forms. But he began the undermining of this fundamental concept by attacking the notion that forms were straightforwardly graspable by the intellect. The forms of substances, at any rate (such as the form of a lion, of an oak, of gold, of water, of air), he claimed were too 'perplexed' to be accessible in any immediate way, and he proposed instead a roundabout route involving a study of the thing's or a stuff's properties (as we should call them today) which would have to be undertaken if their forms were to be grasped.[9]

With Robert Boyle and his generation, however, as the 'learning' gave more and more ground to 'discovery', it became clear that the Scholastic notion of a form could not usefully be distorted in this fashion, and it was effectively discarded. No one notion replaced the form, of course (or else the change would hardly have been substantial). What was constructed, rather, was a new vantage point from which everything looked different.

I am tempted to say that the relationship of the human being to the world was reconceptualized: but that is itself to see things from the new perspective. It is our Modern picture of the human being as an entity distinct from 'the world', and on that account constituting the kind of thing that must have some sort of 'relationship' with the world, that is the seventeenth century innovation.

Following the lead of Descartes, the new thinkers drew screens round the human being, as round a hospital patient. From that point on, the shadows cast on the screens by objects beyond had to take the place of the direct communion with the ordinary things around us that had been assumed before.[10]

The patient surrounded by screens is the mind, and the patient him or herself is the mind's eye. In perception, it is the mind's eye now that does the 'seeing': and what it sees are the images of things as they are thrown up on the screens. The world is accessed in perception only via representations. But perception, understood in this way, is then taken as the model for other

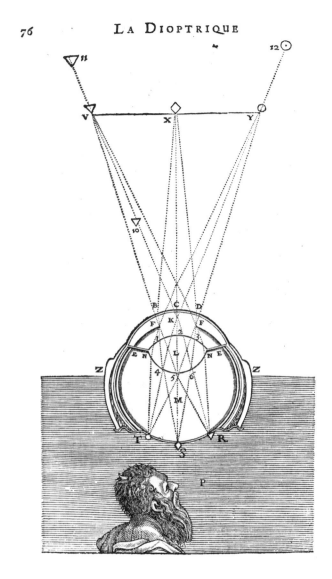

The Modern conception of seeing: from Descartes' *La Dioptrique*

activities: doubting, understanding, affirming, denying, willing, refusing, imagining, feeling, all are now treated as species of one genus – thinking; and thinking is regarded as a function of the inner eye and the representations that pass before it.

The Moderns – Francis Bacon, René Descartes, John Locke, and Thomas Hobbes

There were two prongs, then, to the revolutionary assault. One was to recategorize what had previously been regarded as a variety of different things as, instead, different kinds of one thing; and the other was to establish a representational model of the generic activity – thinking – under which the variety had been subsumed. These two thrusts were indeed sequential. Descartes, who mounted the first, did not accept that thinking was an operation upon representations when it was put to him by Hobbes.[11] But Locke established the point very firmly, by articulating his notion of an 'idea' with forthright bluntness ('an idea is whatsoever is the object of the understanding when a man thinks'), by working the concept into a comprehensive 'philosophy', and by getting his work so widely read.

Thus was the 'mind' invented, the work of Descartes and Locke and the seventeenth century. It was, as Rorty explains, 'a single inner space in which bodily and perceptual sensations [...] mathematical truths, moral rules, the idea of God, moods of depression, and all the rest of what we now call "mental" were objects of quasi-observation.'[12]

The notion of the 'idea' became the new fundamental concept. Where the hylomorphic view had seen perception (for example) in terms of a person sharing the form of the object seen, according to the new perspective the object is represented before the mind by an idea. Ideas are 'mental' entities, the only items with which the mind can deal directly, but they stand for the non-mental things about which the thinker has occasion to think. And insofar as thinking involves manipulation, ideas are what we manipulate.

The 'invention' of the mind, as Rorty puts it,[13] constitutes one of the foundation stones upon which the Modern framework of conceptions is built. The emergence of mathematics as a practical tool of very general utility, itself occasioned by changes in patterns of trade, played a central role in putting it in place. For mathematics provides the paradigm of thought as representational – once it frees itself from the conception that it is about things or lines or shapes. This liberation occurred first in the sixteenth century innovation of François Vieta,[14] who proposed that we should let marks stand as 'representatives' and thus invented a mode of thinking that dealt with *symbols*: and symbols were manifestly different from the plurality of things that they indifferently stood for. Vieta's algebraic symbols were ready colonists of the new territory, the mind.

The rise of modern mathematics is important to us for another reason. It offered a model not only for the new category of thinking in general, but also in its rigour and formalism for the special kind of thinking known as reasoning – which it was Leibniz' ambition to mechanize.

Notes

1 See, for example, Aristotle, *Metaphysics* Z, XVII.
2 On the relation between generality and immateriality see Richard Rorty, *The Mirror of Nature* (Blackwell, Oxford, 1980), p. 31 and throughout Part I.

3 See, for example, A.J. P. Kenny, *The Anatomy of the Soul* (Blackwell, Oxford, 1973), p. 74.
4 See below, p. 65.
5 Cf. Aristotle, *De Anima*, III, 430a, 15; Kenny, *Anatomy of the Soul*, p. 64.
6 Rorty, *Mirror of Nature*, p. 144.
7 See, for example, Kenny, *Anatomy of the Soul*, pp. 62–80.
8 Cf. Rorty, *Mirror of Nature*, pp. 157ff.
9 Francis Bacon, in J.M. Robertson (ed.). *The Philosophical Works of Francis Bacon* (Routledge, London, 1905), p. 95.
10 Plato invoked shadows, but his were the real things of our world, supposed to be less real than the Forms of the eternal world beyond. The objects of mentality, as the seventeenth century conceived it, were simulacra of things rather than things themselves.
11 Descartes, 'Objections and Replies', 3rd set of Objections and Replies, Fourth Objection and Reply, in *The Philosophical Writing of Descartes*, trans. John Cottingham et al. (CUP, Cambridge, 1984), pp. 125, 126.
12 Rorty, *Mirror of Nature*, p. 50.
13 Rorty, *Mirror of Nature*, ch. 1.
14 See below, pp. 41–3.

2 The Rise of Modern Mathematics

For much of the Middle Ages, numbers were obviously a source of discomfort. They could be generally coped with only if they were kept small, and were avoided altogether wherever possible. Even in manuals of technology, like the *De diversis artibus* published about AD 1100, the potential of numbers for securing accuracy and precision was strikingly discounted, and expressions such as 'a bit more' or 'a medium-sized piece' had to serve instead. A typical example of another genre, Abbot Suger's twelfth century *Vita Ludovici Grossi Regis*, contains, apart from a few estimates of military strength where large numbers are used with obvious imprecision, only one reference to a definite number above ten. Abelard's autobiography, from the same century, invokes no number above ten. Those who, like Gerbert of Aurillac (later to become Pope Sylvester II) in the tenth century, attempted to manipulate numbers, recorded with eloquence the great difficulty they encountered. A four page booklet on reckoning cost Gerbert 'almost impossible' toil, he tells us, and he was speaking as one for whom logic had been easy meat: contemporaries speak of the 'tears', 'sweat' and 'mountainous labour' demanded of them by mathematics.[1]

Mathematical advance is perhaps no more easily achieved today, but undoubtedly Gerbert and his contemporaries got less for their pains. Their handicap, an enormous one, was simply the way in which numbers (for arithmetic was seen in the Middle Ages, if not in Ancient Greece, as the heart of mathematics) were written in their time: in Roman numerals. Insofar as people counted at all, they used the same number system as we use today – they counted in tens. The Roman numeral system reflected this fact by giving a different letter or set of letters to each multiple of ten (e.g. 'X', 'L'). But it did little to represent the relationships between such multiples. It went some of the distance. 'XX' is a helpful way of expressing a number which is twice that represented by 'X'. But, for example, 'L' does nothing to display the fact that the number it represents is five times the number represented by 'X'. The consequence was that though it was possible, with difficulty, to perform addition and subtraction, multiplication

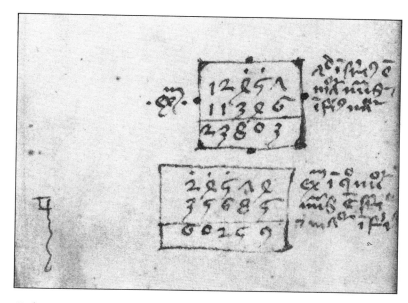

Early use of Arabic numerals for calculation. First half of the fourteenth century (Bodleian Library MS Ashmole 1522 fo. 18r)

was taxing in the extreme.

The Arabic numerals we are familiar with today do of course make these relationships clear: '1' with one '0' ('10') represents 10 to the power 1; '1' with two '0's ('100') represents 10 to the power 2. In the Arabic system, we have symbols for the numbers up to nine, including (crucially) one for zero, and use the position of a digit in a numeral to represent the fact that it stands for units, or tens, or tens of tens, or tens of tens of tens, or whatever. Thus, when we have reached the last of our symbols, '9', and want to carry on counting, we return the digit to zero and put the digit '1' to the left of it (that is, we write '10'). We then proceed by increasing the left digit by one every time a further ten has been counted; and when this digit reaches nine, we return it to zero and start a tally of tens of tens to its immediate left (that is, we write '100'). In this way we can express any number; but, more important, since the rule for counting in Arabic numerals is simple, so are the rules for conducting multiplication and division as well as addition and subtraction.

The Arabic system is not the only way of representing numbers that offers these advantages, however, and in fact it was another one that first released medieval Europe from the conceptual yoke of Roman numerals. Numbers were represented in this alternative system, revivified in the tenth century perhaps by the Gerbert we referred to above, not by marks at all, but by the position of counters on a grid. The device here is the abacus, and like Arabic

7	2	3	0	1	8	9
NUMBER		REPRESENTED				

Abacus

numerals, it represents the number of multiples of ten attaching to a given symbol by the position the symbol takes in an arrangement of symbols (just as '10' represents 1×10 when it stands alone, but $1 \times 10 \times 10$ when it appears in '100').

The success of the abacus in bringing large number computation within the limits of the feasible enlarged the circle of those who could make use of arithmetic, and sharpened the sense of accuracy and precision of those who did so. Then, from the twelfth century on, and reinforcing both these effects, came the spread of Indo-Arabic numerals. They were attractive in the first place perhaps as a way of making a preservable record of numbers and calculations as they appeared on the face of the abacus,[2] but anyway gave, at least over the board abacus (the form it took in medieval Europe), a substantial advantage of speed. Nevertheless, it took until the sixteenth century for those who used the Arabic system of counting, the 'algorists', to win a final triumph, when the multiplication of printing presses and the growing availability of paper made the written mark convenient to teach as well as use.[3]

But well before this, by the thirteenth century in effect, the impact of the abacus and the introduction of Arabic numerals had dissipated the acute sense of discomfort with figures I spoke of, as with some suddenness dates, page numbers, prices – quantities of all kinds – began to proliferate in literature. From that point on two major influences worked gradually to develop mathematics' role: first of course the rise of money, and second the early stirrings of the nation state, concerned increasingly to count soldiers and armaments as well as those under its sway, and to attach importance to political majorities.[4] Thus was an arithmetical mentality established, foreign to the greater part of the middle ages, but fundamental for Renaissance science.

Dead Reckoning

Mathematics played a role in more than one of the activities whose quickening marked the break-up of the medieval world, so that with this acceleration the pressure for easier, faster, more widely applicable mathematical techniques grew and grew. Some pressure had always been exerted – the inadequacy of the calendar in particular had demanded attention throughout the least numerate centuries, and so had the computational needs of the astrologers. But by the sixteenth century demands from new directions were building up. And one of the most significant came from the developing importance, from the European point of view, of overseas trade.

I want to dwell on this particular arena of change a little. The stimulus of the maritime application of mathematics, to navigation in particular, was probably the most important factor in bringing to pass the developments in mathematics that lay at the heart of the scientific revolution, and thus of the framework of ideas through which Leibniz looked out on the world and conceived his plans. But also, the peculiar circumstances in which navigation had to be conducted – that is, of course, on board ship – attracted a special engineering ingenuity to the construction of mathematical aids. Ships at the beginning of the seventeenth century, as the historian of navigation David Waters observes, 'were rapidly becoming the most complex contrivances yet assembled and put together by human hands, while in the navigator's chest was stowed the widest selection of instruments of precision and of books of systematized knowledge in general use'.[5] It is here, therefore, that we find further foundations for Leibniz' project: the navigator's instruments, forerunners, in a sense, of the mechanical calculators which gave him a concrete model for his mechanical reasoner.

For many centuries, shipping the world over stuck very largely to the

An early Stuart navigator's instruments of navigation

coasts. Mariners 'caped' their way to their destinations, sailing from promontory to promontory, without map or chart, with little recourse to compass, relying on their personal experience and a written guide to the landmarks, channels, tides, shallows and other hazards of that particular coastline, known as a 'rutter'. By the sixteenth century, however, the demands of trade were drawing ships out into the open sea. While it was possible, for example, for wine to be brought from Bordeaux to Britain by ships caping along the coast of northern France and crossing to England at the narrowest part of the English Channel, those prepared to brave the Bay of Biscay, open but offering a direct route to Southampton or Bristol, enjoyed a clear advantage.

To keep some sense of where they were, mariners in the sixteenth century relied almost exclusively on 'dead reckoning'. At regular intervals (measured by the passage of fine sand through an orifice – a 'glass') note would be taken of the direction being steered in, the direction and strength of the wind, the speed of the ship as estimated by the eye, and the state of the sea; account would be taken of any known current, of the effect of tide and of any known tendency for that particular ship to steer out of true; and in the light of all these factors an estimate made of the course appropriate to bring the ship home, and the distance still remaining.

The limitations of dead reckoning as a technique for determining position were first experienced acutely by the Portuguese as they ventured ever further down the west coast of Africa during the fourteenth and fifteenth centuries. What was needed was a fixed point that could be referred to at any stage in a voyage, which would thus provide a means of judging how far south of its starting point a ship had sailed. This is just what was provided by the Pole Star, which happens, presumably by chance, to be situated very near the axis about which (as we say now) the earth rotates.[6] The further south a mariner ventured, the lower sank the Pole Star in the sky (that is, its elevation decreased): but it kept its station, directly astern. Its height in the sky therefore amounted to a measure of the distance travelled south.

It was the established belief at this period, of course (at least when navigational matters were being thought about), that the earth took the form of a globe, and there was no difficulty in drawing on the notion of latitude to express in quantitative terms the variation in southerliness that was in question. Largely because they too thought of the earth as spherical and of the heavenly bodies as confined in their movements to the surfaces of spheres, the Ancient Greeks had done much to clarify thinking about the sphere, and had devised the concepts of latitude and longitude to define relative position on the earth's surface.[7] Lines of latitude and longitude began to appear on maps in western Europe in the fourteenth and fifteenth

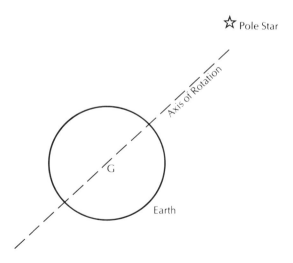

Figure 2.1 The value of the Pole Star in judging latitude: it lies very near the earth's axis of rotation

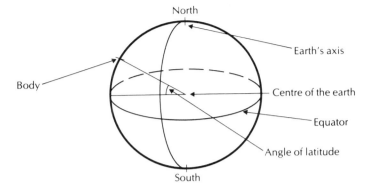

The latitude of a body on the earth's surface is the angle made by a line joining the body to the centre of the earth, and a line joining the equator to the centre of the earth.

Figure 2.2 Latitude: a measure of the degree of southerliness or northerliness of a body on the earth's surface

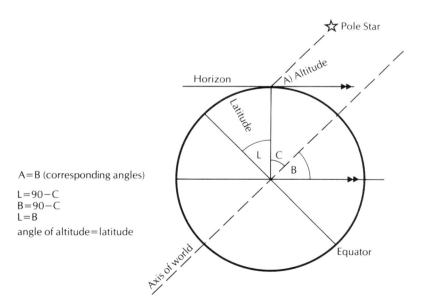

A=B (corresponding angles)

L=90−C
B=90−C
L=B
angle of altitude=latitude

Figure 2.3 Determination of latitude by observation of the Pole Star

centuries, stimulated by the new accessibility of Greek astronomy (in the form of translations of Ptolemy's *Almagest*). By simple Euclidean geometry it followed from the way in which latitude had been defined that measuring the angle of elevation of the Pole Star, and applying certain corrections to account for the lack of coincidence between Pole Star and the true pole, gave the navigator his latitude directly (see figure 2.3). Besides knowledge of the rule governing corrections (the Regiment of the North Star) all that was necessary was an instrument capable of allowing the required observation of the star to be made, and this was provided by either the quadrant or the astrolabe. Operating either instrument was essentially a matter of lining up pointers with the star, and reading off the elevation above the horizon on a scale.

When the equator was crossed in 1481, however, the Pole Star, continuously below the horizon from the Southern hemisphere, could no longer be used to gauge latitude, and other means had to be sought. Recourse was then had to the movement of the sun, which of course was known to cross in its daily path from east to west. At midday, its position would be in the north–south plane, just as the Pole Star indicated the north–south plane in the Northern hemisphere: and just as the elevation of the North Star gave a measure of latitude in the north, so the midday elevation of the sun provided the basis for a measure of latitude in the south. The use of the sun's elevation was more complicated, however, since it was known that the sun could not be construed as orbiting always directly above the earth's equator. Astronomers thought of the sun as orbiting in a plane which made an angle with the plane of the equator, and observations obliged them, moreover, to think of this angle, the angle of 'declination', as subject to daily variation. Navigators had to consult tables (modernized by

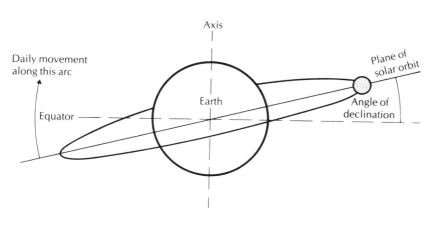

Figure 2.4 Variation in the sun's declination

Declination Tables. From Cortes' *The Art of Navigation* (1561)

Portugal's King John II in 1484) and apply quite complicated rules in order to convert an observation of the sun's meridian altitude into a figure for their ship's latitude.

These complications of determining latitude, however, were as nothing compared to the problem that became acute when the Cape of Good Hope was rounded in 1487: the determination of longitude, of relative position east or west. Because the earth rotates about a north–south axis, the heavens can offer nothing in the way of a fixed point to gauge east–west movement.

On the other hand, of course, it was seen from the first that the apparent steady revolution of the sun about the earth would itself provide an entirely satisfactory reference if only a ship's movement could be rigorously related to it. For example, if an imaginary craft moved west, keeping up with the apparent movement of the sun – so that the sun appeared to stay at its meridian as the craft sped along – the ship would be travelling through 360 degrees of longitude in twenty-four hours, since this is what the sun appears to do. On a real voyage, therefore, one had only to keep accurate time to determine one's longitude easily. The time that elapsed between noon at the home port, which would be given by the ship's clock, and the sun reaching its meridian as seen from the ship would give a measure of the amount of

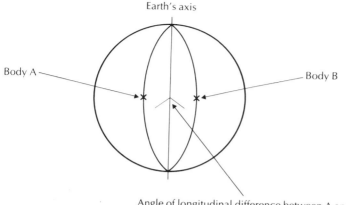

Earth's axis

Body A

Body B

Angle of longitudinal difference between A and B

Difference in longitude is defined as the angle made by the plane containing the first body and the earth's axis, and the plane containing the second body and the earth's axis. (A single agreed reference plane for all measures of longitude – that passing through Greenwich – was established only in the nineteenth century.)

Figure 2.5 Longitude: a measure of two bodies' relative position East or West of each other on the surface of the earth

westerly or easterly movement made. The difficulty was that clocks of the necessary accuracy were not available in the sixteenth century. Waters calculates that to determine longitude to within half a degree after a voyage of six weeks using the clock method the time-keeping error must not be above three seconds a day.[8]

Other ways of comparing time at base and at current position were explored at various stages, but without real success. For example, at the turn of the fifteenth century Columbus had compared the time of an eclipse as observed from his position with the time predicted (as viewed from his home port) in the published tables. Conjunctions between moon and earth were invoked similarly.

But neither approach proved helpful, because of inaccurate almanacs, insufficiently accurate instruments, and insufficiently frequent suitable heavenly phenomena. Perhaps the most sustained effort was devoted to perfecting the method based on sighting the sun's altitude at the moment when the moon crossed its meridian, a project that generated an insatiable demand for lunar tables of greater reliability and accuracy. Attempts to exploit the variation of the magnetic compass, which was observed to alter with longitude, likewise failed to yield results of the required accuracy; and in fact the problem of longitude continued to stimulate research, and to resist solution, until John Harrison devised his maritime chronometers in the eighteenth century.

Dead reckoning, for all its uncertainties, had therefore to suffice for several centuries of busy maritime activity. For great journeys, of which of course many were attempted in the sixteenth century, the only safeguard available was the technique of sailing due south or north until the latitude of the destination was reached, and then attempting to sail along that latitude until landfall.

The point of these ambitious adventures, taking Europeans first down the west coast of Africa, as we have noted, but then north and west too, was not at all academic. It was in the latter part of the sixteenth century that foreign trade first established a significant role in the English economy, with the colonization of St Helena, Jamaica and the east American coast, and it had acquired a similar role earlier for Spain and Portugal. This meant expansion for the merchant marines: but also for the navies, upon whom fell the major responsibility for protecting the new interests. In the seventeenth century, expansion of both overseas trade and the means of protecting it continued. At its close, Pepys' Navy report of 1695 records 200 ships of fifty tons or more, and looks back to a corresponding figure of forty ships in 1607.[9]

This massive expansion of maritime activity appropriated, as R.K. Merton makes clear, a great deal of the time's most brilliant intellectual endeavour.[10] The list of inventors responsible for the state-of-the-art technology in ship-building and naval warfare, as well as long distance navigation, reads like a roll-call of the great thinkers of the scientific renaissance: Boyle, Harriot, Pascal, Leibniz, Napier, among others; and it is now argued on several sides that it was indeed the need to solve practical problems, of which these were the pre-eminent examples, that led to the intellectual achievements of sixteenth and seventeenth century science.

Towards the close of the sixteenth century at any rate the need of the navigators was so acute that they turned – or the ablest of them turned – to mathematics for assistance. For mathematics, in the form of trigonometry, applied to surveying from about 1450[11] and under development from then on as an aid in astronomy (including calendar reckoning), also promised to enable baffled navigators to calculate what they could not observe.

Arithmetical Sailing

The root realization in trigonometry is that if a triangle's angles are kept the same, but its size increased, the lengths of the sides necessarily keep in step with each other. This (see figure 2.6) gives us a way of working out what the unknown length of a side of a triangle must be, provided we know a certain minimum of other facts about it – for example, the lengths of the other two sides, plus one of the angles; or one length and two angles. Trigonometry

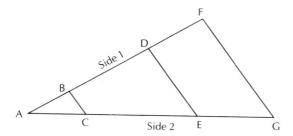

Figure 2.6 Trigonometry: the basic insight

therefore provided mariners with the means of working out distance travelled, as well as movement east or west, if they could only keep track of the compass bearing they were sailing on and observe their latitude (see figure 2.7).

In the Ancient world, the fixed relationships obtaining between the sides

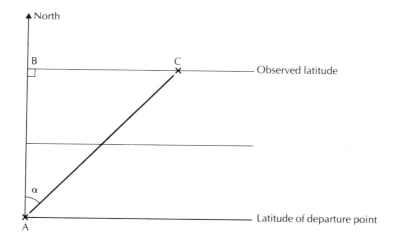

Figure 2.7 Application of trigonometry to navigation

α: compass bearing being sailed upon.
Distance AB would be calculable from observation of latitude at A and C.
Angle ABC, between line of longitude and line of latitude, would be known (i.e. a right angle).

AC, distance travelled, would be calculable; so would BC.

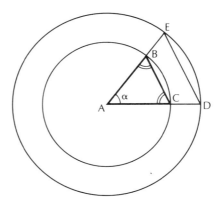

Figure 2.8 Ancient perspective on similar triangles

The fixed ratio determined by the angle α is seen as given by the ratio chord:radius. Thus BC:AC=ED:AD.

of similar triangles (i.e. ones having the same angles) were expressed in terms of triangles drawn in circles (see figure 2.8).

In effect it was the ratio between the lengths BC (the chord subtended at the circumference of the circle by the angle α at its centre) and AC (the circle's radius) that was chosen to express the fixed ratio of lengths determined by α. What was actually done (by Ptolemy), though, was to divide the circle's circumference up into 360 equal parts, and its diameter into 120 equal parts, and to draw up a 'table of chords', expressing for each angle the length of the chord it subtended as a proportion of the length of the diameter.

The modern way of conceptualizing the fixed relationships between the lengths of the sides of similar triangles is in terms of a right-angle triangle. If we imagine a triangle with one angle fixed at 90 degrees, then the fixed relationship implied by a given angle is expressed as a ratio of the lengths of two sides. Since there are three sides there are a total of six ratios, each fixed by the particular angle (see figure 2.9).

Fortunately for the navigators, tables of the most relevant of these functions had been prepared for astronomical purposes by Puerbach and Regiomontus at the close of the fifteenth century, and those who sought to win the navigators over to 'arithmetical' sailing[12] were able simply to reproduce these with explanations of how they were to be used – as, for example, did Thomas Blundeville in his *Exercises*, published in 1594.[13]

The labour and difficulty of drawing on these tables in practice – to solve real navigational problems in the course of a voyage – was of course as nothing compared with the quite awe-inspiring feats of application that were involved in drawing them up in the first place. Still, at a time when the

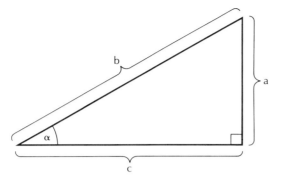

Figure 2.9 Modern perspective on similar triangles

The fixed ratio determined by the angle α is seen as holding between the sides of a right-angled triangle.

Given α, the following six trigonometric ratios are fixed:

$\frac{a}{b}$ (called the sine of α)

$\frac{c}{b}$ (cosine)

$\frac{a}{c}$ (tangent)

$\frac{b}{a}$ (cosecant)

$\frac{b}{c}$ (secant)

$\frac{c}{a}$ (cotangent)

practice was to resort to look-up tables for even simple calculations like the addition of single digit numbers, the demands of working the trigonometrical methods, even with tables supplied, were too much for many navigators, and it was only a tiny elite at the end of the sixteenth century who were able to use them as a practical tool.

At the same time, the inadequacy of existing non-mathematical navigational techniques in a world in which so much hung on moving goods and armaments efficiently about the globe was borne in upon everybody with an interest at stake, and money was forthcoming for various enterprises designed to educate the navigators in the new possibilities. Special lectureships were established for their mathematical education – one in Paris, for example, was reported in 1584 by Hakluyt;[14] another in London in 1588, taken by Thomas Hood. London's Gresham College, where navigation was one of the subjects required to be taught, opened in 1598.

Mathematicians themselves directed their efforts towards devising simplified techniques for applying the new principles, and this resulted in their turning to navigational use an instrument that was first developed for use in

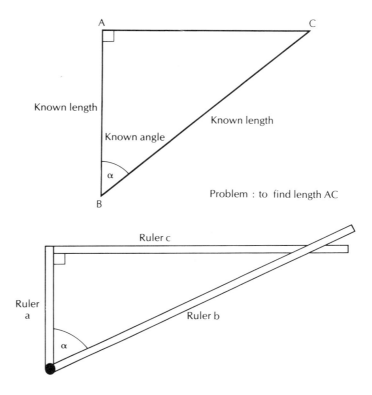

Figure 2.10 Principle of the sector

surveying. The principle of trigonometry – that sides of similar triangles keep their proportion – is perhaps not difficult to imagine expressed in the form of an instrument. Suppose we wished to determine the distance AC (see figure 2.10) without resorting to sine tables and calculations. Could we not construct a kind of model using three rulers, arranged to form a similar triangle to the one in the problem as set? Measuring where ruler b (see figure 2.10) cut across ruler c, and applying an appropriate scale, would give the answer almost directly.

An instrument along these lines was constructed in 1598 by Galileo, and another, independently, by Hood. Known as the 'sector', it was converted from surveying to navigational use by Edmund Gunter, author of one of the seminal works of maritime navigation, *The Description and Use of the Sectore*, published in 1624 (though partially circulating in manuscript for years prior to this).[15] It took the form of a ruler, hinged in the middle, like an old-fashioned carpenter's rule. Scales were engraved on the two arms, and lengths measured off by manipulating a pair of compasses.

The sector could be used to solve all problems of proportion, and not merely those concerned with surveying or navigation. Gunter himself took as one of his examples the problem of working out the interest that would accrue over a sixty month period, if it were known that a forty month period would yield fifty pounds (and assuming a simple rate). The solution involves opening the sector until it forms in effect a triangle with two of its sides in proportion forty to fifty (the ratio of period to interest given in the problem) and, keeping the angle formed by the arms (or legs, as they were actually known) the same, using the scale to read off what the side representing the interest would be if the side representing the period were increased to sixty (see figure 2.11).

A number of different scales (called 'lines') were inscribed on the legs of the instrument so as to ease its use with a range of different problems involving proportion. A 'Line of Superficies' and a 'Line of Solids' facilitated the proportional enlargement or diminishment of surfaces and solids. A 'Line of Inscribed Bodies' made it easy to find what regular solid could be inscribed within a given sphere. A 'Line of Metals' helped establish the proportion between various metals 'in their magnitude and weight'.[16] There were also lines of quadrature, of segments and equated bodies. Nevertheless, it was in making available mathematically sophisticated techniques to the mathematically unsophisticated navigator that the major importance of the sector lay.

Once introduced, trigonometrical techniques exerted a pressure of their own. Position and intended course were now much more conveniently plotted on a surface that was flat than on the spherical globe used by intercontinental navigators hitherto. But since the earth itself remained as spherical as ever, some way had to be found of representing a spherical surface on a flat one.

At first the problem was simply ignored. Lines of longitude were drawn parallel to each other on the 'plane charts', and so were lines of latitude, so that the two crossed each other always at right angles. But the deficiencies of this convention, as of course was well known, were acute, and they grew in proportion with increased latitude. What was needed was some principle of mapping – a rule which would show where, in relation to a given pair of reference points, any particular point on a spherical surface should be represented on a plane one. Indefinitely many such rules are conceivable, but the one that proved generally most useful was that suggested by Mercator in his world map, published in 1569, and promulgated by Edward Wright in his *Certaine Errors* of 1599.[17]

Though the principle Mercator had applied took some working out, the essential idea can be put quite simply. Imagine a sheet of paper rolled into a cylinder and slipped over a globe, so that the axis of the globe lies along the axis of the cylinder. The features on the globe are then transferred to the inner surface of the paper, determining the position that each shall take up by imagining a straight line drawn from the feature as it is on the globe so that it meets the paper at right angles. Unrolling the paper then gives the

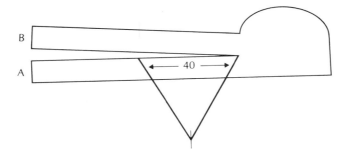

1   Measure off 40 units on scale of arm A with compasses.

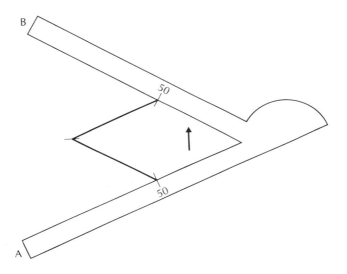

2   Putting one foot of compasses on the 50 units mark of arm A, open sector
    until second foot of compasses falls precisely on the 50 mark of arm B.

Figure 2.11 Using Gunter's sector

chart, prepared on 'Mercator's projection'. On the Mercator chart, lines of
longitude retain their uniform spacing: but lines of latitude, equally spaced
on the globe, become closer and closer together as the degree of latitude
increases.

Working out bearings on the Mercator chart presented no problems, since
the bearing of one point from another, as represented on the globe, transfers

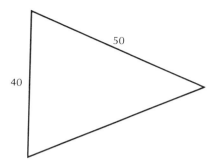

This gives an isosceles triangle with long side in proportion to short side of 50:40.

3 Move one foot of the compasses to the mark of 60 on one of the sector legs, and open the compasses until the second foot falls on the 60 mark of the other leg.

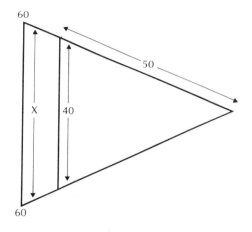

4 Use the scale to read off how wide the compasses are: this gives x, the length of the short side of the isoceles triangle when the long side is 60, and so the answer to the problem set.

without distortion to the chart (one of the great advantages of this projection). Working out distances, however, was more difficult, because what varies from point to point on the Mercator chart is its scale.

The variation in scale can be put in terms of the gradual decrease, as one nears the Poles, of the distance round the earth measured along a line of latitude. At the equator, this distance is the circumference of the earth ($2\pi r$ if r is the earth's radius); at either Pole it is zero. On the Mercator chart prepared as described above, all of these distances are represented by the same length (since the unrolled cylinder of paper is rectangular). What then is the rule that governs the gradual increase in scale? It can be shown that it varies in proportion with the secant of the angle of latitude: and this gives us the ratio by which the scale must be increased before converting distance measured on the chart into actual distance on the surface of the earth. Conversely, it gives us the ratio we need to invoke in constructing a Mercator chart.

Such manipulations were of course capable of being carried out by calculation, but few practical mariners felt equal to the task. It was the sector that brought the new chart within the grasp of the ordinary navigator. Mercator problems were essentially problems of proportion, and the new instrument substituted a few simple and familiar routines with compasses for a complex of unintuitive number juggling (often with figures that would be quite rebarbative even by today's standards).

The invention of logarithms by John Napier sprang out of the same urgent concern to make calculating easier – which tables of logarithms did by reducing multiplication and division to addition and subtraction. Napier first hit on the possibility about 1594, and then spent twenty years calculating the tables of figures necessary to put it to actual use. His *Mirifici Logarithmorum Canonis Descriptio*[18], consisting of tables of logs for sines of every minute of angle, each calculated to seven figures, appeared in 1614. The fundamental observation was to compare the geometric progression

$$1, r, r^2, r^3, \dots$$

with the arithmetic progression formed by the exponents figuring in it:

$$0, 1, 2, 3, \dots$$

Multiplying any two terms in the first progression gives a term whose exponent is the sum of the corresponding terms in the second progression. Although Napier himself had thought primarily of the value logarithmic tables would have for astronomers, they were brought into popular use by one who was inspired by their potential in the navigational context. This was Henry Briggs, who had been a professor at Gresham College since its inception, and who originated the suggestion (in effect – Briggs and his contemporaries could not quite have put it like this) that the most practical basis on which to construct a table of logarithms would be to find the power to which ten should be raised in order to equal the number in question, and to let its logarithm be defined as that power. Logarithms made an enormous impact in every field in which calculations had to be done, and despite the availability of the sector, the major responsibility for transforming navigational practice from an art into a science lies with them.

Napier went on to develop other ideas for facilitating calculation: his 'bones', a system of ivory sticks suitably engraved with numbers which

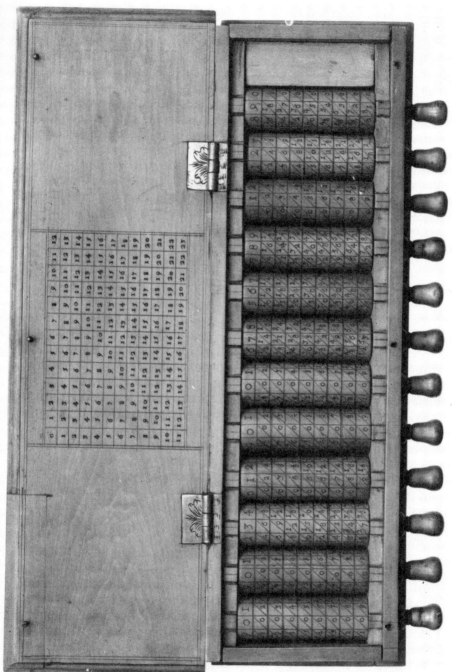

A cylindrical version of Napier's bones

reduced multiplication and division to simple routines of manipulation; and then a semi-mechanized elaboration of them. Others took Napier's revolutionary insight in different directions, the most important of which resulted in the slide rule. Gunter, the man who had converted the sector for navigational use, and another occupant of a Gresham College Chair, saw how by a further conversion a 'mechanical Table of Logarithms' (the phrase is Edmund Wingate's)[19] might be constructed. He needed simply to open his sector out into a single rule and inscribe 'logarithmic' lines upon it. The compasses that served before would also serve with the new instrument to add or subtract lengths measured on a logarithmic scale, which would amount to multiplying or dividing the quantities as marked. The result was Gunter's Scale, first reported in 1624.[20] When attempts were mooted to develop the accuracy of this device by stretching the rule to an unwieldy six feet, William Oughtred responded with the idea of bending a conventionally-sized rule into a circle, and added a disc in the centre, bearing a second scale, to obviate the need for compasses.

The Emergence of Modern Algebra

> As the Mathematical Sciences are the grounds of Navigation, so is Navigation the onley meanes, whereby the excellency of those Arts and Sciences are proved and layde open to the view of the world.

So wrote John Tapp in 1602.[21] But although the demands of navigation were perhaps the most significant, they were not the only ones heeded by mathematics in the ferment of activity around the close of the sixteenth century. Accuracy in surveying – the original stimulant behind the Sector, as I have already mentioned – assumed great importance in an age of multiplying civil engineering projects, and mathematicians were employed in the construction of aqueducts, in drainage schemes (for example, in Fenland), in the construction of ambitious buildings, gardens and water-works, and in the accurate estimation of the value of stands of timber.[22] The financial manipulations of nascent capitalism also drew on mathematicians' services. The 'cossist' tradition of pre-Modern algebra developed and flourished – outside the Schools – as a response to the new problems of trade and exchange encountered by the merchants and bankers of fifteenth and sixteenth century Europe.[23] An early application of logarithms was in the calculation of compound interest (by Briggs in his introduction to an early popularization of logs),[24] and the systematization of accounts and the introduction of double-entry book-keeping reflected their involvement.

Through various channels, then, as the seventeenth century began, mathematics was entering – flooding – into people's lives. It was not the esoteric mystery it had been before the tenth century in the West, nor entirely the preserve of the very highly educated scholar that mathematics remained in the centuries after Gerbert. It was useful, indispensable even, and people of practical ambition did well to acquire its elements.

The importance for Leibniz' project of mathematics' emergence from the shadows is twofold. First, it made people seek ways of easing the pain of mathematical manipulations, leading to the invention of the Sector, logarithms, the slide rule, and the mechanical calculator. This made the construction of a *logical* aid, a reasoning machine, seem feasible, provided that one could show that non-mathematical reasoning was relevantly similar to mathematical – and Leibniz thought this could be shown. But the second effect was much the more profound: the bursting forth of mathematics was accompanied by, and did much to encourage, the idea that mathematical thought constituted the paradigm of thought in general. Galileo said famously that the whole of creation was a book written in the language of mathematics, which had to be learnt if anything was to be understood, and Hobbes declared equally roundly that 'everything done by our mind is a computation'.[25]

The significance of the recognition of mathematical thinking as the model for thinking in general is that mathematical thought, of all the other kinds of what we now call 'thinking', is the most temptingly construable as representational. Faced with concrete problems to do with rates of interest, or angles of fire, or the safe design of buildings, or which direction to sail in, people would have recourse to consultants who would let numbers, or letters, stand for the elements of their problem; perform manipulations; and return their recommendation for the required action. Clearly, numbers or letters were taking the place of coins, stones, ships. Mathematicians let some kinds of things stand for other kinds of things and manipulated the former in place of the latter.

This feature of mathematics was taken even further by the major contribution of the Renaissance to mathematics as such, which was the launch of modern algebra. During the late Middle Ages, algebra of a kind had flourished, much of it outside the universities, as a set of techniques for solving the arithmetic problems of the nascent money economy. But after Vieta, with whom responsibility for the essential innovation rests, it becomes much more than a collection of recipes for solving (mainly commercial) problems. The idea of a *type* of equation is born, and algebra becomes the study of *forms* of mathematical expression – the quadratic equation, for example.

The new way of thinking about algebra which Vieta made possible was grounded in a new way of thinking about numbers. Today, we think of numbers as something rather different from the collections of 'things' – chairs, people, pieces of cake – which can have numbers applied to them. 'Three' is not, for us, a collection of three things, though to say more positively what a number is for us is not easy. For the Ancient Greeks, however, and the medievals, there were just collections of things. In the calculations of everyday, 'numbers' were thought of as collections of concrete objects, though in theoretical discussions it was groupings of

François Vieta, 1540–1603

'measures' or, even more abstractly, 'units', that numbers were considered to be collections of.[26]

This Ancient and medieval conception of number presumably had to do with the fact that calculating was done in those periods by manipulating small objects – pebbles in the case of the Ancient Greeks, beads or counters on the abacus in the numerate centuries of the Middle Ages. In any case, it was a change in the tools of calculation that heralded this conception's end. As I have mentioned before, the reintroduction of the abacus to the West in the tenth century was followed by a new method of calculating, using marks on paper. For some time, the two methods of calculating, working the abacus and making Indo-Arabic signs, existed side by side, their relative merits championed by 'abacists' on the one hand and 'algorists' on the other.[27] But with the invention of printing and the growing availability of paper, particularly in the sixteenth century, the use of written or printed signs eventually (as we know) won out.

At the beginning of this transition, sequences of signs simply took the place of manipulations of counters. But then came the innovation, prepared by the gradual spread of this new technique of doing calculations with signs instead of through physical manipulations: the use of a sign, in a rather special sense, as a representative.[28]

The special sense is one that came from the law courts. Vieta would have been familiar, as a lawyer, with the convention of using a single name (like John an-Oaks, to take one of Wallis' examples cited in O'Neill,[29] or Tommy Atkins) to mean 'any person indefinitely who may be so concerned'. It was just such a convention that gave rise to the sense of 'representation' we are today familiar with in political contexts: a representative as one person who stands for any of a whole category of people.[30] Vieta transferred the concept of 'representative' to number manipulation. A sign, he proposed, might be used to represent indifferently any of a whole range of numbers.[31]

It was not the use of letters to stand for numbers that was new with the Renaissance. This technique is found sporadically in Euclid; and, to much more purpose (to bring out the common form of various equations), in the Alexandrian Greek Diophantus. Moreover, Diophantus also uses letters to stand for unknown numbers. Vieta's innovation was to use a letter as a *symbol* – to use a letter not as a mere stand-in for a number, known or unknown, but to represent any of a whole category of numbers. I will describe later how this enabled him to shift the focus of algebra from the derivation of solutions for particular calculational problems to the study of methods of problem solution in general.[32] But here the point is that Vieta's invention of algebraic symbols – perhaps not too strong a way of describing his seminal contribution, so long as we take 'symbol' in the distinctive sense given above – had the effect of altering the way in which numbers themselves were thought of. When integers were included in expressions of Vieta's 'logistic of species', expressions which also contained the new-style symbols, it became impossible to go on thinking of them as referring to collections of units: 'the new context in which they appear renders the integers themselves symbolic, understood in terms of arithmetical rules.'[33] The non-referential conception of number had been launched.

Notes

1 A. Murray, *Reason and Society in the Middle Ages* (Clarendon, Oxford, 1978), chs. 6 and 7. My chapter is much indebted to this work.
2 Murray, *Reason and Society*, p. 166.
3 E. Eisenstein, *The Printing Press as an Agent of Change* (CUP, Cambridge, 1979), p. 532; and see John O'Neill, *Against Formalism* (unpublished PhD thesis, Lancaster University (UK), 1984), p. 133.
4 Murray, *Reason and Society*, pp. 198, 199.
5 D.W. Waters, *The Art of Navigation in England in Elizabethan and Early Stuart Times* (Hollis & Carter, London, 1958), p. 319. Commander Waters' work is an invaluable resource on its topic.
6 See T.S. Kuhn, *The Copernican Revolution* (Harvard UP, Cambridge, Mass., 1957), for a lucid exposition of the astronomical facts (and so much else!).
7 Hipparchus, in the second century BC, perhaps had the fundamental ideas here, though the distinctiveness of his contribution is obscured by the mediation of Ptolemy, through whose *Almagest* the work of Hipparchus is chiefly known.
8 Waters, *Art of Navigation*, p. 58.

9 Pepys, *Memoirs Relating to the State of the Royal Navy* (London, 1690).

10 R.K. Merton, *Science, Technology and Society in Seventeenth Century England* (Humanities Press, New Jersey, 1970), ch. VII.

11 Morris Kline, *Mathematical Thought from Ancient to Modern Times* (OUP, New York, 1972), p. 237.

12 Davis, *The Seaman's Secrets* (Thomas Dawson, London, 1595).

13 Thomas Blundeville, *Exercises* (John Windet, London, 1594).

14 Hakluyt, Letter to Walsingham, of 1584; part reproduced in Waters, *Art of Navigation*, Appendix 16 B.

15 Edmund Gunter, *The Description and Use of the Sectore* (London, 1624).

16 Gunter, quoted by Waters, *Art of Navigation*, p. 363.

17 Edward Wright, *Certaine Errors* (Valentine Simms, London, 1599).

18 Napier, *Mirifici Logarithmorum Canonis Descriptio* (Andreæ Hart, Edinburgh, 1614).

19 Quoted by Waters, *Art of Navigation*, p. 420.

20 Edmund Wingate, *L'Usage de la Reigle de Proportion en l'Arithmetique et Geometrie* (Paris, 1624).

21 John Tapp, *The Seamans Kalender* (London, 1602).

22 Charles Webster, *The Great Instauration* (Duckworth, London, 1975), p. 350.

23 Salomon Bochner, *Mathematics in the Rise of Science* (Princeton UP, Princeton, 1966), pp. 38, 39.

24 Webster, *Great Instauration*, pp. 350, 414.

25 Thomas Hobbes. This is Leibniz' gloss on *De Corpore* (London, 1655), Pt. I, Art. 2; Leibniz, 'Of the Art of Combinations' in G.H.R. Parkinson (ed.), *Leibniz: Logical Papers* (Clarendon, Oxford, 1966).

26 Jacob Klein, *Greek Mathematical Thought and the Origins of Algebra*, trans. E. Braun (MIT Press, Cambridge, Mass., 1968), p. 213.

27 Eisenstein, *Printing Press*, p. 532; O'Neill, *Against Formalism*, p. 133.

28 O'Neill, *Against Formalism*, p. 134.

29 O'Neill, *Against Formalism*, p. 135.

30 H.F. Pitkin, *The Concept of Representation* (University of California Press, Berkeley, 1967).

31 There is perhaps an anticipation of the idea of one thing representing indifferently any of a category of individuals in Ockham's nominalism: the theory that universals are signs which represent many things. See William and Martha Kneale, *The Development of Logic* (Clarendon Press, Oxford, 1962), p. 266.

32 See below, pp. 93–4.

33 O'Neill, *Against Formalism*, p. 124.

3   Calculating Clocks

The mechanical calculators that began to appear in the seventeenth century took their place naturally alongside logarithms, the bones and the slide rule. They were the fruits of the urgent practical concern to make number handling easier. Their engineering, however, drew on a distinct tradition. They consisted of moving parts, and they were made by clockmakers.

Though the use of weights to drive mechanisms involving geared wheels dates from the Ancient world, time measurement relied, certainly until the middle of the thirteenth century in the West, on keeping track of the movement of the sun, as in the sundial, or on the steady flow of a fluid through an orifice, as in the water clock. The water clock in fact took some very elaborate forms, with complicated arrangements of cords round pulleys, anchored to a float steadily sinking in a water reservoir and bringing in train a puppet show of effects on the clock's facade.[1]

The displacement of the water clock by one which relied on periodic mechanical effects depended on the invention of some means of converting the motion of a falling weight, driving a geared wheel, into a series of increments of equal duration; for of course, left to itself, such a weight simply accelerates toward the ground. What was needed, in other words, was an 'escapement', the earliest known mention of which appeared in a work by Villard de Honnecourt in the middle of the thirteenth century.[2]

By the end of the fourteenth century, we find the 'verge' escapement embodied, for example, in the famous clock finished in 1370 by Henri de Vick. This escapement, in conjunction with the foliot balance, converts what would be the continuous rotation of a weight-driven wheel into a series of equally spaced jerks (which the rest of the mechanism essentially counts). Mechanical clocks then took this form, with improvements restricted to matters of detail, until the introduction of the pendulum in the second half of the seventeenth century.

Something approaching the watch was invented at the beginning of the sixteenth century, when a coiled spring was put in place of the driving weight of the clock: a portable instrument about the size (and shape) of an orange was the result. Because the force exerted by a spring varies as it

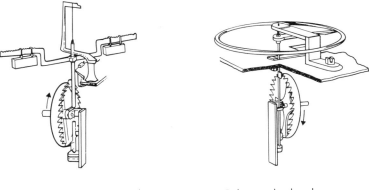

Foliot balance and verge   Balance wheel and verge

Figure 3.1 The verge escapement and foliot balance

The verge escapement works on the principle that the period of oscillation of a T-shaped spindle is effectively independent of variation in an applied torque, so long as the torque remains small in relation to the size of weights carried on the arms of the 'T'. A weight-driven wheel is arranged to apply the torque via teeth around its edge, and the arm of the 'T' is weighted either with a small horizontal circle of metal (the balance wheel) or with a pair of weights (the foliot balance).

Source: Usher, *Mechanical Inventions*, (see note 1) p. 200

unwinds, some mediating mechanism had to be devised so that the actual force bearing on the driving barrel remained constant. First the 'stackfreed', then the 'fusee', invented by Jacob Zech in the second quarter of the sixteenth century, were introduced to this end.

Some of these devices represented invention of the very highest order. Of the fusee, for example, one authority has written that 'perhaps no problem in mechanics has ever been solved so simply and so perfectly'.[3] But the construction of the early mechanical clocks and 'watches', as distinct from their conception, had to be undertaken by craftsmen whose experience had been gained in very much grosser work – in making mill gears, for example,[4] (In fact the great bulk of machinery at the beginning of the seventeenth century was constructed in wood, and continued to be so for the next two centuries.) There was for a long time a gap between idea and realization. It is disputed, for instance, whether the wonderfully elegant spherical devices of the sixteenth century, by which those whose wealth they demonstrated pretended to tell the time, were really very much more than 'wonderfully elegant' in a purely aesthetic sense.[5]

Nevertheless, when the first mechanical calculators came to be con-

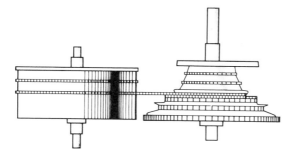

Figure 3.2 Fusee

Source: Usher, *Mechanical Inventions,* (see note 1) p. 306

structed in the seventeenth century, they called for no technical innovation. They depended (except for Napier's device, which was an elaboration of his earlier invention, the bones) on simple trains of gear wheels of a kind that were by then, in clockwork, entirely familiar. In fact the first one we know of (discounting Napier's), reported by its inventor Wilhelm Schickard in a letter to Kepler in 1624, was called a 'clock' – a 'calculating clock'.[6]

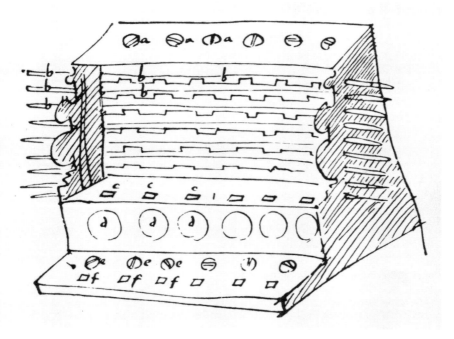

Schickard's own drawings of his "calculating clock", 1624

The basic idea of the gear-train calculator is very simple. Take a single gearwheel with ten teeth, numbered from zero to nine, and fix an index to point to each number successively as the wheel rotates. Initialize by adjusting the wheel so that the index points to the tooth marked zero. Then, if the wheel is rotated by three teeth, and then by a further five, the tooth marked eight will appear under the index. This is the mechanical representation of the addition of five to three to yield eight. (See figure 3.3). To handle the addition of numbers with several digits it is only necessary to arrange a row of similar wheels, interconnected so that when the one first operated upon passes from 9 to 0, the next wheel along is rotated by a single tooth: and so on down the line.

Schickard's machine was lost in a fire and we know of it only through his letter to Kepler, though a reconstruction has been attempted.[7] For the operations of multiplication and division, it seems to have drawn on Napier's scheme to automate the bones, but for addition and subtraction a chain of wheels of the kind outlined above was involved.[8]

Another very early gear-train calculator (completed in 1642, and thought to be indeed the first until the discovery of the Schickard letter in the 1950s)[9] has come down to us in several copies, one of them, now in the *Conservatoire des Arts et Métiers* in Paris, bearing its inventor's signature – that of Blaise Pascal.

In this device we can see the simple principle outlined above clearly realized. It uses the rotation of a 'wheel' to represent the figures zero to nine,

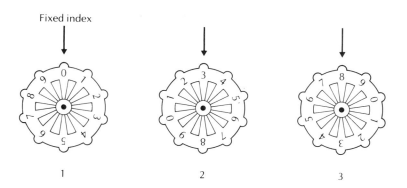

Figure 3.3 Principle of addition by cogwheel

1 The wheel is at zero
2 The wheel is rotated by three teeth: the index points to 3.
3 The wheel is rotated by five more teeth: the index points to 8 (=3+5).

Source: Taton & Flad, *Le Calcul Mécanique*, (see note 8) p. 24

assembling eight such 'wheels' side by side, to represent different orders of ten. The 'wheels' in question actually take the form of hubs, from each of which ten spokes radiate, and the row of eight of these are arranged along the top of the box. The hub and spokes operate a little like a telephone dial. The spaces between the spokes are numbered counter-clockwise from zero to nine, and a stop is fixed to the casing adjacent to the space marked '0'. To enter a given digit, a finger (or 'stylo') is inserted in the space thus marked and the dial rotated clockwise until the finger encounters the stop. Thus the wheel is rotated by the required number of tenths of a revolution (see figure 3.4).

Each dial wheel is connected within the box, via toothed wheels, to a cylinder which is thus caused to rotate in step with the dial wheel. Digits from 0 to 9 are inscribed on the surface of the cylinder, and a window is cut in the box for each cylinder so that as it rotates each digit shows through the window in turn. A number, therefore, is put into the machine by dialling in each digit, using the appropriate dial for the order of ten required, and the number is displayed through the windows.

The chief engineering challenge of this type of calculator is to arrange for the 'carry' to be passed from one wheel to the next smoothly and reliably. Pascal's solution was to have a pin, borne by a wheel which rotates with the lower order cog, acting to raise a weighted pawl gradually. As a whole revolution is completed, the pawl escapes the pin and falls on a ratcheted wheel, connected with the next cog, with sufficient force to rotate it through a tenth of a revolution. In this way the carry is transmitted as a single increment, ensuring that at each stage of any addition a determinate digit is displayed centrally at each window.

The success of this approach – or promise, rather, since there is not much evidence that it worked very well – is that it spreads out the work involved in transmitting the carry over all the addition operations, whether they

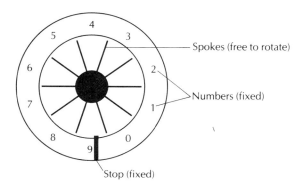

Figure 3.4 Detail of dial on Pascal's box

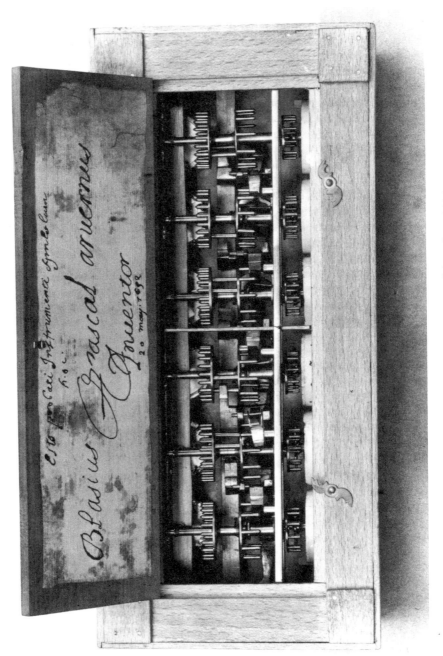

Pascal's Box. This one is in the Musée Nationale des Techniques in Paris and dates from 1654

generate a carry in themselves or not. If this is not done, the extra force that may be required to transmit a carry – since that carry might on occasion cause further carries all down the line – could be completely disproportionate. A similar problem arises in the striking clock, of course, and had been solved similarly by the incremental raising of a pawl in de Vick's clock.[10]

Performing addition using Pascal's machine was straightforward. The first number was dialled in, and then the subsequent ones, and the sum appeared at the windows. To allow subtraction, Pascal used the notion of a digit's complement: the difference between the number represented by the digit and the base of the number system in use. Thus the complement of our 8 is (10 − 8) or 2.

Multiplication could be carried out on the Pascal box (as it was known) only by repeated addition, a weakness addressed by the next contributor to the calculator's development, Leibniz himself. Again, we have more than one surviving example of the machines Leibniz had built, one resting like the ark in an inner sanctum of the fine State Library at Hanover.

It is clear, though, that he also planned machines on different principles, which have not come down to us. In a paper published in 1685, for example, he describes plans for an upgraded Pascal box based on combining a type of variable-toothed gearwheel with a system of pulleys. To build a multiplier out of Pascal's adder, what was needed was an arrangement to enable a given

Leibniz proposed nine pulleys of different sizes (one for each of the numbers 1–9), which were to connect to the variable-toothed wheels (one per digit) through cords or chains. The diameter of the first pulley was to be equal to the diameter of the variable teeth wheel with which it connected: but the diameter of the ninth pulley was to be nine times the diameter of its variable-toothed wheel. When the pulley was rotated just once, the variable-toothed wheel to which it was connected would therefore rotate nine times; when the first pulley was rotated once, its variable-toothed wheel would rotate just once. Diameters for intermediate pulleys would be chosen appropriately to bear the ratios 1:2, 1:3, 1:4, and so on, to the variable-toothed wheel diameter.

Multiplication with this advice would have to be done one multiplier digit at a time. The number to be multiplied (multiplicand) would first be set up by arranging for the appropriate number of teeth to protrude from the appropriate variable-toothed wheels. Then the correct pulley to represent the units digit of the multiplier would be selected, and the system cranked once. The whole multiplier (i.e. variable-toothed wheels and pulley system) would then be moved up an order, as it were, and counts of ten (rather than units) would be added, by a further turn of the crank, once the pulley appropriate to the tens digit had been selected. Further physical shifts would have to be performed for successive orders of ten in the multiplier.

Figure 3.5 Leibniz plan of 1685

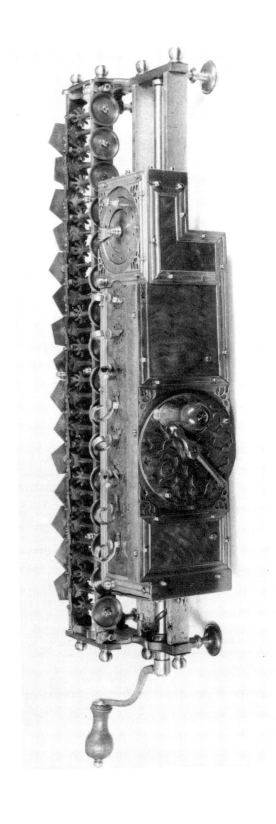

Leibniz' Calculator, now housed in Hanover State Library, W. Germany. Late seventeenth century

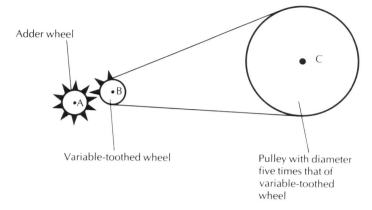

Figure 3.6 Leibniz' Plan of 1685: five × three multiplier

One rotation of C rotates B five times; and each time, the three teeth of the variable-toothed wheel B rotate the adder wheel A by three-tenths of a revolution.

number to be put into the adder repetitively. For example, if 3 is to be multiplied by a number N, Pascal's units wheel needs to be rotated three-tenths of a revolution N times. Leibniz' 1685 solution was to bring into play two devices, one a gearwheel with teeth, the number of which could be varied, the other a system of pulley wheels of graded sizes (see figure 3.5). Multiplication itself was effected by the pulleys, which connected two wheels together with a cord round their unequally sized rims (see figure 3.6). The other principle involved is that of the variable-toothed wheel. Each time these wheels rotated once, the multiplicand would be added into the adder; the pulley system ensured that they rotated the right number of times – that is, the number of the multiplier.

Division could not be performed completely automatically by this machine, but Leibniz describes with great enthusiasm how its powers of multiplication and subtraction might, nevertheless, be used to simplify 'that intricate labyrinth of the common division which is in the case of large numbers the most tedious [procedure] and [the one] most abundant in errors that can be conceived'.[11]

The variable-toothed wheel reappeared much later and very successfully under a different name – the 'Odhner Wheel' – and is not often traced back to Leibniz' 1685 paper.[12] Instead, Leibniz' name is usually associated (as far as calculator technology is concerned) with what is perhaps best referred to as the 'stepped cylinder' (see figure 3.8).

The cylinder bears on its surface nine ridges, parallel to its axis, the first extending almost the length of the cylinder, the one next to it extending not quite as far, and so on until the ninth, corresponding to the number nine, which extends a short distance only. A toothed wheel is arranged to mesh

Stepped cylinders in Leibniz' Hanover calculator

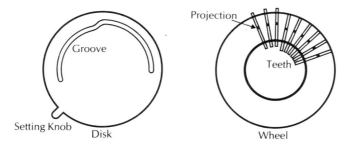

Figure 3.7 Odhner Wheel

Source: F. J. Murray, *The Theory of Mathematical Machines* (Columbia UP, New York, 1961), p. 14

with the ridges of the cylinder, the number of ridges it meshes with depending on the precise point on the cylinder's axis at which it has been located. When the cylinder revolves, therefore, the toothed wheel rotates too, and the degree to which it does so is determined by the number of ridges on the cylinder that its teeth engage. Since this number is itself determined by how far along the cylinder's axle the toothed wheel is fixed, its degree of rotation can be keyed to any number from zero to nine. This is the device that is most commonly known as the 'Leibniz Wheel', though

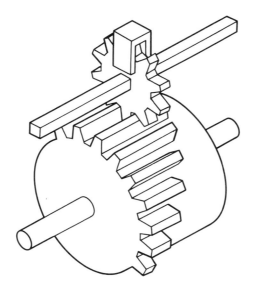

Figure 3.8 Stepped Cylinder

Source: Murray, *Mathematical Machines*, (see Fig 3.7) p. 14

since it is based on a cylinder rather than a wheel, and since Leibniz also invented another 'wheel', this usage can be misleading!

The device proved a good one and was at the heart of the first commercially successful reckoning machine, the Thomas Arithmometer.[13] It also figures in the original Leibniz machines that have come down to us. Several stepped cylinders are ranged in parallel, one for each digit, and they are used to feed numbers into a Pascal box which functions as the adder, as in the 1685 plan.

Motivation and Impact

I have said that these machines were assembled in a context in which there was much concern to make the application of mathematics in a wide variety of different practical fields easier and more efficient. It would be wrong to suggest, however, that their invention was prompted by sharply focused practical needs, or seized upon for practical exploitation the moment they were announced. Leibniz, certainly a man of affairs, and writing nearer the end of the seventeenth century than the other inventors, saw the practical potential in very well-defined terms. Not only, he says, will the mechanical calculator facilitate the construction of all manner of scientifically useful tables; it will also (conferring what he recognizes as the ultimate accolade) be of immediate commercial utility to 'managers of financial affairs, the administration of others' estates, merchants, surveyors, geographers, navigators, astronomers, and [those connected with] any of the crafts that use mathematics.'[14]

But as for the earlier inventors, Schickard and Pascal, though they made gestures towards practicality (as do those modern commentators who suggest, for example, that Pascal's motivation was to construct an aid for his tax-collector father),[15] it is clear that the pleasure they and their contemporaries found in their achievements had more to do with the fascination exerted in seventeenth century minds by mechanical contrivances. 'Surely,' writes Schickard to Kepler of his machine, 'you will beam when you see how [it] accumulates left carries of tens and hundreds by itself',[16] though unfortunately Kepler was going to have to wait for his treat, because the copy being made for him had been lost (in the fire) and Schickard's mechanic now had higher priorities than to construct a replacement. Pascal reveals that artisans up and down the country were making bowdlerized copies of his machines, which had no hope of working but which nevertheless attracted interest when displayed as 'novelties'.[17] Pepys' comment on another calculator, announced by the prolific inventor Sir Samuel Morland in 1666, was that it was 'very pretty, but not very useful'.[18]

This reminds us that the world in which these machines were conceived and admired was one very much taken with the excitement of 'automata' and mechanical devices of all kinds. We know how much Descartes, for example, was fascinated by the automata he encountered 'in the gardens of our kings', and though these would have been based on water-flow, their sophisticated capacity to simulate spontaneous movement and to generate sounds may well have suggested to him the idea that animals might be nothing but mechanisms.[19] The furnishing of public gardens with devices of this kind shows clearly that Descartes' interest in automata was not at all unusual: and so does the furnishing of several great cities of Europe with cathedral clocks like that at Strasbourg, built in the 1570s, with its revolving globe and calendar, its display of the current planetary movements and lunar phases, and its parade of moving figures striking hours and quarter-hours. These creations clearly dazzled the imaginations of the crowds drawn to them, including those of the early apologists of science, Locke and Boyle, and bear perhaps some real responsibility for the new, enormously influential metaphysics of substance (with its invocation of underlying 'corpuscular mechanisms') that such writers articulated.[20]

The first mechanical calculators, then, take their place in a world in which both mathematical aids and mechanical devices attracted great interest. In both fields they had powerful competition, and their impact was for that reason not at all revolutionary. We have only come to learn of Schickard's device in the last few decades. Interest was certainly expressed in Pascal's machines at the time;[21] but not enough, apparently, for any news of it to reach the very well-informed Leibniz by the time he began to plan a machine of his own around 1670.[22] In fact their fate rather bears out Taylor's bleak judgement on sixteenth- and seventeenth-century mathematical arts and practices in general – that for the most part they ended in 'disappointment and failure'.[23] It is not enough to suggest (as is also suggested to explain Babbage's disappointments in the nineteenth century) that they demanded too much of the engineering techniques of the time. Certainly it remains true that the explosion of interest in mechanisms that dated from the mid-fourteenth century expressed itself to begin with almost exclusively in wood: there was, for example, practically no metal-turning before the end of the eighteenth century,[24] and the non-functioning model[25] that Leibniz brought to London's Royal Society in 1672/3 was made of wood.[26] There is, not surprisingly therefore, evidence that the earliest machines were not at all reliable, and the saga of Leibniz' Sinclairesque announcements of impending success (especially to the Royal Society) before he was really justified in making them testifies to the fact that he was indeed working at the frontiers. Nevertheless, the machine that sits in Hanover still works, and works well, conveying indeed an air of well-engineered sturdiness.

Two factors must be taken in conjunction with any difficulty on the engineering side. The first is the availability of logarithms and the slide rule, which proved more flexible and convenient for most of the purposes Leibniz listed as calling for mechanical assistance. And the second is the turn science and European culture generally made after Leibniz, a great man in so many fields, had been (with some obloquy) buried: a turn away from mathematics,

Strasbourg Cathedral clock, built 1570—4

away from mechanics, towards areas where calculators were less useful, and people less fascinated by them.

Before their eclipse, however, these machines had supported Leibniz in his concept of a mechanical reasoner. I shall now turn to the final part of the structure which gave substance to this idea, beliefs about reasoning itself.

Notes

1 A.P. Usher, *A History of Mechanical Inventions* (Harvard UP, Cambridge, Mass., 1962), pp. 189–191. An invaluable summary account of clock history.

2 Usher, *Mechanical Inventions*, p. 193

3 G. Baillie, quoted by Lyn White, *Medieval Technology and Social Change* (Clarendon, Oxford, 1962), p. 128.

4 Usher, *Mechanical Inventions*, p. 207.

5 Usher, *Mechanical Inventions*, p. 308.

6 Schickard, letter to Kepler, reported in B. von Freytag-Loringhoff, 'Eine Tubinger Rechenmaschine aus dem Jahre 1623', *Heimatkundliche Blatter fur den Kreis Tubingen*, Vol. II, Pt. 3, July 1957, pp. 25–8.

7 By von Freytag-Loringhoff, 'Eine Tubinger Rechenmaschine', pp. 25–8.

8 A clear account of its workings is to be found in R. Taton and J.P. Flad, *Le Calcul Mécanique* (Paris, 1963), pp. 24–8.

9 Jean-Paul Flad, 'L'Horloge à Calcul (1623) de l'Astronome W. Schickard', *Chiffres*, 1 (1958), pp. 143–8.

10 Usher, *Mechanical Inventions*, p. 201.

11 Leibniz, in D.E. Smith (ed.), *A Source Book of Mathematics* (McGraw-Hill, New York, 1929), p. 178.

12 But see R. Mehmke and M. d'Ocagne, 'Calculs Numériques', *Encyclopédie des Sciences Mathématiques Pures et Appliquées*, Edition Française: Tome 1, Vol. 4 (1908), Fascicule 2, p. 250; and F. Cajori, *History of Mathematics* (Macmillan, New York, 1961), p. 485.

13 See below, p. 99.

14 Leibniz, in Smith, *Source Book*, pp. 173–81.

15 See, for example, Herman H. Goldstine, *The Computer from Pascal to von Neumann* (Princeton UP, Princeton, 1972), p. 8.

16 Schickard's letter to Kepler, reproduced in Flad, 'L'Horloge à Calcul'.

17 Blaise Pascal, in Smith, *Source book*, p. 171.

18 Pepys, entry for 14 March 1668, in R. Latham and W. Matthews (eds), *Diary of Samuel Pepys* (Bell & Hyman, London, 1976); Samuel Morland, *A Description of the Use of Two Arithmetic Instruments* (London, 1673).

19 J. Jaynes, 'The Problem of Animate Motion in the Seventeenth Century', *Journal of the History of Ideas*, 31 (1970).

20 See, for example, R.S. Woolhouse, *Locke's Philosophy of Science and Knowledge* (Blackwell, Oxford, 1971), p. 112.

21 Jacques Payen, 'Les Exemplaires Conservés de la Machine de Pascal', *Revue d'Histoire des Sciences*, 16 (1963), pp. 161–78.

22 The chronology of Leibniz' various ideas for machines and actual models is difficult to get clear. See J.E. Hofmann, *Leibniz in Paris, 1672–6* (CUP, Cambridge, 1974), pp. 22ff; but also Leibniz' paper dated 1685 in Smith, *Source Book*, together with Smith's introduction.

23 E.G.R. Taylor, *The Mathematical Practitioners of Tudor and Stuart England* (CUP, Cambridge, 1967), p. 3.

24 Maurice Daumas (ed.), *A History of Technology and Invention* (Murray, London, 1980), Vol. II, p. 80.

25 Some imply that it did function. See Hofmann, *Leibniz in Paris*, p. 23.

26 A.R. and M.B. Hall (eds), *The Correspondence of Henry Oldenburg* (Madison et al., and University of Wisconsin Press, 1965–84), Vol. IX, p. 493.

4 Reasoning and its Rules

Traditional Logic and Reasoning

The Ancient Greeks not only reasoned about the shapes and numbers of things: they also turned their attention on to the processes of reasoning themselves. As far as reasoning about shapes (and lines and volumes) was concerned, for example, Euclid was able to organize what was known into a deductive system, in which the mass of truths was displayed as following in systematic fashion from a small number of elementary axioms. Reasoning about the relations between different categories of things also attracted their interest: the relation, for example, between being a man and being an animal. They tried to articulate the rules which governed validity in arguments which depended on 'category membership' (as we might put it) of this kind, an effort which involved analysing them into components of various kinds, and attempting to say how the components must be related to each other if validity were to be achieved.

Take the following argument as an example:

> Every animal is a living thing,
> and every man is an animal,
> therefore every man is a living thing.

This was analysed into premises and conclusion, each of which was said to consist of two 'terms' (*man, living things*) linked by the expression 'Every … is …' (the dots holding a place for terms). Other expressions that were considered to enter into arguments of the same general type were:

Some … is/are …
('Some animals are four-legged creatures');

No … is/are …
('No man is a four-legged creature');

Some … is/are not …
('Some animals are not men').

Arguments made up of these components, and following the pattern of the one given above, were categorized as 'syllogisms', and the logic that articulates the rules that govern their validity is sometimes known as the 'logic of terms'. It was on this type of argument, apart from those found in geometry and arithmetic, that the Ancient Greeks concentrated, pre-eminently in the person of Aristotle.

At the same time, of course, they actually *used* many more types of argument, types that hung on components not distinguished in the logic of terms. One of these was given particular attention by the Stoics, working about a century after Aristotle. Here is an example:[1]

> Either every man is a living thing or there are animals that are not living things,
> But it is not the case that there are animals that are not living things,
> Therefore every man is a living thing.

Here, the argument is carried by the phrases

> Either ... or,

and

> It is not the case that ...,

and what these phrases relate are not classes of things as in the syllogism (*men, living things*), but statements or propositions. Study of this kind of argument is now known as the 'logic of propositions'. It was developed by logicians around the turn of this century – most notably by Gottlob Frege in his *Begriffsschrift* of 1879, and by Bertrand Russell and A.N. Whitehead in their *Principia Mathematica* of 1910 – as the foundation on which a very general and very powerful logic, the 'predicate logic', might be built. Much earlier, it had attracted the attention of some of the ablest medieval thinkers, particularly Ockham and Buridan, writing in the early fourteenth century. The study of logic was therefore a flourishing (academic) enterprise in the heart of the Middle Ages, and it was conceived of as the attempt to articulate the rules that arguments had to follow if they were to be valid.

Logic and Learning

It is often thought that because observation and experimentation attracted little attention in medieval writings, and reason, including logic, a good deal more, the medievals looked exclusively to reason to help them extend their knowledge of the world. On this basis it is easy to go on to agree with Locke that the logic of the syllogism 'at best, is but the art of fencing with the little knowledge we have, without making any addition to it.[2] It seemed to Locke, as it seems to us, almost incredible that syllogistic reasoning might be looked upon as a means of *discovery*.

It was so looked upon, no doubt, by some of Scholasticism's last defenders; but it is very misleading to think that it was there at the centre. The fact is that discovery, the extension of human knowledge, was not a central concern to the medieval world, and its philosophers gave it scant attention. It is not that Aquinas rejected observation and experimentation and put some other techniques in their place – syllogistic reasoning, for example. It is simply that discovery was so low a priority that thought about it was but weakly articulated.

Aquinas gives the impression, nonetheless, that for him finding out new things, or correcting factual mistakes, is something that can be done by some kind of 'reflection'. He thinks at any rate that 'human reasoning [...] starts from certain truths quite simply understood, namely first principles'[3] – for example, the Euclidean proposition that things that are equal to the same thing are also equal to one another. These principles may be used, on the one hand, to establish further principles, and this I think is Aquinas' conception of the nature of logic and mathematics. On the other hand, it is these basic principles that also form the basis for establishing new facts – for example, for determining whether Ptolemy was right about planetary motion involving epicycles.[4]

Albertus Magnus, 1193–1280

Ptolemy's model of the universe (as presented by Andreae Cellarii in 1666)

The puzzle of how thinkers like Aquinas might have thought of facts concerning the world about us as discoverable without recourse to what we should now call 'experience' is eased if we take seriously two features of their outlook. The first is that while we think in terms of phenomena being governed by 'laws' which it is science's business to establish, the medievals, following Aristotle, thought the behaviour of a thing flowed from whatever 'tendencies' of behaviour were inherent in it. Insofar as people needed to extend their understanding of things, therefore, their aim should have been to identify things' 'tendencies' (which would amount to discovering the things' essential characters).

Then secondly, alongside this, we must bear in mind the account of what it is to 'see' a thing – the hylomorphic account – that was also accepted by these thinkers: seeing was a matter of 'grasping' the form of the thing seen, and involved a relationship so intimate as to amount to a kind of identity. From this perspective, the thing seen is not conceived of as out there in a world distinct from the person seeing it, but as directly accessible; and the difficulty perhaps lies not so much in explaining how knowledge of a thing can be obtained by reflection alone, but in explaining why reflection is ever necessary: for how, when we are sharing the form of a thing, can there be aspects of it of which we are ignorant?[5] It is for this reason that commentators find it difficult to tell in the course of Aquinas' discussion whether he is referring to the acquisition of knowledge, or to seeing.[6]

The most significant point remains, however, that for the bulk of the Middle Ages and for the dominant medieval thinkers, to acquire knowledge was to learn *what others already knew*: and while this was deemed very important, the possibility of extending human knowledge was not. The question of what methods might be effective in pursuing such a possibility therefore went unaddressed. When 'method' in connection with the acquisition of knowledge was spoken of, for example, it was transmission of knowledge in teaching that was meant.

But then, in the fifteenth century, there began to develop a pregnant ambiguity between, on the one hand, the method of teaching, and on the other, the method of finding new things out. Once this new interest claimed general attention, it was possible to look back and see work in which answers had already been articulated, but in dark corners, well away from centre stage. For there were, throughout the Middle Ages, weaker voices, not opposing the neo-Aristotelian orthodoxy but putting a dissenting emphasis on some of its elements, who persisted in the search for new knowledge, and who looked very seriously to observation and even to experiment in their quest. The possibility of checking postulated principles against what might be observed, and indeed of contriving observations specially for this purpose, is seen, for example, by the twelfth-century writer Adelard of Bath, as well as in a much more developed way by Robert Grosseteste, the thirteenth-century thinker who had been described as the founder of the tradition of scientific thought in medieval Oxford.[7]

By the time Bacon issued his clarion call for fact-gathering in 1620, the formal study of reason's rules, logic, had suffered a considerable decline form its apogee under Ockham, Buridan and Burleigh in the early fourteenth century. For one thing, the rise of humanism may have created a distracting interest in other types of writing.[8] But for another, as is clear from the case of mathematics, there developed an anxiety from this point on that academic knowledge and skills should be turned to assist with practical problems – flowing, I think, from the beginnings of the sense that life might be *changed*. As this perspective began to be articulated, the study of validity no longer seemed self-justifying, but worthwhile only in virtue of the help it could be expected to give when it came to the actual deployment of arguments in some field of application. Logic began to be hyphenated with rhetoric.

The first to sound this note with real power was Rudolph Agricola, at the end of the fifteenth century. In the next it was taken up by Petrus Ramus, and he became one of the most influential logicians of the intellectual world into which broke the new significance of discovery. When Bacon's *Novum*

Organum was published in 1620, Ramus' book, first published in 1555, was not by any means the only textbook of logic adopted in the universities of Europe. Pre-Ramist late medieval works were still widely available (especially the *Summulae Logicales* of Peter of Spain); there were works written from the point of view which sought reform of traditional logic in a so-called 'Aristotelian', not a Ramist, direction (represented by the '*Dialectices Philippi Melanchthonis Libri IV*' of 1534); and there were also textbooks which simply drew on these traditions eclectically.[9] Nevertheless, the educational thinking which provided the context within which these works were studied looked to the *application* of logic at the beginning of the seventeenth century in a way that it had not done at the beginning of the fifteenth.

At the beginning of this 'reformist' movement, when Agricola wrote *De Inventione Dialectica*, it was clear in what field logic was deemed to have its

Petrus Ramus, 1515–72

main application: in the teaching of undergraduates. Whatever the discipline, it was held, the application of logical principles would bring system and order, enhancing the efficiency with which matter was both presented and learnt.[10] At a time, that is to say, when 'learning' meant almost exclusively the transmission of knowledge, the usefulness of logic lay in facilitating learning. But 'learning', as I have intimated, was to develop an ambiguity over the next hundred years: it was to come to stand for the discovery of entirely new knowledge as well as for the passing of knowledge from one person or generation to another. The question then became: what part should logic play in acquiring learning of this newer kind – in adding to the stock of human knowledge? This was the issue that confronted – and divided – logic's apologists.

Logic and Discovery

Some were accused of simply ignoring the issue, a charge laid, for example, against Ramus.[11] Others, like the mid-sixteenth century scholar Jacobus Zabarella, looked to traditional logic (the syllogistic, together with such work on the other argument types as had been carried out by the early fourteenth century logicians), and maintained that, if properly applied, this represented the required means of discovery. Radicals constituted a third party, with Bacon in the van, who advocated not something entirely new but something entirely neglected by the then current intellectual establishment: that the route to new knowledge lay in assembling as many facts in a given field as one could, and drawing general truths from these. (This procedure, known as 'induction', had been recognized by Aristotle as centrally important to discovery, and neglected by those for whom discovery was unimportant.)

If the third position was that of the new men of science, the first two represented the positions they were most concerned to oppose: on the one hand the position that discovery could simply be neglected; and on the other, the view that the best means to discovery, granted its importance, was the application of established principles of valid argumentation.

At the same time the substance of the logic that was currently taught in the Schools was not, since the impact of Ramism, the exquisite structure of rigour and precision it had been in the past. It was now seen more as the source of the skills necessary to be victorious – or rather to appear to be victorious – in disputation, and Ramus himself seems to have won much of his popularity by the short cuts he offered to intellectual prestige.[12] It is striking that the pressure towards usefulness that catapulted mathematics into spectacular progress at the same time reduced logic to a shadow of its former glory.

All this means that it would be wrong to suggest that the butt of the criticism deployed by Bacon, Boyle, Locke and others was straightforwardly the pure study of validity as pursued by a long line of medieval logicians,

PETRI HISPANI

SVMMVLAE LOGICALES

C V M

VERSORII PARISIENSIS

C L A R I S S I M A

EXPOSITIONE.

Paruorum item Logicalium eidem Petro Hispano ascriptum opus,
nuper in partes ac capita distinctum

QVAE OMNIA A MARTIANO ROTA

Viro Clariss. infinitis ferè erroribus, summo studio,
ac maxima sunt diligentia castigata.

Duos demum Indices nunc primum excogitatos, quorum alter singulorum
textuum ac capitum, alter verò, eorum, quæ in toto opere scitu
digna habentur, imprimi curauimus.

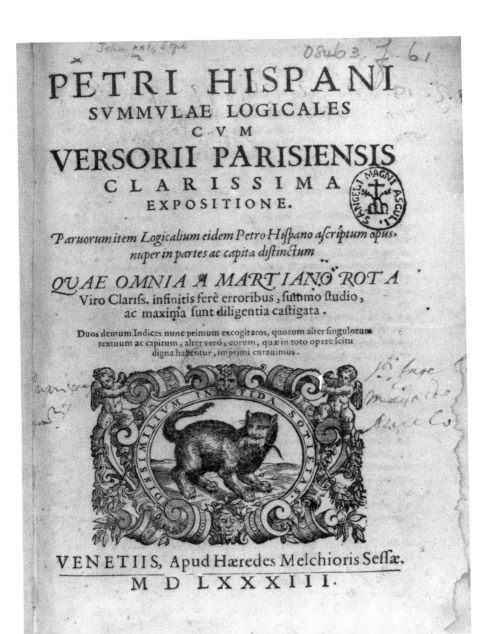

DISSIMILIVM INFIDA SOCIETAS.

VENETIIS, Apud Hæredes Melchioris Sessæ.

M D LXXXIII.

Peter of Spain's *Summae Logicales*, title page. First published late thirteenth century

from Alcuin in the eighth century, through Abelard in the early twelfth, John of Salisbury in the later twelfth, William of Shyreswood in the thirteenth, to Ockham, Buridan and Burleigh in the fourteenth. They were commenting primarily on the role of logic in the newly important programme of discovery; and in any case the 'logic' they had been taught, and saw being taught, was not the logic that had been.

Notes

1 A.N. Prior, *Formal Logic* (Clarendon, Oxford, 1962), p. 3.
2 Locke, *Human Understanding*, IV, 17, vi.
3 Thomas Aquinas, *Summa Theologiae*, IA 79, 8.
4 Aquinas, *Theologiae*, IA, 32, 1, ad 2.
5 F.C. Copleston, *Aquinas* (Penguin, Harmondsworth, 1955); P.T.Geach 'Aquinas', in Elizabeth Anscombe and Peter Geach, *Three Philosophers* (OUP, Oxford, 1961); Kenny, *Anatomy of the Soul*, pp. 62–80.
6 Kenny, *Anatomy of the Soul*, pp. 62–80.
7 A.C.Crombie, *Augustine to Galileo* (Heinemann, London, 1970), p. 27.
8 E.J. Ashworth, *Language and Logic in the Post-Medieval Period* (Reidel, Dordrecht, 1974), pp. 21, 22.
9 Ashworth, *Language and Logic*, ch. 1.
10 Lisa Jardine, *Francis Bacon* (CUP, Cambridge, 1974), p. 5; W.S. Howell, *Eighteenth Century British Logic and Rhetoric* (Princeton UP, Princeton, 1971), p. 19.
11 Jardine, *Bacon*, p. 53.
12 Ashworth, *Language and Logic*, p. 16.

5 Leibniz: Mechanizing Reason

When we encounter the attacks of Moderns like Locke on 'logic', one thing we must bear in mind, therefore, is that they were attacking a view about the utility of logic in the process of discovery. But there is another point too. They were operating with a conception of reason that was different from the one assumed in the medieval period.

If thinking, for Locke,[1] was watching ideas parade before the mind, reasoning was spotting any connections that might exist between them.[2] For Leibniz, it was specifically the identification of identities among ideas.[3] For Hobbes, another pioneer, it was reckoning: 'adding and subtracting, of the consequences of general names agreed upon for the marking and signifying of our thoughts'.[4] In other words, reason was not exempt, as of course it could not be, from the conceptual upheaval that affected every other central concept when, in the seventeenth century, the long hegemony of Aristotle in Europe came to its end.[5]

It is important to see that this new conception of reason does nothing to force one to the conclusion that logic is useless for this purpose or that. Certainly Locke thought it was useless for the purpose of extending our knowledge of things, and rather left it to be understood that it was good for nothing else either:

> I am apt to think that he who shall employ all the force of his reason only in brandishing of syllogisms will discover very little of that mass of knowledge which lies yet concealed in the secret recesses of nature, and which, I am apt to think, native rustic reason (as it formerly has done) is likelier to open a way to and add to the common stock of mankind, rather than any scholastic proceeding by the strict rules of mode and figure.[6]

On the other hand, at least for some purposes, Leibniz thought it of great utility. What is there more useful, he asked, than the project of bringing clarity and system to the all-important processes of reason, which is logic's true business:

> if praise is given to the men who have determined the number of regular bodies – which is of no use, except insofar as it is pleasant to contemplate...

how much better will it be to bring under mathematical laws human reasoning, which is the most excellent and useful thing we have. Logicians are not to be blamed because they have pursued these tasks, but because they have wearied boys with them.[7]

Leibniz' recommendation was that, far from being disparaged, logic as the systematization of reasoning should be mastered – and, indeed, once mastered, mechanized. Perhaps because he was more familiar with mathematics than Locke was, Leibniz saw glimpses of a profound continuity between mathematics, with its already proven track record, and the logic that Locke so despised.

These different emphases on the significance of logic are associated with differences over the role of reason, particularly its role in discovery. But we must not miss the reconceptualization of reason that forms the common ground. Reason, for Aquinas, was the power that enabled the intellect to move 'from one thing understood to another'.[8] But for the Moderns it is an instrument for the inspection of representations, to use Leibnizian terminology; or, in Lockean terminology, of ideas; or, for the nominalist Hobbes, of words.

All three of these concepts of reason are concerned with representation in our terms, for along with the new ways of thinking about reason, and about thinking itself, there came also a new way of thinking about words. The sixteenth century had already done much to undermine the medieval view of language 'as a thing inscribed in the fabric of the world'[9] in which words were united to things by the relationship of resemblance. But with the seventeenth century comes the seminal separation of language from the world which Foucault holds responsible for that 'immense reorganization of culture' which separates us from the medieval world,[10] and in which we are still caught.

Words, says Locke in 1690, are 'the signs of internal conceptions', 'marks for the ideas within [man's] own mind.'[11] thus, words were themselves seen now as representations, representing ideas, and it was in virtue of their standing for ideas that words had meaning. Alike in being representations, in many ways words and ideas were treated as equivalent to each other. 'The language of the Classical age,' as Foucault puts it, 'is caught in the grid of thought, woven into the very fabric it is unrolling. It is not an exterior effect of thought, but thought itself.'[12] Thus when Hobbes surmises that reasoning might be 'simply the joining together and linking of names or labels',[13] the essential conception of reason as concerned not with things but with representations he shares with Locke.

This, then, was the framework that supported Leibniz' thoughts about a reasoning machine. For one thing, there was the mechanical calculator, presenting a challenge to contemporary engineering technique, but one that Leibniz had himself demonstrated could be met. But much more significant, the spectacular rise of mathematics had set up a new paradigm for activities of other kinds. There was now an understanding not only of reasoning, but of seeing and feeling as well, which saw them as operations on representations. All that was necessary was to find mechanical expressions of the various representations involved; and, just as mechanical representations of numbers yielded the mechanical calculator, so might be conceived (as Hobbes, for example, was not afraid to conjecture) machines capable of emotion and even sensation – but also, more soberly to our thinking, of reason.

Leibniz' Account of Concepts

In working on the feasibility of mechanical reasoning Leibniz contributed to the new framework of ideas. In particular, he developed a representative account of 'concepts'.

Hobbes had suggested that it was possible for one representation to relate to another in the way that one part of a package relates to the package as a whole. Then: 'When a man reasoneth, he does nothing else but conceive a sum total, from addition of parcels; or conceive of a remainder, from subtraction of one sum from another'.[14] This was the picture that Leibniz elaborated.[15] When we say something true, in Leibniz' view, we are very often simply bringing out what is already there in the representation of the subject we are talking about. In terms of one of his own examples, when we say that 'man is an animal', we are, he thinks, doing no more than bringing out the fact that the representation *animal* is contained in the representation *man*.

Because it contains component representations in this way, Leibniz calls *man* a complex representation. He thinks *animal* complex in this sense too, since it contains the representation *living thing*; and also that, in its turn, the representation *living thing* contains component representations as well. But ultimately he thinks such regresses come to an end and we encounter representations which are simple: while they may be contained in representations, they themselves contain none. He called these unanalysable representations 'first terms', and his suggestion was that a complete list of them would represent a kind of alphabet out of which all other concepts were constructed.

An Ideal Language

The fact that a certain representation is contained in a certain other, Leibniz claimed, is usually obscured by ordinary language: it is not obvious from the words used, for example, that *man* contains *animal*. He argued that thinking, as well as communication across languages, would be very much aided if this situation were rectified. In this sentiment, Leibniz was registering a familiar preoccupation of his period. Once it had become established that thinking was a matter of the inner eye inspecting representations, language, which represented those representations to the thinker, and to those he or she wished to communicate with, took the guise of a glass that could distort the objects viewed through it. If you believed, like Leibniz, that thoughts had to reflect the natures of things if they were to be sound, you might put this by saying that a perfect language would be one that reflected accurately the structure of the thoughts it was used to express. John Wilkins and George Delgarno, both working in the mid-seventeenth century, were two of the many who took up the challenge of devising such a language, and reached the point of publishing proposals.[16]

Leibniz' contribution was to look towards a 'universal polygraphy' in which a complex representation was symbolized by stringing together the signs that severally stood for the various component simple representations it contained. In this way, to anyone who was familiar with the signs of the simple representations, the correct analysis of every complex representation would be immediately apparent. Leibniz also recommended that the signs for the simples be designed, to the extent that this was feasible, so as to picture what they represented, rather in the manner of the Chinese ideographs. Though there would therefore be choice – and indeed scope for ingenuity – in determining the signs for the 'first terms', the 'words' in Leibniz' 'characteristica universalis' for all other representations would simply follow from these basic terms.

Such a system of writing Leibniz set about devising in his *De Arte Combinatoria*, apparently taking some inspiration from the colourful thirteenth century visionary Raymond Lull,[17] and concentrating on the symbolization of geometrical notions. It would, he thought, if well-conceived, address the imperfections of ordinary languages by bypassing them, since it would be 'intelligible to anyone who reads it, whatever language he knows'. Thus would it meet the aspirations of those who sought 'a universal writing'.[18]

New Perspective on Knowledge

Leibniz thought, as I have explained, that a perfect system of writing would present to the reader the correct analysis into component simple representations of each of the complex representations it expressed. That way, thoughts would be represented without distortion. But what of the accuracy of the representing done by thoughts themselves?

Leibniz continued to speak, as many of the new thinkers continued to speak, in terms of kinds of stuff and things having 'essences', and his assumption was that it was these essences that must be accurately reflected in their representations. It was part of, or at least flowed from, the essence or nature of gold, for example, that it should dissolve in some acids but not in others, just as it flowed from a creature's being a horse that it should have four legs.

There are many cases, Leibniz thought, in which it was by no means obvious what a thing's or a substance's nature was; and then induction – involving what we now call empirical research – was called for in order to

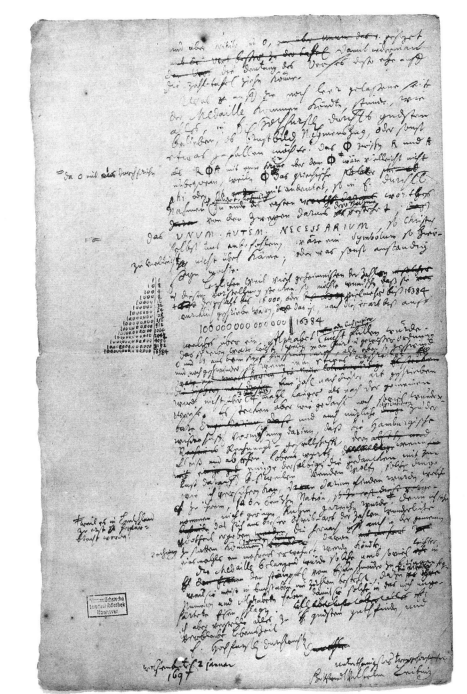

Part of a letter sent by Leibniz to the Duke of Braunschweig-Wolfenbüttel describing the development of the dual system

advance knowledge on this score. Particular historical truths (for instance, 'Augustus was emperor of Rome') are one kind of example, and there are also truths which he thinks can only be arrived at by observation (he gives the example, 'All European adults have a knowledge of God'.[19]

Once our knowledge of things' essential natures was complete we would be in a position to allocate to each its correct representation: that is, one consisting of just those simple representations which corresponded to what our research had discovered or confirmed to be the several essential qualities of the thing. That indeed would bring the scientific enterprise to fulfillment: not only would our knowledge be complete, but it would be laid out with maximum clarity in language.

Leibniz' Work in Logic

Leibniz thought that it was the way in which some representations contained others that made reasoning possible. He held that the proposition 'Every animal is a living thing', for example, expressed the fact that the representation or 'concept' *animal* included the concept *living thing*. Likewise, 'Every man is a living thing' is to be understood, he thought, as saying that the concept *man* includes the concept *living thing*. Thus he thinks we may rewrite

> Every animal is a living thing,
> and every man is an animal,
> therefore every man is a living thing

as

> *Animal* includes *living thing*,
> and *man* includes *animal*,
> therefore *man* includes *living thing*.

Analysed in this way, this syllogism is valid in virtue of a property of the 'inclusion' relation, namely that if one thing includes a second, and a third includes the first, then the third also includes the second; or as Leibniz put it, 'An includer of an includer is an includer of what is included'.[20]

Leibniz held that the remaining forms of judgement that entered into the types of argument treated by the traditional syllogistic – which was the framework his thought in logic both encountered and retained – likewise amounted to assertions about concepts 'including' and 'not including' (or 'excluding') each other; thus 'No just man is unhappy' was considered to amount to 'The just man excludes the unhappy man'.[21]

He does not leave 'inclusion' to be understood intuitively. He defines it in terms of sameness or 'coincidence', itself defined by saying that 'those terms are "the same" of which one can be substituted for the other without loss of truth'.[22]

The inclusion relation, or 'being contained in', is then given like this:

> If several terms taken together coincide with one, any one of those several terms is said to 'be in' or to 'be contained in' that one term, and the one term itself is said to be the 'container'.[23]

Thus Leibniz believes that arguing rests ultimately on statements of identity:

> The primary truths of reason are those which I call by the general name of identical because it appears that they do nothing but repeat the same thing, without teaching us anything.[24]

By giving precise definitions of his terms and by exploring the ways which various syllogisms can be deduced from others, Leibniz is clearly attempting to set out logic as a system. Take, for example the following syllogisms:

> I   No A is a B,
> but every C is a B,
> therefore no C is an A

and

> II   No B is an A,
> but every C is a B,
> therefore no C is an A.

These differ only in the first premise, so that if these premises were equivalent, we could deduce the validity of one of the arguments from the validity of the other. The principle that asserts the equivalence between the two premises here – that if no A is a B, then no B is an A – was called by the medieval logicians 'simple conversion'. What we have, therefore, is an example of one syllogism being deducible from another, given the validity of an additional rule.

Writing

> 'Eab' for 'No... is a ...',

and

> 'Acb' for 'Every... is a ...'

we can say:

> Eab, Acb   →   Eca
> Eab   →   Eba   (simple conversion)
> Eba, Acb   →   Eca

Many relationships like this obtain between the syllogisms, and logicians, ever since a beginning on syllogistic logic was made, have been drawn to the project of systematizing them – most satisfyingly done, perhaps, by identifying a small number of syllogisms and auxiliary rules and showing that the validity of all the rest follows from the validity of these only. This is the project known as the 'axiomatization' of syllogistic logic.

The first object of axiomatization was of course not syllogistic reasoning but reasoning about shapes and volumes. The Ancient Egyptians, we know, discovered formulae which enabled them to calculate geometrical functions that were of practical importance to them, like the volume of a truncated pyramid. But the Ancient Greeks were the first to show how these truths of geometry could be organized into a deductive system. Thus it was Euclid's *Elements* that demonstrated that all the then established geometrical truths could be deduced from a very small number of propositions, including some rules of inference, whose truth appears intuitively obvious.

One of the contributions Leibniz made to the development of logic was to take the axiomatization of the syllogistic further. Aristotle had taken one possible axiomatization almost to completion, but what Leibniz did was not so much take up the system as Aristotle had left it, but devise new methods which pointed towards a more economical system than Aristotle's. (Combining both approaches, modern logicians have shown that it is possible to base the whole of syllogistic logic on just four axioms, plus some principles from the propositional logic.)[25]

Seen in conjunction with his project to push to a conclusion research into the nature of things and of the stuffs of which they are made, Leibniz' logical endeavours can be regarded as preparing the way for what amounted to the axiomatization of science as a whole. He wanted to do for things in general what Euclid had done for volumes and shapes.

But we cannot assume that by 'science' Leibniz meant quite what we mean by the term. It was for him, for one thing, an enterprise that was capable of being completed within a few decades, if only people would organize themselves properly. With this in mind, for example, he launched several initiatives aimed at bringing the work of learned societies into co-operation, laying plans also for compiling the knowledge assembled into a comprehensive encyclopaedia. This is not how we think of science today. If we are forced to consider whether it might one day be complete, we are likely to concede the possibility only at the expense of pushing the completion date well into the indefinite future.

The fact is that for Leibniz – and his contemporaries, for Descartes and Bacon, for example, likewise looked towards science as a finite project – science was directed at the analysis of the nature of things and the stuffs of which things were made. He accepted that complete analysis was beyond human powers, and that science would be forever imperfect on that account. But for that degree of analysis that did fall within human powers the task of completion was finite, and when done, there would be nothing left for

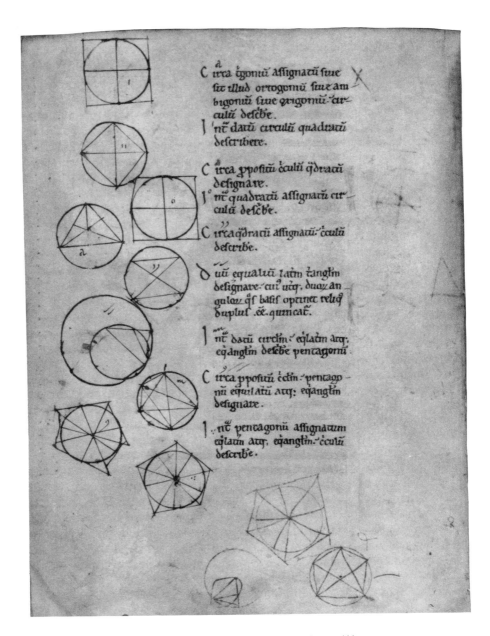

Circa trigonū assignatū siue
sit illud ortogoniū siue am-
bigoniū siue oxigoniū circulū descbe.

Int datū circulū quadratū
describere.

Circa ppositū oculū qdratū
designare.

Int quadratū assignatū circulū descbe.

Circa qdratū assignatū oculū
describe.

duū equaliū latim tanglm
designare cui utq̄ duor an-
gulor qs basis optinet reliq̄
duplus ee qurncat.

Int datū circlm eqlatm atq̄
eqanglm descbe pentagoniū.

Circa ppositū eclm pentagoniū equilatū atq̄ eqanglm
designare.

Int pentagoniū assignatum
eqlatm atq̄ eqanglm oculū
describe.

From the translation of Euclid by Adelard of Bath, early twelfth century

science to undertake; except (if one considered that this fell within the purview of science itself) to design the concepts of the perfect language that would then be possible, so that each representation reflected accurately the qualities of which research had shown its subject to be made up. As Foucault puts it in his inimitable way, 'The limit of knowledge would be the perfect transparency of representations to the signs by which they are ordered.'[26]

Once science had completed its task, all the knowledge available to human beings would be stored, not only in the encyclopaedia, but in language. And by that time too, if Leibniz' ambition was to be fulfilled, the setting out of logic as a deductive system would likewise be complete. Leibniz' advice to disputants locked in what had hitherto been protracted and irresoluble controversy – that they should take up their pens and 'calculate' – would at this point become appropriate. For suppose that we are agreed on certain facts but disagree on whether such and such a putative conclusion follows from those facts. If we call the body of agreed facts 'p' and the proposition under contention 'q', then we can say that our difference is over whether p entails q. But in a deductive system there is another way of putting this, namely: can 'p entails q' be proved within the system?

Leibniz said little that was explicit on this score. The line of thought sketched here, including the imputation to Leibniz of the thesis that in the logical system towards which he was working there would be a definite procedure for checking out whether any given proposition was provable or not, must be conjectural. So too must be the question of how such quasi-mechanical procedures were to be converted into the real thing, into mechanisms of wood and metal. In spite of Hobbes' characterization of reasoning as nothing but addition and subtraction, the operation of anything along these lines invented by Leibniz would presumably have had the recognition of identities as its basis.

What we can say at any rate is that these two fundamental theoretical orientations of Leibniz' (logic viewed as a deductive system on the one hand, and concepts viewed as lists of properties on the other), together with the proven feasibility of mechanical calculators, created framework enough for the idea of a mechanical reasoner to be conceivable, even though it amounted for Leibniz to little more than a gleam in the eye.

Notes

1 See above, pp. 1, 15–18.
2 Locke, *Human Understanding*, IV, ch. XVII.
3 See, for example, Leibniz, 'A Mathematics of Reason', in Parkinson, *Logical Papers*; Gerhardt, *Die Philosophischen Schriften*, vi, p. 413.
4 Hobbes, *Leviathan* (London, 1651), ch. 5. On the new notion of reason see A. MacIntyre, *After Virtue* (Duckworth, London, 1981), pp. 51–52.
5 In 1632, according to John Laird, *Hobbes* (Russell & Russell, New York, 1968), p. 90.

6 Locke, *Human Understanding*, IV, ch. XVII, paragraph 6.

7 Leibniz, 'Of the Mathematical Determination of Syllogistic Forms', in Parkinson, *Logical Papers*, p. 105

8 Aquinas, *Summa Theologiae*, IA 79, 8.

9 Michel Foucault, *The Order of Things* (Tavistock, London, 1970), p. 43.

10 Foucault, *Order of Things*, p. 43.

11 Locke, *Human Understanding*, III, 1, ii.

12 Foucault, *Order of Things*, p. 78. Logicians encountered the need to distinguish between talking about a word (as in "*Homo*" is a noun) and using the word in the ordinary way. (We speak today of the 'use/mention distinction'.) But the branch of logic, the '*proprietates terminorum*', which attempted to clarify this and related distinctions, came to very little, though it attracted considerable interest in its day (the twelfth century). See W. and M. Kneale, *Development of Logic*, pp. 273, 274.

There is another context in which we might expect logicians to have been forced into taking a position on the relation between words and the world, and that is when they confronted, as from earliest times they did, the 'problem of universals'. But though we might put it in terms of how certain kinds of word relate to the world, this was not how it was put in the Ancient world, if only because the Ancient Greeks had no conceptual resources with which to make the required distinction (*Development of Logic*, pp. 26, 27). Nor was it put in this way by the medievals, for whom 'terms' were not simply words (*Development of Logic*, p. 266).

13 Descartes, 'Objections and Replies', Third Set of Objections and Replies, Fourth Objection (by Hobbes), in *Philosophical Writings*, trans. Cottingham, p. 125.

14 Hobbes, *Leviathan*, ch. 5.

15 For example, In 'Of the Art of Combination', in Parkinson, *Logical Papers*, ch. 1.

16 L. J. Cohen, 'On the Project of a Universal Character', *Mind*, LXIII (1954), pp. 49–63.

17 Martin Gardner, *Logic Machines and Diagrams* (Harvester, Brighton, 1983), ch. 1.

18 Leibniz, 'Of the Art of Combination', in Parkinson *Logical Papers*, p. 10.

19 Leibniz, 'Of the Art of Combination', in Parkinson *Logical Papers*, pp. 5, 6.

20 Leibniz, 'An Intensional Account of Immediate Inference and the Syllogism', in Parkinson, *Logical Papers*, p. 113.

21 Leibniz, 'An Intensional Account', in Parkinson, *Logical Papers*, p. 112; Hidé Ishiguro, *Leibniz's Philosophy of Logic and Language* (Duckworth, London, 1972), pp. 39 ff.

22 Leibniz, 'A Study in the Plus–Minus Calculus', in Parkinson, *Logical Papers*, p. 122.

23 Leibniz, 'Plus–Minus Calculus', in Parkinson, *Logical Papers*, p. 122.

24 Leibniz, *New Essays on the Human Understanding*, trans. A. G. Langley (Macmillan, London, 1896), IV, ch. 2, section 1.

25 Prior, *Formal Logic*, p. 121.

26 Foucault, *Order of Things*, p. 76.

6 The Failure of Leibniz' Project

In one sense Leibniz' plans for reducing argument to a set of uncontroversial procedures and embodying these procedures in a mechanical reasoner are realized in the predicate calculus on the one hand, and in the modern computer programmed to operate the rules of this calculus on the other. But only in a sense. If something like his objectives have been achieved, the strategy he sketched out for achieving them proved entirely unsound.

His conception of the nature of representations is perhaps the easiest to fault from our contemporary perspective. Leibniz' picture of an 'alphabet of thought' providing the basic conceptual atoms out of which all complex representations in language are built, and his account of reasoning as founded on the inclusion relation that may obtain between such entities, is now judged ill-conceived. It oversimplifies, as we understood it, the nature of our concepts, gets wrong the relationship between language and the world, and is mistaken about the basis of reasoning.[1] So the fact that both project and the thinking about language and logic that informed it came to nothing in the decades following their promulgation we may find unsurprising.

Yet there is much to explain. It was not the case that people inspected Leibniz' work and found it wanting, or that variations on his approach were tried which ran into the sand. The fact is that his work, though it sprang from a quick sense of practicality and need, failed to find a real audience for a hundred and fifty years. The obscurity Leibniz himself fell into towards the close of his life, and, in the end, the unregarded passing of one who had moved in the brilliant centre of European life, symbolizes something of a break in the times.[2]

To begin with the concrete, there is the question of why nothing much came, in the decades following his death, of Leibniz' most tangible legacy, his mechanical calculator.

The Calculator – its Powers and Rivals

Leibniz had identified two types of task with which the mechanical calculator should help. On the one hand there were the great variety of everyday calculations that even then came the way of administrators, managers and merchants, as well as geographers, navigators and astronomers. On the other, he foresaw a developing need for the preparation, and revision, of a wide variety of numerical tables, for the everday use of the people just mentioned and others: tables of geometrical functions, of ellipses, parabolas and hyperbolas, as well as of circles, squares, cubes, combinations, variations, and progressions.[3]

Over a century later, Babbage, as we shall see, was urging the enormous utility of his own Difference Engine on grounds that compliment Leibniz' prescience. The tables that Leibniz had thought would be needed (and more) had by Babbage's time been constructed, but at enormous cost in terms of human effort and by means that were grossly vulnerable to human error. Established tables needed correction and development, and new ones were required. Babbage's Engine, once constructed, would have enabled such tasks to be carried through cheaply and without error; and thus have set tabulation on an entirely different footing.

The most telling potential of the machine was its promise to eliminate error, because this was something no amount of non-mechanical ingenuity seemed capable of achieving. For example, near the end of the eighteenth century the new French Republic determined to have an authoritative set of logarithmic and trigonometrical tables prepared, partly with the aim of encouraging the spread of the decimal system.[3] They were to be drawn up 'with such accuracy that they should form a monument of calculation the most vast and imposing that had ever been executed, or even conceived',[5] and a project was set up which involved half a dozen eminent mathematicians at the head of the enterprise, another eight or ten properly qualified mathematicians as middle management, as it were, and nearly a hundred operatives restricted to the performance of simple additions. Each number was calculated by at least two independent 'computers' (as the human adders were called before they became redundant), and then a third party checked that the results were identical. But when it is possible, as it is in such work, for the same mistake to be made by two – or more – independent human calculators, errors are bound to creep in; and when the work is on such a scale (the body of these tables occupied, in manuscript, seventeen folio volumes) the creeping gives way to a brazen march.

The tables drawn up by this project, masterminded by de Prony, were never put to the test of general use, since their publication was abandoned. But, to take a different example, in the first edition of tables published for the use of navigators by the Board of Longitude in 1767, more than a thousand mistakes were identified by a single individual user; and in another set published by the same Board, more than a thousand errors were listed as acknowledged errata (an errata list which, of course, contained errata of its own).[6]

It is clear that simple adders like Pascal's would have had little to contribute to an operation designed along the lines of de Prony's project. Even in a mechanically reliable form, they would have offered no speed advantage (on the contrary) over the mental addition of the human computer, and little extra safeguard against error. It can be no surprise, therefore, that no use appears to have been made of them, either in the monumental exercise mounted by the French Republic, or in the innumerable lesser tabulations that were published between the times of Leibniz and Babbage, especially around the end of the eighteenth century.[7]

It might seem that machines capable of multiplication (directly, not simply by repeated addition), like that of Leibniz himself, would have offered advantages of speed; but in table production, where each successive entry can be calculated by simple addition, it is not clear how a multiplier might assist. What is clear is that they were not used, at any rate at all extensively, and indeed that they were not well known. In his *Memoir* of 1842 (the first published description of Babbage's planned Analytical Engine), the Italian mathematician Menabrea suggests that multipliers might have something to offer tabulation, but is clearly under the impression that all existing machines are incapable of multiplication except by repeated addition.[8]

Just as Leibniz correctly forecast a growing need for mathematical tables, so he was right to think that practical people would increasingly feel the need for help with the calculations their everyday business now entailed. Everyday business of this kind increased dramatically after Leibniz, with the great expansion of production, trade and engineering subsumed under the 'industrial revolution', and with the military action that the colonizing powers of Europe were engaged in from the middle of the eighteenth century. But once again, the mechanical calculator was passed over, this time because alternative aids were preferred: logarithms, in the form of tables on the one hand, and embodied in the bones and the slide rule on the other.

Though the bones made a tremendous impact when introduced in 1617, it was the tables and the rule that came in the longer run to answer the needs of those who needed to calculate. The tables were valued particularly by those

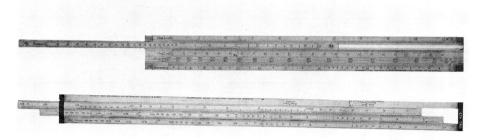

Thomas Dixon's slide rule (top) and Charles Hoare's reversible slide rule (bottom)

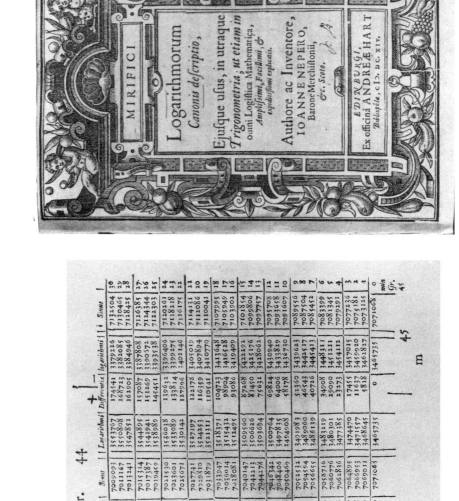

Logarithms from Napier's *Mirifici Logarithmorum*

Title page of Napier's *Mirifici Logarithmorum*

who depended on greater accuracy, and who could have their tables by them (mariners, for example, and astronomers);[9] the slide rule was favoured by those for whom accuracy was less important and handiness more (for example, surveyors and engineers).

These points, then, help explain why the calculator remained pretty well undeveloped during the eighteenth century: it did not quite address the need for efficient and error-free tabulation, and where it might have been useful, other aids were more convenient.

Eighteenth-Century Science

Changes in the overall cast of thought in the generation after Isaac Newton (who died in 1727) are also relevant – to the fate of Leibniz's logical and quasi-logical work as well as to the dearth of interest in his arithmetic machine.

There were shifts within science flowing partly, if pardoxically, from the achievement of Newton himself. Far from inspiring in the new generation a passion for pursuing physics, Newton's successes registered with people as having brought that part of science to a very satisfactory conclusion; and they turned to areas where it appeared that much more work needed to be done.

'Natural history' was the first major beneficiary, with Georges Buffon, Director of the *Jardin du Roi* in Paris, hailed as the 'Pliny and Aristotle of France'.[10] Carolus Linnaeus in Sweden, setting forth the order to be discerned in nature, was regarded as the only greater figure in eighteenth-century science. But neither natural history, nor early chemistry, which also attracted eighteenth-century genius in the shape of Antoine Lavoisier, found much use for mathematics, nor for the mathematical aid represented by the mechanical calculator.[11]

The study of mathematics itself underwent a partial eclipse. In France, the impetus largely continued, with the potential of the calculus being exploited by a number of brilliant contributors (Leonhard Euler, Joseph Lagrange, Pierre Laplace); yet even there, there was a loss of confidence towards the end of the century. In 1781 Lagrange wrote to Jean d'Alembert:

> It appears to me also that the mine [of mathematics] is already very deep and that unless one discovers new veins it will be necessary sooner or later to abandon it [...] it is not impossible that the chairs of geometry [i.e. mathematics] in the Academy will one day become what the chairs of Arabic presently are in the universities.[12]

In post-Newtonian Britain, however, mathematics fell into a miserable decline. Again, Newton is himself usually held particularly responsible, though for a much more down-to-earth reason. A fierce dispute had arisen between intellectuals on either side of the English Channel when Newton and Leibniz (adopted by the French) both claimed priority in the invention

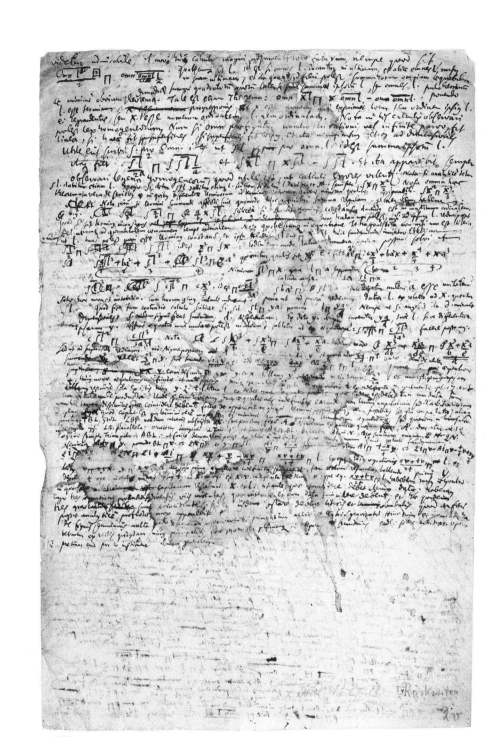

Calculus notations — manuscripts by Leibniz (left) and Newton (right)

terminos $-2azy\dot{y} + 4y^3\dot{y}$ in $y^\mu z^\nu$ in quibus fluxionem ultimam $\ddot{y}$
reperitur, mutoqʒ fluxionem illam in primam $\dot{y}$ Et terminos
$-2azy\dot{y} + 4y^3\dot{y}$ in $y^\mu z^\nu$. Dein colligo horum fluxiones usqʒ ad ultimam
$\dot{y}$ et aufero. Termini $4y^{\mu+3}z^\nu\dot{y}$ fluxiones $4\mu+12y^{\mu+2}z^\nu$
$\dot{y}^2 + 4\nu y^{\mu+3}z^{\nu-1}\dot{y} + 4y^{\mu+3}z^\nu\ddot{y}$ deinde $\overline{4\mu+12}\times\overline{\mu+2} y^{\mu+1}z^\nu\dot{y}^3 +$
$+\overline{\mu+3}\times 8\nu y^{\mu+2}z^{\nu-1}\dot{y}^2 + \overline{\mu+3}\times 12 y^{\mu+2}z^\nu\dot{y}\ddot{y} + \overline{\nu-1}\times 4\nu y^{\mu+3}z^{\nu-2}\dot{y}$
$+8\nu y^{\mu+3}z^{\nu-1}\ddot{y} + 4y^{\mu+3}z^\nu\dddot{y}$. Et hæc posterior fluxio de æquatio-
ne sublata delere debet terminos relativos $4\dot{y}\dot{y}^3 + 36\dot{y}\ddot{y}y^2 +$
$24y\dot{y}^3$ in $y^\mu z^\nu$. Collatis igitur terminis homogeneis animadverto
quod terminus per fluxionem solam $\dot{y}$ multiplicatus evanescere
debet ideoqʒ ejus coefficiens 8ν + ν = 0. Animadverto etiam
etiam quod ex æqualitate terminorum qui per $\dot{y}\ddot{y}$ mul-
tiplicantur prodit coefficientium æquatio $\mu+3\times 12 = 36$ et inde $\mu = 0$. Deleo
igitur ubiqʒ dignitatum exponentes
μ et ν et sic terminis adservatis evadunt $-2azy\dot{y} + 4y^3\dot{y}$.
Horum fluxionis prima sunt $-6ay\dot{y} - 4a\dot{y}^2 - 2azy\ddot{y} - 4ay\ddot{y}$
$+24y\dot{y}^3 + 36\dot{y}\ddot{y}y^2 + 4y^3\ddot{y}$. Secundas Has aufero ex æquatione proposita et r fluxio ablatitia delet
terminos illos relativos et manet æquationis pars
$24z - 6ay^2 - 6ay\dot{y} - 2ay\ddot{y} - azy\ddot{y}$, ac termini adservati fiunt
$-2azy\dot{y} + 4y^3\dot{y}$.

excerpe terminum quemvis in qua fluxio ultima reperitur.
muta fluxionem illam ultimam in primam, multiplica hunc terminum per dignitatem indefinitam y^τ & collige facti fluxionem
illam in qua ipsius y fluxio penultima in primam ducitur.
& Multiplica hunc terminum per dignitatem fictitiam $y^\tau z^{t}$, et
sit $\epsilon z^\sigma y^\tau\dot{y}$ terminus qui producitur. Pone $\overline{\tau+1}\times\epsilon z^\sigma y^{\tau-2}$
$\overline{\tau+1}\times\tau\epsilon z^\sigma y^{\tau-2}\dot{y}^2 = P$ si sæpius y fluxio secunda $\ddot{y}$ est fluxionum ultima vel $3\tau\epsilon z^\sigma y^{\tau-2}\dot{y}\ddot{y} = P$ si fluxio tertia $\dddot{y}$ est fluxionum ultima vel $4\tau\epsilon z^\sigma y^{\tau-2}\dot{y}\dddot{y} = P$ si $\ddddot{y}$ est fluxio ultima
vel $5\tau\epsilon z^\sigma y^{\tau-2}\dot{y}\ddddot{y} = P$ si $\ddddot{y}$ est fluxionum ultima et sic deinceps
et ponendo terminos P æquales homogeneis terminos æquationis per
$y^\tau z^t$ multiplicata, determina dignitatum exponentes ν, et μ.

Postea assumendo datam quamvis d-pone d sit $\sigma-2\times\sigma-1$
$\sigma t d z^{\sigma-2} y^\tau = R$ et $\sigma t d z^{\sigma-1} y^{\tau-1}\dot{y} = S$ si &c vel $\sigma-2\times\sigma-1\times\sigma t d z^{\sigma-3}$
$y^\tau = R$ et $2\overline{\sigma t+\varepsilon\sigma}\times z^{\sigma-2} y^{\tau-1}\dot{y} = S$ si &c vel $\sigma-3\times\sigma-2\times\sigma-1\times$
$\sigma t d z^{\sigma-4} y^\tau = R$ et $3\overline{\sigma t+\varepsilon\sigma}\times z^{\sigma-3} y^{\tau-1}\dot{y} = S$ &c si &c.
Confer etiam terminos vel $\overline{\sigma t+\varepsilon\sigma}\times z^{\sigma-1} y^{\tau-1}\dot{y} = S$. $\overline{\sigma t+3\varepsilon\sigma}\times z^{\sigma-1}$
$y^{\tau-1}\dot{y} = S$. $\overline{\sigma t+3\varepsilon\sigma}\times z^{\sigma-1} y^{\tau-1}\dot{y} = S$. Et $\sigma-1, d z^{\sigma-2} y^\tau = R$
$\sigma-1,$

of the infinitesimal calculus. British and French mathematicians for decades afterwards would have nothing to do with each other, because of nationalistic feeling. And because the Leibnizian symbolism was much more convenient to think with, it was the French who made all the progress: in neglecting British work they missed very little, while the British, in neglecting French work, missed a great deal.[13]

Whether it is right to blame this effect simply on jingoistic sentiment is questionable, especially since the first bridge between French and British mathematics after the divide was built in circumstances of heightened national feeling – while the two countries were actually at war.[14] It may be more relevant to note that the calibre of thinker attracted to mathematics in Britain during the period of its isolation was in fact not high. When powerful thinkers again began to take an interest in the field, as they did with the beginning of the nineteenth century, jingoism was not allowed to stop either the Leibnizian reform of the calculus notation in particular (effected by Babbage), or the free communication of ideas in general.

Whatever the causes, when Babbage went up to Cambridge in 1810 he found mathematics there in a very sorry state. It figured prominently, and controversially, on the syllabus, but exclusively as a mental exercise in the education of professional men. On its own account it was being pursued hardly at all, and a contemporary of Babbage, looking back over the last seventy years of the eighteenth century, could see no notable British contributions to mathematics whatsoever.[15]

If there were shifts within science during the eighteenth century, there were also shifts in the relationship between science and other affairs. In the early days of London's Royal Society, for example, the pursuit of science was very closely linked to practical problems. But with the development of the new production methods – machinery driven by coal-fired steam engines in factories located in towns – which marked the growing industrial revolution, this Baconian connection was lost. All the early seminal inventions, starting with the steam engine itself, were made by practical people without benefit of science. 'We know not who gave currency to the phrase of the invention of the steam engine being one of the noblest gifts that science ever made to mankind,' writes Robert Meikleham in 1824. 'The fact is that science, or scientific men, never had anything to do with the matter.'[16]

Indeed, if science had been of practical importance in early industrial development, the revolution would have begun in France, where not just mathematics but science and scientific education were so much stronger than in Britain.[17] In Britain, the decline in practical significance of science was reflected in the character of the once illustrious Royal Society, which after a succession of Presidents of impeccable scientific credentials settled for one Martin Folkes in 1741, and launched upon a period in which its affairs were run (badly) by people for whom science was an amusement and not an intellectual summons.

Later, it is true, after the first flush of industrialization, a Baconian stress on the practical importance of science returned. In Britain, about the end of the eighteenth century, a series of specialized scientific societies were formed to bypass the obstruction that the Royal Society had come to represent; a movement concerned with the scientific education of skilled workpeople set up a network of 'mechanics' institutes' up and down the country; the new University of London gave mathematics, physics and chemistry important places in the curriculum; and scientific concerns began to stir in Oxford and Cambridge.[18] In France, a similar consciousness resulted in the foundation of the *Ecole Polytechnique* in 1794 and the *Ecole Centrale des Arts et Manufactures* in 1829.[19] In short, the critics' case (prosecuted as vigorously by Babbage as by anyone else) that continued progress in industry depended on a scientifically informed technology began to be heeded. But such a flurry of foundations and reforms makes the point very clearly that for the bulk of the century, science and industry had gone their separate ways.

The brilliant hopes of Leibniz, for his calculator, which sunk in obscurity, and indeed for science, which failed to yield the universal knowledge and rationality he thought lay within its power, thus came to very little – at least within the time scale of decades he anticipated for their success. His contributions to logic and philosophy fared no better, the great majority of his papers remaining unread and unpublished until the nineteenth century. But then came a renewal of interest in mathematics, or perhaps rather a shift in the focus of interest of mathematicians: there developed a concern with mathematics as a structure, and a concern that that structure should be well founded. Leibniz' work became relevant once more, and projects not unrelated to his own seemed reasonable again.

Notes

1 A recent collection of Liebniz criticism is R. S. Woodhouse, *Leibniz: Metaphysics and Philosophy of Science* (OUP, Oxford, 1981).
2 E. J. Aiton, *Leibniz, A Biography* (Adam Hilger Ltd., Bristol, 1985).
3 Leibniz, in Smith, *Source Book*, pp. 180, 181.
4 L. F. Menabrea, 'Sketch of the Analytical Engine invented by Charles Babbage', in P. and E. Morrison (eds), *Charles Babbage and his Calculating Engines* (Dover, New York, 1961), p. 227.
5 Dionysius Lardner, in P. and E. Morrison, *Calculating Engines*, p. 174.
6 Lardner, in P. and E. Morrison, *Calculating Engines*, p. 176.
7 In part listed by Lardner, in P. and E. Morrison, *Calculating Engines*, pp. 167–73.
8 Menabrea, 'Sketch', P. and E. Morrison, *Calculating Engines*, pp. 225, 226.
9 And those involved in business: Webster, *Great Instauration* p. 414.
10 Quoted in J. Lyon and P.R. Sloan (eds), *From Natural History to the History of Nature* (University of Notre Dame Press, Notre Dame, 1981), p. 8.
11 R. E. Schofield, *Mechanism and Materialism* (Princeton UP, Princeton, 1970) p. 94; see also A. O. Lovejoy, *Essays in the History of Ideas* (John Hopkins Press, Baltimore, 1948), pp. 235–7.

12 Lagrange, quoted in Kline, *Mathematical Thought*, p. 623.
13 J. M. Dubbey, *The Mathematical Work of Charles Babbage* (CUP, Cambridge, 1978), pp. 11, 12; Kline, *Mathematical Thought*, p. 622.
14 Dubbey, *Mathematical Work of Babbage*, p. 12.
15 Dubbey, *Mathematical Work of Babbage*, p. 11; D. S. L. Cardwell, *The Organization of Science in England* (Heinemann, London, 1972), p. 20.
16 Quoted by A. Wolf, *A History of Science, Technology and Philosophy in the Eighteenth Century* (Allen & Unwin, London, 1938), p. 611.
17 Cardwell, *Organization of Science*, pp. 25ff.
18 Cardwell, *Organization of Science*, ch. 3.
19 Cardwell, *Organization of Science*, pp. 26, 27.

Part II

Babbage's Project

7 Towards the Analytical Engine

In the 1830s, Babbage conceived of building a machine with the power 'to combine together general symbols in successions of unlimited variety and extent.[1] It was to be first a calculator, with powers that encompassed the whole of arithmetic; but beyond that, it was to be the embodiment of a newly reconstituted algebra, now conceived of as 'the science of general reasoning.'[2] Thus was the Leibnizian theme reintroduced, when the eighteenth century divertissment was done.

Algebra Refined

As I explained earlier,[3] algebra of a kind was practised prior to the seventeenth century, largely outside the universities by consultants hired to help with commercial problems to do with rates of exchange, interest and the like. The expert would select from among his formulae the one appropriate for the problem in hand, substitute the numbers provided by the client for the letters which held a place for them in the formula, and apply arithmetic rules to determine the value for which the letter for the 'unknown' stood.

In the sixteenth century, Vieta introduced letters for coefficients too, and in doing so introduced into algebra the idea of a letter representing indifferently any of an entire category of numbers. I have noted already that this innovation resulted in the Ancient and medieval referential conception of number giving way to the idea of a number as in some sense a symbol. But there were other effects. By putting letters for coefficients in equations, Vieta focused attention on a new level of generality. In the old style, putting letters for numbers in equations brought out the fact that different problems might share the same form: that is, they might be solved by the application of the same formula, with different substitutions for the letters. But by putting letters also for coefficients, Vieta exposed the fact that there was a higher level of generality at which equations with different coefficients might nonetheless share a common form. Thus was born the idea of a *type* of equation – for example, the cubic, or the quadratic – and the project of studying the properties of the type, as distinct from studying or simply using this formula or that. This amounted to a shift from problem-solving to a concern with methods of problem-solving.[4]

There was yet another level or dimension of generality that the new 'logistic of species' opened up. In seeing that letters may sensibly be used to represent any of a whole category of numbers, Vieta also saw that there was no need to restrict the things letters could symbolize to numbers. He regarded them in fact as symbolizing magnitudes of all kinds, of which numbers were one sort. The other sort he had in mind were geometric magnitudes – lines, for example, and areas – and thus he thought of himself as developing a tool that would be useful to arithmetic and geometry alike. We have in Vieta, therefore, and in Descartes, who took these ideas further, the concept of a system of symbols that could be useful in different domains, depending on how on a particular occasion one chose to interpret the symbols – as numbers in some applications, as geometrical magnitudes in others.[5]

It was a further step to think of the possibility of a symbol-system capable of being interpreted in ways that included items other than magnitudes: the step seen by Leibniz. His visionary thought had been that there must be a single order, which might be expressed as a set of symbols subject to a set of rules for their combination, underlying not only the algebra developed by Vieta and Descartes, and not only geometry, but also logic (as well as the sciences of probabilities and series): a 'universal mathematics'.

In their seventeenth century beginning, the rules of combination to which the symbols of the new algebra were considered to be subject were simply taken over from arithmetic: the rules of addition, subtraction, multiplication and division (to which Vieta added the rule of homogeneity, to ensure that squares were added only to squares, cubes to cubes, etc.). As algebra was pressed into wider and wider use, different types of numbers were assumed to be valid interpretations for its formulae – signed integers (-1, $+2$), fractional numbers ($\frac{1}{2}$, $\frac{1}{10}$), irrational numbers ($\sqrt{2}$, π), complex numbers (numbers of the form [$a + bi$], where a and b are real numbers and $i = \sqrt{-1}$) – without any justification being offered for the legitimacy of so doing. It was being assumed that the properties of these other types of numbers were such as to make the ordinary rules of integer arithmetic apply to them, but during the eighteenth century intuition was left to carry the burden of this assumption.[6] Because of the boldness of these moves, the period in which they took place is known, somewhat archly, as the 'heroic' age of mathematics.

The algebra that Babbage first encountered, therefore, as he prepared to go up to Cambridge in the first decade of the nineteenth century, was subtle, powerful – and without foundation. There was the beginning of the sense of its constituting an autonomous symbol-system, but only insofar as it was recognized as interpretable in terms of numbers or geometrical magnitudes alike; for though Leibniz had indeed taken this thought further, his ideas on this score, as on most others, had gone pretty well unnoticed. As for the way in which the rules for integer arithmetic were simply applied to the other kinds of number, there was a growing sense of unease. 'Much has been heard,' writes Robert Woodhouse in 1801, 'of the science of quantity being vitiated with jargon, absurdity and mystery, and perplexed with paradox and contradiction,' for which 'the introduction of impossible quantities' (that is, roots of negative numbers) was blamed.[7]

Babbage was himself instrumental in developing a defence of algebra from charges of this kind. What resulted from his work, though, and that of the circle he gathered round him when he arrived in Cambridge, was effectively a new understanding of what algebra was.[8]

The innovation was to see that there was no need to justify the manipulations of symbols in terms of the rules that governed integer arithmetic – provided that one took seriously the nature of symbols as symbols. If one could only show that the rules followed in manipulating the symbols were valid, any kind of dependence of algebra on integer arithmetic would cease. Indeed the relationship between the two would be reversed, since then the validity of arithmetic would flow from the fact that numbers and numerical operations would constitute one possible interpretation of the symbol-system that algebra would be.

Could the independent validity of the rules of algebra be demonstrated? The first task was to give them a precise articulation, for as yet mathematicians had been conducting algebra on the basis of an intuitive transfer of rules from integer arithmetic. As for authentication, the only approach seemed to be axiomatization, reducing the demand on intuition to the acknowledgement of a minimal number of simple 'incontrovertible' propositions.

In his 1830 *Treatise on Algebra*, Peacock began the task of giving formal expression to the commonly invoked rules. He set out the commutative law of addition, for example; that is, whatever a and b are, adding the first to the second yields the same result as adding the second to the first:

$$a + b = b + a$$

He also set out the associative law of addition:

$$(a + b) + c = a + (b + c)$$

and the commutative and associative laws of multiplication:

$$a \times b = b \times a$$
$$(a \times b) \times c = a \times (b \times c)$$

Others, like D. F. Gregory and Augustus de Morgan, brought into focus other laws and explored their mutual relationships.[9]

The algebra thus taking shape was the 'analysis' that Babbage devised his great Engine to body forth.[10] It was a symbol-system that owed its conception to the 'suggesting science'[11] of arithmetic, but which in maturity was defined in terms of rules (for manipulating symbols) which owed nothing to arithmetic. Arithmetic rules, like the rules of geometry, were rather to be seen as particular interpretations of algebraic rules, to which belonged, therefore, the greater generality. These were fields, at the time insufficiently analysed, which one day would come to be seen as further spheres of application for the new science. Ada Lovelace pressed the logic of the conception to its conclusion: if there were laws in *any* sphere governing the changes to which the relationships between items in that sphere were subject, they would of necessity be special cases of the general laws identified and systematized by algebra (or the 'science of operations' as she called it).

This did not mean, though Lovelace's words sometimes suggest the opposite, that algebra was conceived of as destined to displace physics. The claim is only that its laws define a language in which physical laws might be

George Peacock, 1791–1858

accurately expressed. In an ideal language, the laws that govern which transformations of statements are legitimate must be the laws of reason, for if we assert B on the basis of A, the justification must take the form of showing that it is reasonable to do so. Algebra in the new style was, in fact, conceived of as the project of systematizing the laws of reason itself: 'the science of general reasoning by symbolic language', as Peacock says.[12]

Thus in a sense Leibniz' project is returned to, but with a shift. Leibniz' ideal language was based on the idea of devising terms that represented the list of properties belonging to the thing the term was to refer to. Algebra, viewed as an ideal language, was not conceived along those lines. It was ideal not because its terms had meanings that accurately reflected the groupings of properties that things possessed, but in virtue of the validity of the rules that governed which transformations of formulae were allowed. (If we understand statements as equations, this amounts to rules of syntax.) The items related in the formulae are for algebra empty of meaning.

Is what we see emerging here algebra as understood today? Not quite, for absent from the conception of Babbage, of Peacock, and of the others, is any notion that the rules of algebra might be other than what they are. We are witnessing but a stage in the maturation of the notion of a 'symbol'. For Babbage and his circle the innovation was to see more clearly than even Leibniz had done that there could be a symbol-system defined by rules, quite independent of arithmetic's or geometry's, which were capable of being interpreted not only as they are in arithmetic and in geometry, but in other ways too. What was to come – with William Hamilton in 1844, Hermann Grassmann in 1844, and then others – was the idea that it made sense to think of developing different symbol-systems, altering the traditional algebra's rules in various ways and creating a variety of alternative ones.

Nevertheless, the development of algebra in the hands of Babbage and Peacock and their circle of reformers represents a clear advance towards the formalization of our instruments of thought. It constitutes the conceptual background against which Babbage's great project makes sense.

The Calculator in the Eighteenth Century

Like Leibniz before him – and Turing and von Neumann afterwards – Babbage could think engineering as well as mathematics. He helped to bring about the new conception of algebra which created the theoretical framework for the conception of his 'Analytical' (that is, algebraical) machine: but also partly his responsibility were the refinements of engineering technique that allowed such a machine to be conceived in concrete terms.

Though their impact was small throughout the eighteenth century, mechanical calculators had continued, after Leibniz, to be the subject of experimentation, with inventors for the most part devising variations on themes introduced by Leibniz himself.[13] The basis of eighteenth century machines, as of Leibniz', was the Pascalian adder: a set of wheels, each representing a different order of ten, linked by a carrying mechanism so that as each completes a rotation it moves the one representing the next, higher order of ten through a tenth of a revolution. It was this carrying mechanism, in a way the most challenging problem of the whole design task, that several further machines attempted to improve – for example, those of Lépine (1725), Hillerin de Boistissandeau (1730), and Jacob Pereire (1751). Others attempted to make it easier and more reliable to set numbers up in the machine. C. L. Gersten, for example, devised in 1720 an arrangement whereby the operator slid a rack, engaging with a cogwheel, along a graduated scale.[14]

Other inventors directed their attention to the mechanism whereby the multiplicand was successively added into the adder. One of Leibniz' devices for this was to have the multiplicand represented by the number of teeth projecting from a variable-toothed wheel, with each revolution of that wheel advancing the adder wheel by N tenths of a revolution, where N is the multiplier.[15] This was the principle taken up by the Italian G. Poleni, in a device described in 1709. Constructed in wood, it had the incidental advantage of being easily broken up when it failed to fulfill the hopes of its disappointed inventor.[16] Despite this inauspicious early history, the

Brunsviga calculating machine, 1892

variable-toothed wheel was to be returned to several times and in the end, having become known as the Odhner Wheel after the granting of a patent to W. T. Odhner in 1891, came to play a major role in commercial machines around the end of the nineteenth century. It was the basis of the Brunsviga calculating machine, for example, of which over twenty thousand were produced between 1892 and 1912.[17]

No less influential was Leibniz' stepped cylinder.[18] The English Viscount Mahon, later Earl Stanhope, who was one of the few serious scientists during the dog days of London's eighteenth century Royal Society, used this as the basis for a machine he had built in 1775,[19] while in Germany one Matthew Hahn incorporated into a machine of circular design, subsequently improved by fellow-countryman J. H. Müller.[20]

The commercial career of the stepped cylinder, however, was launched in 1820 when it was used as the basis of a machine designed by the manager of an insurance company, Chevalier Chas. X. Thomas de Colmar, in Alsace. Thomas was the first to attempt the production of calculators on a businesslike footing, and as the 'Thomas Arithmometer' his machine underwent a protracted programme of development. Under one form or

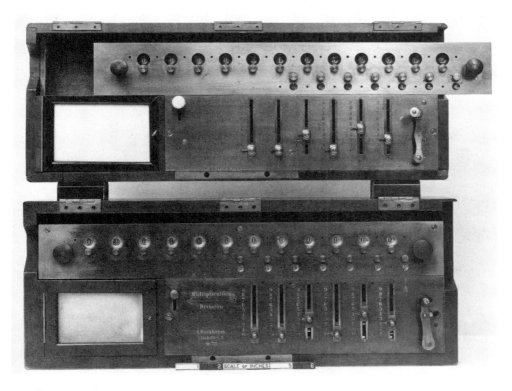

Thomas Arithmometer

other it acheived widespread use. Baxandall's catalogue of the calculating machines held by the London Science Muesum reports that it was still in production in 1926.[21]

A different approach, this time not to be found in Leibniz, was taken by Jacob Leupold in a design published in 1727. The Pascalian adder wheel system was retained, but where other devices had found ways of varying the number of effective teeth on the device carrying the multiplicand, Leupold conceived of having a fixed number of teeth engaging with the adder

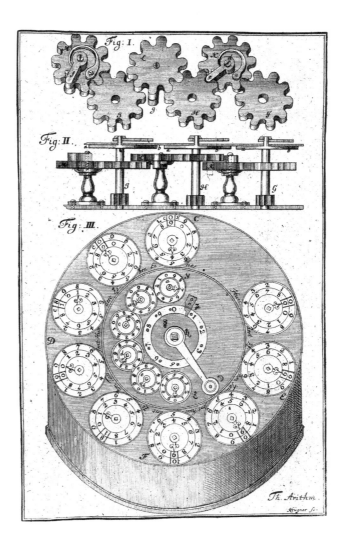

Leupold's calculating machine

Figure 7.1 Leupold's calculator

The adder wheels are arranged around the perimeter of a circle. The operator turns a handle which swings round, within the circle, a curved piece of metal bearing teeth along one edge, rather like a saw. If there was nothing to prevent it, these teeth would engage each of the adder cogs in turn and rotate each by a single complete revolution. However, the saw is held out of contact with the cogs by a spring, so that if nothing acts against the spring no wheels will be advanced at all. Pieces of metal fixed adjacent to each adder cog provide the action against the spring. They bear on a strip of metal which projects from the saw like a spine. As the saw swings round, the spine encounters each projection in turn, and in each case its teeth are pushed into contact with an adder cog, which is thus turned. The degree to which an adder cog is turned thus depends on the length of the metal spine carried by the saw. In fact this spine is cut to a 'staircase' profile, so that the length encountered by a given projection depends on its vertical elevation. This elevation can be varied by the operator, and it is by this means that the different digits of the multiplicand are represented in the machine and fed with each revolution of the saw into the adder.

If the multiplier is a single figure number, a multiplication is completed by rotating the handle that number of times. But tens can be added efficiently by single turns of the handle, by the simple expedient of rotating the sequence of projections as already set, relative to the sequence of adder wheels; so that, for example, 30 may be added instead of 3 by having the projection which has been set at 3 force the saw against the tens adder wheel instead of the units one. Leibniz' arrangement in this respect was similar.

Table 1 Beginning of the table of differences for squares

Number X	Square of the number X^2	Column of first differences D^1	Column of second differences D^2
1	1		
2	4	3	
3	9	5	2
4	16	7	2
5	25	9	2
6	36	11	2
7	49	13	2
8	64	15	2
9	81	17	2
10	100	19	2

intermittently, withdrawing when it had engaged the number of teeth required by the multiplicand. A second machine by Stanhope was based on a similar principle.[22]

Difference Engines

Babbage's own first contributions to mechanical calculation broke away from this tradition of searching for a reliable and speedy desk calculator, which by the time he arrived at Cambridge, in 1810, had yet to issue in any kind of commercial success. What he sought to mechanize (to have produced 'by steam')[23] was the preparation of mathematical tables, and there was an established method of performing the necessary calculations using addition only. This was the method used in the great tabulation project of the new French Republic, under de Prony,[24] and it enabled the bulk of the dauntingly vast chore to be performed by people with very little mathematical ability.[25]

Suppose, to take a simple case, the project is to calculate a table of the function $f(x) = x^2$, or in other words a table of squares. Suppose we begin to write the whole numbers 0, 1, 2, 3, ... N in a column, and in an adjacent column their squares. Then, we subtract the square of one from the square of two, the square of two from the square of three, and so on, writing the results in a third column, the column of the first differences. We then take the figures of this third column and subject them to the same operation: that is, working down the column we take the first figure from the second, the second from the third, the third from the fourth, and so on: entering the results in a fourth column, the column of the second differences (see table 1).

The differences listed in the final column are clearly the same; and this gives us a way of generating the table of the squares of numbers. If we started with the column of second differences we could work out what the figures in the column of first differences must be (by adding one to two to give three, three to two to give five, five to two to give seven, and so on); and then work out figures for the column of squares (by adding one to three to give four, four to five to give nine, nine to seven to give sixteen, and so on). This is perhaps a complicated way of working out squares (at least for small numbers!), but it is a procedure which depends on nothing more mathematically demanding than simple addition.

Rather more important, however, is the fact that the same 'method of differences' can be applied to the tabulation of any polynomial – an expression of the form

$$a + bx + cx^2 + \ldots + dx^n,$$

where n is any positive whole number. The more complicated the expression, the more columns of differences there will be before we reach a column in which all the differences are the same, but it *will* be reached in the end. (In fact, the number of columns of differences will be equal to the highest power to which the term x in the formula is raised – that is, in the expression given, n.) And it had been shown by Karl Weierstrass in the 1870s that most mathematical or physical functions are expressible as polynomials. Such expressions may be approximations only, but the approximation can be to any desired degree of accuracy. If the object was the calculation of a table, therefore, the method of differences provided a means by which the main burden of the chore could be carried by people capable of simple addition only : or, as Babbage saw, by an adding machine.

We know that Babbage was not the first to have this idea, though he himself probably did not realize it.[26] The J. H. Müller who developed Hahn's circular calculator had made the same proposal thirty-eight years earlier, and had made a vain approach to his government for funds to put the plan into effect.[27] Babbage's proposal was successful, a fact which reflects the turn taken by thought patterns at the beginning of the nineteenth century, already evidenced in the transformation of algebra in which Babbage also played such a central part.

Babbage's own approach to winning financial support was by no means politically naive. He completed a working model of the calculating part of the proposed engine, and on this basis in July of 1822 circulated among influential 'savants' (the term displaced by 'scientists') an open letter nominally addressed to the President of the Royal Society, Sir Humphrey Davy. The ground was thus well prepared for the British government to receive his bid for funding and to follow its usual course, as regards scientific projects, of asking the Royal Society for its comments. Within a month a favorable reply had been received, and in an interview with the Chancellor of the Exchequer, Babbage was delighted to be promised substantial support to begin developing his model into the Difference Engine proper.[28]

The proposal had had its detractors – Robert Peel, for one, later to become Prime Minister and to bear some responsibility for the tangle of frustration Babbage's affairs eventually got into. But the story up to this point is not the stereotype of an ignorant and shortsighted government blind to scientific potential. The government received Babbage's bid, took expert advice, and extended support, all within a timetable that would put our own Research Councils to shame.[29]

This in itself might need something of an explanation if what is often said were true, namely that government financial support for a scientific project was unprecedented.[30] But it is forgotten that what counted for much of the eighteenth century as the most significant kind of scientific research was the exploration of the living world, and proposals that the government should support expeditions of one kind or another in pursuit of this concern were certainly not unknown. It was, moreover, to the Royal Society (for long years dominated by naturalist Sir Joseph Banks) that they looked.[31]

It is true, nevertheless, that with the new century, projects of a different kind began to be referred. They originated in the main from the Admiralty, and it is tempting to link them with the hostilities with France, opened in 1793 and not resolved until 1815. The British navy, engaged in maintaining the most far-flung empire that the world has ever known, might be expected to be concerned with whatever technological developments it might turn to advantage. But the navy had been under fierce challenge, and therefore under great pressure to develop, throughout the eighteenth century, as European avarice steadily extended its ambitions. Why was it that only at the turn of the century did its interest in science begin to quicken?

The navy's new interest in science, and the government's sympathetic response to Babbage, were part of a general revival of Baconianism which began about the turn of the century, and which was linked with the contemporary flowering of political radicalism. The cause of science in Britain was advanced by the Benthamites, by the progressive school of thinkers behind the *Edinburgh Review*, by the radical sentiment that promoted the mechanics' institutes, and by those who looked to science to alleviate the lot of the people bearing the brunt of industrialization;[32] and it was opposed by the high aristocracy and the Anglican clergy, those who considered that 'science and learning, if universally diffused, would speedily overturn the best constituted government on earth.'[33] In France, whence some of Britain's reformers drew part of their zeal,[34] the well-funded professionalization of science looked very much like the sweeping of the revolutionary broom.[35]

Unfortunately for this account of the change that led to Babbage's project for a difference engine being funded, whereas Müller's had not, support for Babbage came not from the reformed government of Melbourne, but the reactionary one of Wellington.[36] But funded it was; and by the end of 1832 the central part of Babbage's plan had been realized, to the extent that he was able to entertain his dinner-party guests with it. It was not the completed engine, but it was the central part, and it worked perfectly: as indeed it does today.

It is sometimes suggested that Babbage's plans went ahead of technical feasibility,[37] but as regards the Difference Engine, at any rate, this is not so. It is true that the engineering involved was state of the art: novel problems had to be solved, and novel techniques and indeed tools designed to solve them. With such challenges in mind, Babbage had at an early stage launched the subsidiary and staggeringly ambitious project of surveying the entire gamut of contemporary machinery and manufacturing processes, to provide a stock of ideas upon which the design of the Difference Engine might draw. (A small part of the results was published in 1832 as *The Economy of Manufactures*.) In the reverse direction, a host of technical advances made in the construction of the Engine subsequently proved their usefulness elsewhere.[38]

Babbage's biographer Anthony Hyman comments that the working portion of the Engine constitutes in itself 'an engineering triumph ... one of the finest achievements of the first half of the century,' and adds: 'If the full

Engine planned by Babbage had been completed it would have been the wonder of nineteenth century precision engineering.'[39] The structure of the Difference Engine was not at all complicated in outline. Numbers were to be represented on wheels, as in the machines of the Pascal tradition, but the wheels for successive digits of the same number were to be piled up in columns instead of set out horizontally. Facing the machine, one would have seen the column on which the 'result' appeared on the far left. Next to the right would have been the column holding the first difference; next to the right again, the column holding the second difference; and so on, until the seventh column from the left, representing the sixth constant difference, which was to be the highest order of difference within the capacity of the machine. Each column was to be eighteen wheels high (according to Lardner;[40] Baxandall[41] says twenty), accommodating an eighteen digit number, with the units represented on the lowermost wheel (so that the number was to be read from the top down).

(The operator would have begun a tabulation by entering the relevant constant difference on the column furthest to the left, and the orders of difference appropriate to the particular formula under tabulation on the appropriate difference columns, and would then have turned a handle twice clockwise and twice counter-clockwise. This would effect the required additions: the number on column eight to the number on column seven, the number on column seven to the number on column six, and so on, with the figure that was to be created in the table appearing on the column furthest to the right. There was an auxiliary mechanism, to which Babbage in his ambition to eliminate error (half the project, after all) attached much importance, which took the result figure and impressed it on a copper plate. The required tabulation could thus be printed from the plate directly, without the intervention of any fallible human copying process. (Like many before and since, Babbage seems to have thought the complete elimination of error a feasible ambition: such a dangerous thought.) A good impression of the machine as it would have been can be gained from the cut-down version Babbage asked his engineer, Joseph Clement, to assemble in 1832,[42] which can now be seen in the London Science Museum – although this is very much smaller than the dimensions (ten feet by ten feet by five feet) envisaged for the Engine proper. The version exhibited has a capacity for two orders of difference (and a third if it did not exceed the number nine) and for five-digit numbers only. But it featured an automatic printing facility, and specimens of its printed output are also exhibited.[43]

As to the key mechanism involved, the addition of a number represented on one wheel to the number represented on the wheel adjacent is accomplished by the device of a withdrawable bolt. The first wheel (the one carrying the number to be added) is rotated through a complete revolution. At the commencement of the movement a bolt is shot which locks it to the second wheel (the one which is to carry the resulting sum). But the first wheel carries with it a wedge, in a position that is governed by the number represented on it. When the two wheels have revolved in unison to just that extent which corresponds to the number being added, the bolt runs up against the wedge and is pushed out. The first wheel then completes its revolution, but out of gear with the second, which thus ends up bearing the sum.

 The problem of perfecting an efficient carrying mechanism is one that involved Babbage in protracted thought over many years.[44] Imperfectly efficient solutions were not difficult to arrive at. His general approach, adapted on mechanical grounds, was to have the carrying performed as a separate operation after the primary addition had taken place, and the threat of inefficiency arose from the fact that once one round of carrying had been conducted another might be required, depending on whether in the first round any nines had been incremented. In the second round, however, it was always possible that still other nines would be incremented, so that a further round would be necessary; and so on. The number of carrying rounds might conceivably amount to the number of digits in the number being added.[45] Babbage clearly felt very keenly the disproportionate amount of machine time carrying might therefore occupy, and it was this that drove him from improvement to improvement. Eventually he devised a mechanism which he describes as capable of 'foreseeing' which carriages would be necessary:

> A toothed wheel had the ten digits marked upon its edge; between the nine and the zero a projecting tooth was placed. Whenever any wheel, in receiving addition, passed from nine to zero, the projecting tooth pushed over a certain lever. Thus, as soon as nine seconds of time required for addition were ended, every carriage which had become due was indicated by the altered position of its lever. An arm now went round which was so contrived that the act of replacing that lever caused the carriage which its position indicated to be made to the next figure above. But this figure might be a nine, in which case, in passing to zero, it would put over its lever, and so on. By placing the arms spirally round an axis, these successive carriages were accomplished.[46]

Babbage's own part in the Difference Engine project ran into the sand about 1833, under personal circumstances sometimes quite erroneously thought to reflect badly on Babbage's temperament, and worth recounting on that account.

Prior to the crisis, work on the Engine had gone on in the workshop of Babbage's engineer, Clement. This occasioned Babbage a good deal of inconvenience, since his own house was four miles distant; and partly for this reason, partly perhaps with the idea of keeping a closer eye on Clement (whom he with reason distrusted), Babbage tried to insist on moving both machine and engineer to new premises, specially built by the government, adjacent to his own house. Clement, who, according to one who had worked for him, saw the advantages of working under minimum supervision at a pace that would extend the project indefinitely,[47] refused to cooperate.

In the background was an unstable political situation which made

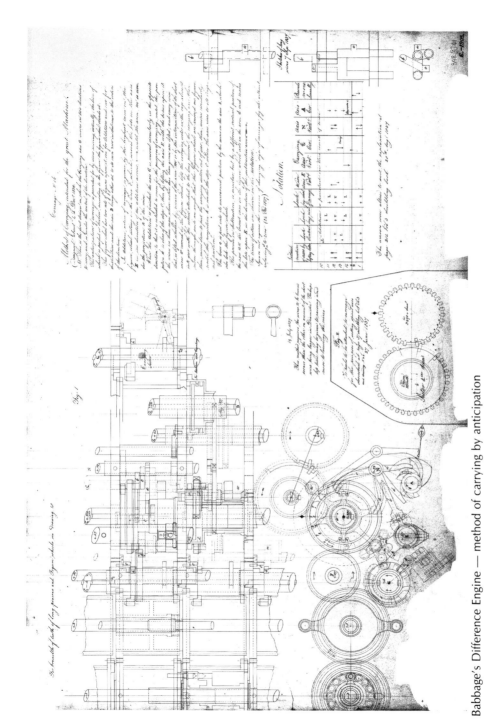

Babbage's Difference Engine — method of carrying by anticipation

Babbage's Difference Engine — truncated version in the Science Museum, London

The Scheutz' Difference Engine, Science Museum, London

continuing funding greatly troublesome, and, from 1834, impossible. In the foreground, however, at least in Babbage's mind, a much more positive development tended in the same direction: a new enthusiasm. For it was at this point, around 1833, that he began to see how it might be possible to build a more powerful machine, capable not simply of addition and tabulation, nor indeed restricted to arithmetic, but enjoying the generality of 'the general science of reasoning' – algebra itself.

With administrative and financial frustration without, and the sapping of the drive within, the Difference Engine project claimed less and less of Babbage's attention, and when it was brought to a successful conclusion the triumph was not directly Babbage's – though to his great credit, he derived much pleasure from it nonetheless. An account of the Difference Engine by one of Babbage's contemporaries, Dionysius Lardner, appeared in the *Edinburgh Review* of 1834, and stimulated the interest of a Swedish printer by the name of George Scheutz. After a great deal of effort, and invoking rather different mechanical principles from those Babbage had proposed, Scheutz and his son Edward succeeded in completing the construction of a Difference Engine in 1853. They brought it to London for exhibition in 1854, and found Babbage filled not with envy, as they feared, but, large man that he was, entirely with warmth and admiration.[48]

The Scheutz machine worked, and was bought by the Dudley Observatory at Albany, New York, for the production of astronomical tables. The fact that the British government had in the end discontinued its support for Babbage's work, in 1842, did not stop them making use of a copy of the Scheutz engine taken by the engineers Donkin & Co. It was installed in Somerset House and used by the Registrar-General to produce life-expectancy tables. (This copy is now in the London Science Museum; the original is in the Smithsonian.)[49]

The question that is often raised in connection with the Difference Engine project is why it was never brought to a successful conclusion. This rather overlooks the fact that it *was* completed – by Scheutz and son: and the real question that arises (though I myself do not offer an answer) is why, in view of the claims made for them (by no means only by Babbage), the working machine successfully built by Scheutz and his son made so modest an impact on practical tabulation once they had become available. An enormous number of tables were in fact prepared towards the end of the nineteenth century, and after the beginning of the next, but negligible use of the Scheutz machines was made.

For Babbage's seminal project, however, the algebra machine or Analytical Engine, the ultimate fate of the earlier idea was incidental. The significant preparations were two: first, the articulation of new ideas about algebra, towards which we have seen Babbage himself contributed importantly; and second, the development of engineering techniques to the point where they allowed the much greater – and by any standards quite daunting – complexity of the new proposal to be thought of, by Babbage at least, as feasible. By 1833 both these conditions had been met.

Notes

1 Ada (Lady) Lovelace, notes to her translation of Menabrea, 'Sketch', in P. and E. Morrison, *Calculating Engines*, p. 252.

2 George Peacock, 'Report on the Recent Progress and Present State of Certain Branches of Analysis', *Report of the Third Meeting of the British Association for the Advancement of Science, 1833*, pp. 185–352 (London).

3 See above, p. 41.

4 Edward Mahoney, 'The Beginnings of Algebraic Thought in the Seventeenth Century', in Stephen Gaukroger (ed.), *Descartes (Philosophy, Mathematics and Physics* (Harvester Press, Brighton, 1980), ch. 5.; O'Neill, *Against Formalism*, ch. 6, section 3.

5 O'Neill, *Against Formalism*, pp. 111–113.

6 O'Neill, *Against Formalism*, pp. 111, 112; Kline, *Mathematical Thought*, pp. 426–34.

7 Woodhouse, 'On the Necessary Truth of Certain Conclusions by Means of Imaginary Quantities', *Philosophical Transactions of the Royal Society*, 91 (London, 1801), p. 89.

8 Major responsibility for the new orientation is usually assigned to Babbage's friend Peacock, though the new picture was first drawn by Babbage himself in an unpublished essay which almost certainly provided Peacock's inspiration. See Dubbey, *Mathematical Work of Babbage*, ch. 5.

9 Kline, *Mathematical Thought*, pp. 774, 775.

10 Woodhouse, 'On the Independence of the Analytical and Geometrical Methods of Investigation; and on the Advantages of their Separation', *Philosophical Transactions of the Royal Society*, 92 (London, 1802), p. 87n.

11 Peacock's phrase. See Dubbey, *Mathematical Work of Babbage*, p. 101.

12 Quoted by Dubbey, *Mathematical Work of Babbage*, p. 100.

13 General treatments of eighteenth century calculators are given in: Maurice d'Ocagne, *Le Calcul Simplifié* (Gauthier-Villars, Paris, 1905); Taton and Flad, *Le Calcul Mécanique*; Wolf, *History*; Mehmke and d'Ocagne, 'Calculs Numériques'.

14 Wolf, *History*, p. 655.

15 See above, pp. 51–3.

16 Wolf, *Hisotry*, p. 657.

17 D. Baxandall, *Catalogue of the Collections in the Science Museum: Mathematics: Calculating Machines and Instruments* (HMSO, London, 1926), p. 49.

18 See above, pp. 53–6.

19 Wolf, *History*, p. 658; Baxandall, *Catalogue* p. 18.

20 Both machines are extant. See d'Ocagne, *Le Calcul Simplifié*, pp. 46, 47. Wolf unaccountably suggests that nothing is known of how either machine worked (*History*, p. 659).

21 Mehmke and d'Ocagne, 'Calculs Numériques', p. 254; d'Ocagne, *Le Calcul Simplifié*, p. 46; Baxandall, *Catalogue*, p. 20.

22 Leupold, *Theatrum Arithmetico-geometricum* (Leipzig, 1727); Wolf, *History*, p. 657.

23 Anthony Hyman, *Charles Babbage: Pioneer of the Computer* (OUP, Oxford, 1982), p. 49.

24 See above, p. 82.

25 In fact, apparently the less the better – see Lardner, in P. and E. Morrison, *Calculating Engines*, p. 174n.

26 Brian Randell, *The Origins of Digital Computers* (Springer-Verlag, Berlin, 1975, p. 3.

27 d'Ocagne, *Le Calcul Simplifié*, p. 74; Ph. E. Klipstein, *Beschreibung einer neu erfundenen Rechenmaschine* (Barrentrapp Söhn und Wenner, Frankfurt, 1786); Wolf, *History*, pp. 654–60.

28 I defer to the convention of using capitals in 'Difference Engine' (and in 'Analytical Engine'), which after all gives honour where honour is due.

29 Hyman, *Babbage*, pp. 52, 53.

30 Goldstine, *The Computer from Pascal*, p. 14; Hyman, *Babbage*, p. 53

31 Sir Henry Lyons, *The Royal Society, 1660–1940* (CUP, Cambridge, 1944).

32 Cardwell, *The Organization of Science*, p. 43.

33 Patrick Colquhoun, quoted by Cardwell, *Organization of Science*, p. 38.

34 Hyman, *Babbage*, p. 90.

35 Cardwell, *Organization of Science*, pp. 25–8.

36 Hyman, *Babbage*, p. 87.

37 See, for example, Randell, *Origins*, p. 3.

38 Lardner, in P. and E. Morrison, *Calculating Engines*, p. 261.

39 Hyman, *Babbage*, p. 128.

40 Lardner, in P. and E. Morrison, *Calculating Engines*, p. 305.

41 Baxandall, *Catalogue*, p. 32.

42 Babbage, *Passages from the Life of a Philosopher* (London, 1864), p. 82.

43 A description of the cut-down version, including its printing facility, is provided in Babbage, *Passages from the Life*, pp. 63–7.

44 Babbage, *Passages from the Life*, pp. 62, 63.

45 Babbage, *Passages from the Life*, p. 62.

46 Babbage, *Passages from the Life*, p. 62.

47 Hyman, *Babbage*, p. 131.

48 Hyman, *Babbage*, p. 240.

49 For some details of the Scheutz story, see R. C. Archibald, 'P. G. Scheutz – Biography and Bibliography', *Mathematics of Computation*, 2 (1947), pp. 238–45.

8   Babbage: Mechanizing Mathematics

The Difference Engine was capable of performing operations on numbers put into it at the beginning of a calculation. The operator would 'put into its columns the series of numbers constituting the first terms of the several orders of differences for whatever is the particular table under consideration.'[1] The Engine would then perform the required sequence of additions and output the results.

But might not a way be devised of allowing the machine to use its own output as the input for a further calculation? This was Babbage's seminal idea, the thought of a Difference Engine 'eating its own tail'.[2]

Babbage's work on this project, resulting not in an Engine certainly, but in a series of conceptions which all but define the computer as we know it today, ushered in a new phase in the evolution of machines capable of supporting 'thought'. The Difference Engine brought to culmination the eighteenth century concern with tabulation. It was a special purpose adding machine, brilliantly executed, but no conceptual explosion. It attracted funding, and it was brought, in a way (via Scheutz and son), to a successful and useful conclusion. But the Analytical Engine was of a different order: too advanced to attract governmental support, utterly innovative in conception, it pointed forward to the twentieth century when much of what Babbage had in mind was to achieve realization. Babbage, therefore, does not represent a chapter in 'the story of the computer'. He completes one, and starts another.

It is not possible to give a straightforward description of the Analytical Engine because, although his son was able to use some of the drawings to build a 'mill' that worked (stickily) in 1889,[3] the Analytical Engine as such was never constructed. Moreover, as Hyman points out, it is a mistake to think of Babbage as ever launching its actual construction. His efforts constituted instead an elaborate research and development programme, in which designs for the various sub-mechanisms were devised, tested, refined, and often supplanted by improved designs based on superior principles. Hyman goes so far as to say that what Babbage had in mind was not one machine at all, but a whole series: 'Analytical Engine' was conceived of, he suggests, as the name of a category of machines, like the modern term 'computer'. I do not myself see the evidence for this, except for indications that Babbage, if he had ever constructed an Analytical Engine, would have had plenty of ideas for his next project. Babbage's manuscript of 1837, Menabrea's paper of 1842, Lovelace's notes to this paper, and Henry Babbage's account of 1888[4] all speak unequivocally of a particular engine: though, equally obviously, its design underwent substantial revisions as the years went by. From these sources, and from the large quantity of drawings and annotations that represented the output of Babbage's great project, a clear and in many respects immensely detailed picture of what might have been emerges: and it is easiest to describe the picture as though it were the article itself.

The Analytical Engine: Control

At the heart of the new machine, in one sense, is a 'central processor' or mill. It is to the mill that numbers are brought, it is within the mill that they are

Babbage's Analytical Engine – the Mill. Science Museum, London

operated upon, and it is from the mill that the results emerge. Connected to it is a store, the receptacle of numbers prior to being passed to the mill, and of numbers resulting from the operations in the mill. Numbers are represented, as in the Difference Engine, on columns of wheels, only now these are forty-one wheels high, and the topmost wheel represents the sign of the number stored below.[5] When passed to the mill via the 'ingress axis' (a kind of input buffer), numbers can be subjected to multiplication by invoking a stored multiplication table, as well as to addition. Subtraction, as in the Difference Engine, is done by the addition of complements,[6] and division by successive subtraction. Extraction of roots is also provided. Via another buffer (the 'egress axis'), the result is passed back to one of the columns making up the store.

In another sense, however, none of this lies at the heart of the new machine: for its innovation is in the arrangement for sequencing these operations automatically – the control mechanism, whereby the machine is told which numbers from the store to operate upon, what that operation shall be, and whereabouts in the store the result should be put. Babbage's preparatory exercise[7] in scouring Europe for ideas for his engines provided him with an approach to this problem which might well have been missed by a more cloistered thinker. He simply used the system of sequence control that Joseph Jacquard had perfected for the loom.

The pattern in a damask or other brocaded material is produced in the process of weaving it, by altering which warp (lengthwise) threads are covered by the weft (widthwise threads). Where no pattern is involved, the warp threads are set up on the loom with alternate ones raised to allow passage for the shuttle carrying the weft. After one passage, the raised warp threads are lowered, and the remainder raised. The shuttle passes back: and then the whole cycle is repeated. To introduce a textured pattern, all that is necessary is to vary which warp threads are raised. If a number of adjacent warp threads is left lowered, the whole batch of them will be covered by the weft thread, and this will appear as a line on the finished cloth. By varying the threads lowered for the next pass, and for subsequent ones, the line can be developed into an area, shaped by whatever regime of raising and lowering is adopted.

Prior to the eighteenth century, the operator and his or her assistant followed a chart in selecting which threads were to be raised for any particular passage of the shuttle, and then raised them by hand. Such a process took time, perhaps weeks of preparation before the shuttle was even thrown. Jacquard's idea – consolidating and developing earlier innovations by Bouchon and Falcon, and ideas by Vaucanson[7] – was to have the raising of each thread controlled by a lever, and to have the levers, for each passage of the shuttle, selected automatically.

It was in fact impractical and unnecessary to have a separate lever for each thread, and the arrangement adopted was for each lever to control a cluster of threads, which thus acted together. Jacquard connected the levers to rods

Jacquard's loom – an example from the 1870s

in such a way that each lever was operated by pressing on the end of the rod in which it terminated. These rods he brought together, in a parallel bundle of rectangular cross-section. This meant that if a rectangular plate was taken and pushed flat against the bundle end, all the levers would be operated: and also that if there were any holes in such a plate, any rod end aligned with such a hole would not be pushed forward when the plate was advanced, since it would simply pass through the hole. The pattern of threads raised for any particular passage of the shuttle would thus be determined by the pattern of holes in the plate; and by having a whole series of plates, each

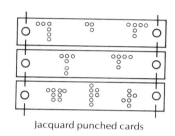

Jacquard punched cards

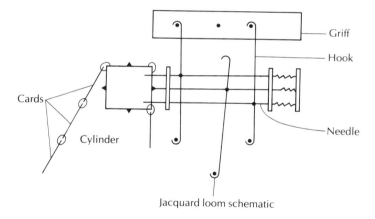

Jacquard loom schematic

Jacquard needle

Figure 8.1 Details of the Jacquard loom

Source: S. Fernbach & A. H. Taub (eds) *Computers & their Role in the Physical Sciences* (Gordon & Breach, New York, 1970) p. 35

with its set pattern of holes of which a new one came into operation with each successive throw, an overall pattern in the cloth could be achieved. The plates were often in fact made of pasteboard strung together with tape hinges. Babbage had in his possession a portrait of Jacquard himself, woven in silk on a loom fitted with his device. Five feet square, it had required 2,400 cards, each with capacity for 1,050 holes.[8]

It was this punched-card control device that Babbage applied to solve the automatic sequencing problem for his new Engine. One sequence of cards, the operation cards, dictates which operation the machine should next perform; and another (bearing on a separate set of levers), the variable cards, tells it on which columns to find the numbers to be operated upon, and where to put the result. These two sequences are to be set up beforehand by

Joseph Jacquard, a portrait woven in silk on one of his looms. Victoria and Albert Museum

the machine's operator, in the light of the formula to be calculated, but even so a further arrangement is necessary to ensure that the machine's working through one set of cards meshed with its working through the other set. This central co-ordination is provided by what Babbage called the 'barrels': a series of upright cylinders carrying the necessary instructions coded in the patterning of studs protruding from their outer surfaces. Each barrel, Babbage explains,

> is divided into about seventy rings, the circumference of each ring being divided into about eighty parts. A stud may be fixed on any one or more of these portions of each ring. Thus each barrel presents about eighty vertical columns every one of which contains a different combination of fixed studs.
>
> These barrels have two movements:
>
> 1st: They can advance horizontally by a parallel motion of their axis.
>
> 2nd: They can turn in either direction and to any extent on their axis. When the barrels advance horizontally these studs act on levers which cause various movements in the mill, the stud belonging to each ring giving a different order.[9]

Thus the mill may be set by the advance of a barrel to accept a number in the input buffer (the ingress axis), to give off whatever number it holds to the output buffer (egress axis), or to clear itself. But other movements are also controlled by the advancing movement of a barrel: the turning mechanism for the variable cards may be activated, and so also may that of the operation cards. Finally, the advance may instruct the barrel itself (or some other barrel) to turn on its axis, thus bringing into play a different column of studs, should a further advance be instructed.

Babbage gives the example of an addition, which involves the action of two barrels. The first step is that the appropriate operation card is turned, which orders the barrels to rotate so as to bring into play the vertical line of studs that commences addition; and one of the studs activates a mechanism which brings the next card into position. As the main drive continues to rotate, the barrels now advance, which causes the ingress wheels to take up the number specified on the variable card, and the barrels themselves to rotate, after their advance, so as to bring into play the next vertical line of studs required by addition. A further variable card is also turned, which specifies the second number to participate in the addition. With the third turn of the main drive this number is placed on to the ingress axis, and the barrels rotate to the third vertical required for addition. At this point Babbage's description comes to an end (it is taken from a manuscript he had not prepared for publication), but we may guess that with the next advance, the addition takes place and perhaps a variable card is turned to specify the column on which is to be stored the result.

For the serious scientific purposes Babbage planned for it, the new Engine had to be able to manipulate not only fractional and whole numbers but signed integers (−1, +3) as well. It needed, for example, to be able to multiply a negative number with a negative number and attach the 'right' sign to the result. For this purpose, Babbage placed an extra wheel at the top of every column of the store: just like the others below it, but bearing on its circumference the signs '+' and '−'; '+' in place of all the even numbers, '−' in place of all the odd. The sign of the number stored is thus indicated by the sign displayed by the topmost wheel of the column on which it is stored. If we consider the multiplication of one such signed number by another, we need only arrange for the numbers represented by the sign wheels to be added together, and the correct sign for the resultant number will be generated. This is because an even number added to an odd number gives an odd number, in a way exactly parallel to that in which a positive number multiplied by a negative number gives a negative number. Moreover, two numbers of the same kind (either both even or both odd) multiplied together give an even number, in a way exactly parallel to that in which two numbers of the same sign (either both positive or both negative) multiplied together give a positive number.

The rule for handling the 'number' on the sign wheel of any number being multiplied is then clear: add it to the 'number' on the sign wheel of the other number involved, and store the result on the sign wheel of the column holding the result. Rules for keeping the signs right during processes of addition, subtraction and division are different, but just as mechanical.

The Analytical Engine: Powers

The machine's potential for performing algebra (as algebra was being redefined by Babbage and his circle) begins in its capacity to place a number, once calculated, in store, so that it could take part in a subsequent operation. For this entailed instructing the machine to operate not on a specific number, but on whatever number came to be generated by the machine in a certain preceding operation. It had to be told: look at such and such a column of the store and operate on the number, whatever it is, that you find there. It had to be given the power, in other words, to handle variables.

Menabrea gives the following example. Suppose we wish to have calculated the value of x and y, given the remaining quantities in the following equations:

$$mx + ny = d$$
$$m^1x + n^1y = d^1$$

The operator works out that the expression for x, for example, is:

$$\frac{dn^1 - d^1n}{n^1m - nm^1}$$

The operator then places the known values (m, n, d, m^1, n^1, d^1) in the store, and instructs the machine to conduct the following sequence of operations:

> multiply d and n^1
> multiply d^1 and n
> multiply n^1 and m
> multiply n and m^1
> subtract d^1n from dn^1
> subtract nm^1 from n^1m
> divide $dn^1 - d^1n$ by $n^1m - nm^1$

This is the result sought, the value for x.[10]

This was to employ analysis to solve arithmetic problems, however, and left out of the account algebraic manipulations in a pure sense, which involved retaining symbols as such but subjecting them to legitimate transformations. For example, it might be desired to multiply

$$A + A_1 \cos \theta + A_2 \cos 2\theta + A_3 \cos 3\theta + \dots$$

by

$$B + B_1 \cos \theta$$

The result of such a calculation can in general be expressed as a series, in which each term consists of the variable raised to a certain power, and a coefficient, a number by which the term involving the variable is to be multiplied. In the example above, the result could be expressed as:

$$C_0 + C_1 \cos \theta + C_2 \cos 2\theta + C_3 \cos 3\theta + \dots$$

Formulating such a series correctly, given the expressions of which the product is to be found, is therefore a matter of 'the formation of coefficients according to certain laws', and 'the distribution of these with respect to the variables'.[11]

The 'programmer' has to plan out which variable's coefficient is to be represented on which column and label the columns appropriately, but with the right set of instructions the correct coefficients would be calculable. Lovelace observes that with a few modifications (troublesome in practice, though not at all so in principle), the manual labelling and reading off could be dispensed with and the result printed out in full algebraic style.[12] Babbage's Analytical Engine was therefore to be more than a 'manufactory of figures',[13] immensely useful though that promised to be. It constituted in fact the 'material and mechanical representative' of analysis, its powers 'coextensive with our knowledge of the laws of analysis itself'.[14] But there was more.

While the point of the sign-wheel device was clearly to enable the machine to perform arithmetic with signed numbers, it actually endowed the machine with a much more general capacity, namely to represent and manipulate symbols which might have nothing to do with arithmetic. For signs are of course not numbers. What Babbage had done was to find for each sign an arithmetical rule which yielded the same transformation as the rule governing that sign. This was a technique that would work for any symbol, provided only that an equivalent arithmetic rule, or perhaps pattern of rules, could be found. It would work, for example, for the symbols for logical operations that were being articulated, even as Babbage worked, by George Boole (as we shall see in the next chapter).

The generality of the Analytical Engine's powers was not wholly unappreciated by its early enthusiasts, though much of the claim they made for its ultimate significance rested on their belief in the importance of mathematics as 'the language through which we can alone adequately express the great facts of the natural world':

> Those who view mathematical science, not merely as a vast body of abstract and immutable truths, whose intrinsic beauty, symmetry and logical completeness, when regarded in their connexion together as a whole, entitle them to a prominent place in the interest of all profound and logical minds, but as possessing a yet deeper interest for the human race, when it is remembered that this science constitutes the language through which we can alone adequately express the great facts of the natural world, and those unceasing changes of mutual relationship which, visibly or invisibly, consciously or unconsciously to our immediate physical perceptions, are interminably going on in the agencies of the creation we live amidst: those who thus think on mathematical truth as the instrument through which the weak mind of man can most effectually read his Creator's works, will regard with especial interest all that can tend to facilitate the translation of its principles into explicit practical forms.[15]

This is to say that it is because of its mathematical powers that the Engine must be seen to be of high importance, because scientific truths about the universe are expressible only, or best, in the language of mathematics. But Lovelace was one who also had the idea that algebra, as Babbage and his circle were redefining it,[16] would develop into a science that went beyond mathematics. She envisaged a symbol-system that would represent a language in which might be expressed the laws governing the changes to which any relationship between two things – any two things – were subject. It might be possible, for example, for a machine capable of embodying this language (that is, the Analytical Engine) to compose music: if only it were to turn out that 'the fundamental relations of pitched sounds in the science of harmony and of musical composition' were expressible in the universal language she was envisaging, 'the engine might compose elaborate and scientific pieces of music of any degree of complexity or extent.'[17]

A 'science of operations' would have as its task the articulation of such a language, which, if the ideal were achieved, would provide a means of expressing laws governing 'any process which alters the mutual relation of two or more things, be this relation of what kind it may.'[18] It was this prospect that conferred on the Engine, in Lovelace's eyes, an importance that went beyond even that of an all-competent mathematical machine.

The sign-wheel device, in conferring the capacity to handle non-mathematical symbols and operations, was on these grounds alone a portentous feature. But there was a further aspect to its significance. It was the sign-wheel that made possible what we now call 'conditional branching'. This was the capacity that impressed the machine's early admirers the most. They could understand how a machine might be got to

Ada, Lady Lovelace, 1815–52

proceed automatically through a predetermined sequence of operations: but Babbage claimed that his would be capable of choosing, at key points in a calculation, which of several alternative continuation sequences would be correct in the light of the result so far achieved: and this seemed extraordinary in a machine. Once the sign-wheel had been devised, however, a means of decision making was straightforward. The arrangement was simply to have a lever bearing on the sign-wheel of the column storing the number resulting from the key calculation, fixed so that it registered any change from positive to negative. Movement of the lever could then be used to switch the machine into whatever continuation sequence had been planned as appropriate.

This, then, was Babbage's conception, and he thought it through in very considerable detail. In 1879 the British Association set up a committee to work through the drawings Babbage had left behind him when he died and determined the feasibility of bringing the Analytical Engine to realization. Though lauding his achievement, however, the committee did not consider the machine could be built. Babbage's son, as I have mentioned above, had a cut-down version of the central mill constructed in the eighties which functioned for purposes of demonstration after a fashion, and this is now to be seen in London's Science Museum. But when the enthusiasm of Babbage himself finally expired, his project, as an engineering venture, fell into suspended animation: until new needs and new resources to meet them woke it with a start in the thirties of the next century.

With the analytical part of the project, however, there was continuous progress. That is, the line of thought begun by Peacock, Gregory and Babbage himself, articulating a symbol-system of which not only magnitudes but domains beyond mathematics might be interpretations, and which might thus be handled by the Analytical Engine, was pursued with great brilliance first by Boole, and then by Frege. The new domain which they managed thus to formalize was logic.

Notes

1 Lovelace, notes to Menabrea, 'Sketch', in P. and E. Morrison, *Calculating Engines*, p. 253.
2 Babbage, quoted by Hyman, *Babbage* p. 164.
3 Hyman, *Babbage*, p. 254.
4 All reprinted in P. and E. Morrison, *Calculating Engines*.
5 See below, pp. 119–20.
6 See below, p. 51.
7 Usher, *Mechanical Inventions*, pp. 290–2.
8 P. and E. Morrison, *Calculating Engines*, p. xxxv. For a fuller description of the Jacquard loom and its history see Usher, *Mechanical Inventions*, pp. 284–95.
9 Babbage, *Passages from the Life*, p. 190.
10 Menabrea, 'Sketch', in P. and E. Morrison, *Calculating Engines*, p. 234.
11 Menabrea, 'Sketch', in P. and E. Morrison, *Calculating Engines*, p. 240. The example is given by Lovelace, notes to Menabrea, 'Sketch', in P. and E. Morrison, *Calculating Engines*, p. 272.

12 Lovelace, notes to Menabrea, 'Sketch', in P. and E. Morrison, *Calculating Engines*, p. 273.

13 Menabrea, 'Sketch', in P. and E. Morrison, *Calculating Engines*, p. 244.

14 Lovelace, notes to Menabrea, 'Sketch', in P. and E. Morrison, *Calculating Engines*, p. 251.

15 Lovelace, notes to Menabrea, 'Sketch', in P. and E. Morrison, *Calculating Engines*, p. 251.

16 See above, pp. 95–7

17 Lovelace, notes to Menabrea, 'Sketch', in P. and E. Morrison, *Calculating Engines*, p. 249.

18 Lovelace, notes to Menabrea, 'Sketch', in P. and E. Morrison, *Calculating Engines*, p. 247.

9   The Formalization of Logic

It was mathematician George Boole who first saw, against the background of the development of algebra towards greater abstraction I have spoken of, how logic might be a possible interpretation of the symbol-system called algebra.

It is true, he says, that hitherto 'the expression of magnitude, or of operations upon magnitude, has been the express object for which the symbols of Analysis [algebra] have been invented, and for which their laws have been investigated,'[1] but this does not mean that interpretations of algebra can only be quantitative (that is, only have to do with mathematics). He goes on to develop a way of interpreting algebraic expressions as

George Boole, 1815—64

statements about classes of things – a way which enables the established rules of syllogistic reasoning to be expressed algebraically.

This was the objective towards which Leibniz had laboured, of course. He had made a variety of attempts, none of them satisfactory.[2] Boole's success was based on the notion of two extreme categories: the category to which everything whatever belonged, known as the 'universal' class; and the 'null' class, the class which has no members whatever.[3]

The syllogistic was already an attempt to systematize arguments that depended on the relationship between categories of things, but the idea of a category embracing everything, and the idea of a completely empty category, were innovations. They enabled Boole to think of the categories invoked by the syllogistic (all A, or some B, etc.) as produced by making selections out of the universal class.[4] Thus he defined the symbols x, y, z … as standing for operations of selection. x applied to the universal class selected a certain subclass of things, y another. Once a first selection out of the universal class had been made using one selector (or 'operator'), a further selection could be made out of the resulting subclass using a second selector, and so on. Boole's symbol for the universal class was '1', and he wrote 'y(1)' for the subclass resulting from the operation on the universal class of the selector 'y'. But he then employed a shorthand for 'y(1)', viz. 'y' on its own. 'xy' then represented the class resulting when, first, y selects from the universal class, and then x selects from the result. (Without the shorthand it would read x(y(1)).)

This gave him a way of expressing classes. But in syllogisms classes are related to each other – a pair in each of the premises and another in the conclusion: a premise might say, for example, 'All As are Bs'. How were these relationships to be expressed?

If we introduce the sign '=' to mean 'has the same members as', we can express one of the classical propositions straightaway:

$$xy = 0$$

This says that when x selects from the class that results from y selecting from the universal class, the answer is nothing. But this will only be the case when the classes selected from the universal set by x and y are mutually exclusive. '$xy = 0$' is thus a way of expressing the traditional formula 'No As are Bs'.

To express the contradictory of this, namely that 'Some As are Bs', Boole introduces the symbol 'v' to refer to the class that has at least one member (though this brings confusion – there is not just one class that has at least one member). He thus writes

$$xy = v$$

saying that there is at least one item that is selected by both y and x, or that 'Some As are Bs'.

One more definition is required before the other two traditional forms of proposition in the syllogism are expressible, and this is the symbol '$-$'. One class minus a second is defined as standing for the class of things that remain unselected when the selector that generates the second class is applied to the first.

$$1 - y$$

thus represents the complement of y. When x and y both select the same things from the universal class, x selecting from the complement of y will select nothing. Thus, corresponding to

All As are Bs,

Boole can write

$$x(1 - y) = 0$$

And the contradictory of this, namely

Some As are not Bs,

is expressible as

$$x(1 - y) = v$$

In summary:[5]

Proposition	Boolean symbolization
All As are Bs	$x(1 - y) = 0$
No As are Bs	$xy = 0$
Some As are Bs	$xy = v$
Some As are not Bs	$x(1 - y) = v$

Is this a successful symbolization of the traditional propositions of the syllogistic? We see when we use it to express arguments. Below is set out an example of a syllogism, alongside the Boolean symbolization of the component propositions:[6]

All As are Bs:	$y(1 - x) = 0$	or	$(1 - x)\, y = 0$ (1)
All Cs are As:	$z(1 - y) = 0$	or	$zy - z = 0$ (2)

Therefore

All Cs are Bs:	$z(1 - x) = 0$	(3)

The triumph of the Boolean symbolization is that simply by invoking the recognized laws of (numerical) algebra we can show that (3) follows from (1) and (2). (1) relates y and x, and allows us to write an expresson for y. We can then substitute this for y in (2). And that gives us an expression relating x and z, which is (3), the conclusion.[7]

Boole shows, in his 1847 pamphlet *The Mathematical Analysis of Logic*, how the various forms of syllogism may all be expressed as propositions cast in Boolean symbolism, which can be shown to follow from other such propositions if only the explicit rules which he sets out are followed. He gives proofs, on the same basis, for many of the principles of the syllogistic established by Aristotle and the medieval logicians, showing how they can be set out as theorems of his system.

The rules of the calculus Boole had thus established are not quite those of the algebra of ordinary arithmetic. The difference lay in the axiom of the logical calculus that if you select according to a principle from the universal set and then use that same principle to select from the result, you do not alter the first selection. That is,

$$xx = x$$

or, in general, and using the notation of powers in the usual way,

$$x^2 = x$$

This is clearly different from the rule of the familiar numerical algebra covering multiplication.

As Boole himself saw, however, this difference is eliminated if a further rule is introduced, laying it down that x, y, z, ... may carry one of only two possible values, 0 and 1.

$$1 \times 1 = 1$$

just as

$$0 \times 0 = 0$$

and, in general,

$$x^n = x$$

But a system with this stipulation does not take us away from arithmetic altogether. The arithmetic we are used to is based on counting in tens, but the fundamentals are not changed if we count, for example, in sixteens (the hexadecimal system) or hundreds (a suggestion once pursued for calculators) or twos (the binary system). Binary arithmetic is, precisely, a system in which only two possible values are allowed each number variable. Boole's calculus, understood as having this condition built in, becomes an algebra for expressing two-valued or binary arithmetic, as well as an algebra capable of expressing the syllogistic:

> Let us conceive, then, of an algebra in which the symbols x, y, z etc. admit indifferently of the values 0 and 1, and of these values alone. The laws, the axioms, and the processes, of such an Algebra will be identical in their whole extent with the laws, the axioms, and the processes of an Algebra of Logic. Differences of interpretation will alone divide them.[8]

The potential of binary arithmetic was not explored until the 1930s.[9] Once Boole had devised his calculus, laying emphasis on the distinction between the formal system that the calculus constituted and its interpretation as the syllogistic, he explored other possible interpretations. One of the most influential was to propose that the symbols X, Y, Z, ... might be used to stand for propositions, and the elective symbols x, y, z, ... to represent whether or not the relevant proposition was true. Truth on this scheme was be represented by '1' and falsity by '0'. Then 'x = 1' would mean that the proposition X was true, and 'x = 0' that it was false.[10]

As the syllogistic came to be abandoned, or rather subsumed under a more general logic, this notion of propositions possessing a 'truth-value' was made much of; first by Frege, who invented the term itself, and in the next century by Ludwig Wittgenstein, Lucasiewicz and Emil Post.[11] Boole's achievement was not so much to launch this particular idea as to establish what perhaps only Leibniz before him had felt – the possibility of articulating logic as a formal system, whose principles could be displayed as deducible from a set of explicitly stated axioms and rules, exactly on the pattern of geometry in mathematics. This was a tremendous advance for logic, and of course it brought the mechanization of such deduction as logic had managed to systematize within reach. The logician and philosopher W. S. Jevons was the first to have an actual machine built that realized the potential Boole's ideas represented. He was at once Boole's champion, being among the first to hail him as the successor in logic to Aristotle himself,[12] and his critic, condemning his 'mathematical' symbolization and identifying weaknesses in his construal of the logical operator 'or'. His machine, accordingly, makes no use of Boole's logical algebra.

Jevons' basic notion is to let A, B, C, ... stand for classes, and a, b, c, ... stand for their complements.[13] But because a thing is thought of as belonging to a class in virtue of an attribute it shares with the other members, A, B, C, ... are often treated as standing for attributes. In understanding his system it is in fact easiest, if a little loose, to think directly in terms of attributes. 'A', then, might stand for being made of iron, and 'a' for not being made of iron.

What Jevons proposes is that syllogistic premises can be regarded as ruling out certain combinations of attributes. For example, 'All things made of iron and metallic' rules out the possible combination of being made of iron and being non-metallic. Syllogistic reasoning then appears as working out what combinations of attributes remain possible once the ones ruled out by the premises have been deleted. This turns out to be none too difficult, since for small numbers of attributes, at any rate, the number of possible combinations to check against the premises is not very large. There are only eight ways, for example, in which three attributes may conceivably be combined, and in Jevons' symbolism they are written:

ABC	(iron, metallic, an element)
ABc	(iron, metallic, but not an element)
AbC	(iron, non-metallic, an element)
Abc	etc.
aBC	
aBc	
abC	
abc	

If we suppose, for instance, that we wish to work out what can be deduced from the two premises 'All A is B' and 'No B is C', we proceed by crossing out AbC and Abc because of the first premise, and ABC and aBC because of the second. The remaining combinations are thus revealed as consistent with the premises, and any statement asserting a relation between the attributes concerned which is compatible with them constitutes a valid inference from the premises (such as the conclusion that 'No A is C').

Jevons' logical machine, which, following the venerable tradition, he had made by a clockmaker in 1869, has the general form of a cash-register.[14] The upright part of the machine consists of two rows of wooden rods, each bearing a symbol for a term. The rows are placed back-to-back, and doors on either side enclose them, except that the symbols are visible through a horizontal slit. The rods are capable of vertical movement in a way that is controlled by the horizontal keyboard to which they are linked, so that symbols may appear or disappear from view depending on the keys pressed. The keys themselves allow the premises of an argument to be put in. In the middle there is a key for the copula (the 'is' of a premise) and on either side a key for each term, one for conjunction ('and') and another for disjunction ('or'). Other keys are marked 'FULL STOP' and 'FINIS'. As each premise is keyed in, levers working on pins projecting from the vertical rods move the latter up or down in such a way that the combinations of attributes ruled out as impossible by the premise in question are eliminated from view. The combinations of attributes that remain visible through the slit once all the premises have been put in represents the conclusion.

A graphical version of the logic machine was developed by John Venn and became known as 'Venn diagrams'. Within a square to represent the universe of discourse (which was generally what Boole meant by 'universe'),

= Conjunction (and)
⊃ Implication ("If . . . then . . . ")
v Disjunction, alternation ("Either . . . or . . . or both")
≢ Exclusive disjunction, non-equivalence ("Either . . . or . . .but not both")
≡ Equivalence ("If and only if . . . then . . . ")
| Non-conjunction ("Not both . . . and . . . ")
~ Negation ("Not")

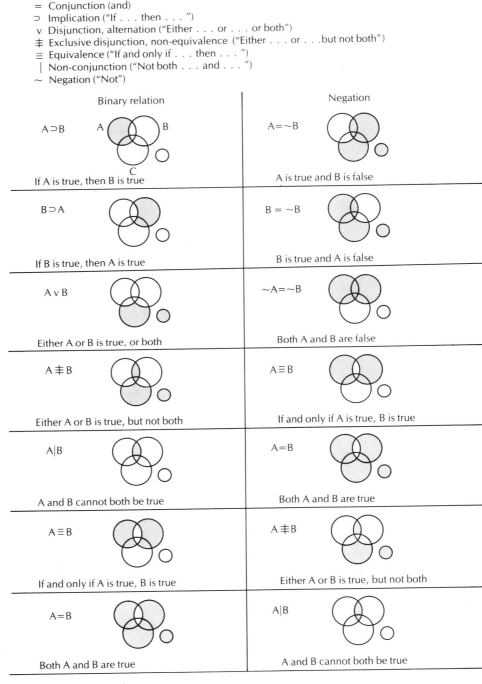

Binary relation	Negation
A⊃B A, B, C — If A is true, then B is true	A=~B — A is true and B is false
B⊃A — If B is true, then A is true	B = ~B — B is true and A is false
A v B — Either A or B is true, or both	~A=~B — Both A and B are false
A ≢ B — Either A or B is true, but not both	A≡B — If and only if A is true, B is true
A|B — A and B cannot both be true	A=B — Both A and B are true
A≡B — If and only if A is true, B is true	A≢B — Either A or B is true, but not both
A=B — Both A and B are true	A|B — A and B cannot both be true

Figure 9.1 Venn diagrams

Source: Gardner *Logic Machines* (see note 17, p. 80 above) p. 52

Venn drew overlapping circles to represent the different possible combinations of classes (or, as Jevons used the notion, attributes) and then added shading to show which possibilities any given premise excluded.[15]

An improved form of Jevons' machine was devised by the American Allan Marquand in 1881, and soon afterwards he designed (but probably did not quite build) an electrical version, using electromagnets, multiway switches and a rheostat.[16]

A plea has been made for recognising Jevons as a seminal figure in the development of mechanizing logic.[17] Certainly he invented a pioneering machine, and indeed inspired a line of logical machines, culminating perhaps in the electrical relay device Ferranti built[18] for Manchester University's philosophy department as a teaching aid (this as late as 1950). His influence, however, went against the parallel that Boole saw between binary arithmetic and class (and propositional) logic, and thus against the development of the predicate logic upon which the greatest potential of modern machines depends. His machine stimulated a series of developments, built by psychologists (Benjamin Burack, 1936), philosophers (Wolfe Mays, 1949, and Roger Holmes, 1954), and logicians and their students (William Burkhart and Theodore Kalin, 1947), which used electricity as it became readily controllable, and culminated in an explosion of interest in mid-century.[19] But logic came of age and began to be *generally* useful only when the Boolean point, that the propositional calculus was

W. Stanley Jevons, 1835–82

isomorphic with the calculus of binary arithmetic, was returned to, and the logical powers of the big binary calculators began to be explored. At this point, the distinctively 'logical' machines in the Jevons tradition were decisively superceded.

Looking only at the logical tradition behind Boole's achievement, there seems an astonishing temporal distance between Boole and the person whose work he was pretty well alone in taking up – Leibniz. The obvious question seems to be this: what could it have been that brought Boole at his time and place to be moved by Leibniz' concerns and to pursue lines Leibniz had begun, when others for such a long time had found other lines of thought under the heading 'logic' more challenging? This, however, is not the most appropriate question, because Boole was a mathematician, and it was from that tradition that he received both framework and stimulus. By logicians he was regarded as the agent of 'a foreign power' set to 'annex the sacred province of logic [...] to the already over-grown empire of mathematics.'[20] As a mathematician he takes his place very naturally in the succession of

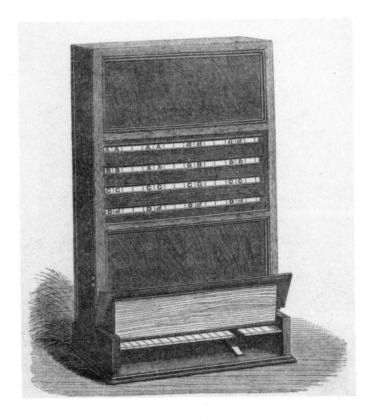

Jevons' logical piano, 1870

thinkers who advanced throughout the nineteenth century the idea of formalization.

Notes

1 Boole, *The Mathematical Analysis of Logic* (Cambridge, 1847), reprinted Oxford, 1948; in Rush Rhees (ed.), *Studies in Logic and Probability* (Watts & Co., London, 1952), p. 49.
2 See Parkinson, *Logical Papers*, pp. xlvii, xlviii.
3 W. and M. Kneale, *Development of Logic*, p. 408.
4 Boole, *The Laws of Thought* (London, 1854); *Mathematical Analysis;* in Rhees, *Studies in Logic*, pp. 49–124.
5 Boole, in Rhees, *Studies in Logic*, p. 69.
6 Boole, in Rhees, *Studies in Logic*, p. 74.
7 In general, from two equations of the form

$$ay + ab = 0$$
$$a^1y + b^1 = 0$$

we can derive by elimination

$$ab^1 - a^1b = 0$$

I think, *pace* the Kneales (*Development of Logic*, p. 417) that this proof involves 'division' – $y = xy / x$. Boole, in Rhees, *Studies in Logic*, p. 74.
8 Boole, *Laws of Thought*, pp. 37, 38.
9 See below, pp. 152ff.
10 Boole, in Rhees, *Studies in Logic*, pp. 88–107.
11 W. and M. Kneale, *Development of Logic*, p. 413; Alonzo Church, *Introduction to Mathematical Logic* (Princeton UP, Princeton, 1956), p. 162.
12 W. S. Jevons, *The Principles of Science* (Dover, New York, 1958), p. 113.
13 Jevons, 'On the Mechanical Performance of Logical Inference', *Philosophical Transactions of the Royal Society*, CLX (1870), pp. 497–518.
14 Before there were cash-registers, it was thought to look like a 'small piano': though I have never seen cash-registers likened to small pianos. A case of 'A is like B and B is like C, but A is not like C'?
15 W. and M. Kneale, *Development of Logic*, p. 420, 1; Gardner, *Logic Machines*, ch 5, pp. 91–103.
16 Wolfe Mays and Desmond Henry, 'Exhibition of the Work of W. Stanley Jevons', *Nature*, 170 (1952), pp. 696, 697.
17 Mays and Henry, 'Jevons and Logic', *Mind*, LXII (1953), pp. 484–505.
18 Wolfe, Mays and D. G. Prinz, 'A Relay Machine for the Demonstration of Symbolic Logic', *Nature*, 165 (1950), p. 197.
19 Gardner, *Logic Machines*, ch 8, pp. 125–155.
20 Hugh McColl, 'Symbolic Reasoning', *Mind*, 5 (1880), p. 46.

10 Machines for Science and Commerce

Babbage's project had to wait some time for fulfilment, but as far as its mathematical powers were concerned at any rate, fulfilled it was. Suddenly, in a single decade of the present century, developments in a number of different centres, and in a number of different contexts, converged on the modern computer. In Berlin, Konrad Zuse applied to patent an electromechanical automatic calculator in 1936. In 1937, work began on another electromechanical device in the Bell Telephone Laboratories in New York. That year, in Harvard, Howard Aiken proposed a giant automatic calculator based on cobbling together commercially available electromechanical accounting machines. In Ohio, John V. Atanasoff was working towards an automatic calculator on electronic principles throughout the second half of the decade. And, again in 1936, there was a development of what seems an utterly different kind: three theoreticians, Alan Turing, Emil Post and Alonzo Church, working independently both of each other and of the machine builders just mentioned, published different but (as it was later shown) equivalent definitions of what it was to be 'computable'.

These events of the 1930s, in striking parallel to those of the 1830s, marked not so much one developing story as the denouement of one and the prologue of another. Much of what had animated Babbage remained intelligible and inspirational – his ambition to build a powerful, automatic, fast, error-free calculator, which, because of numerical analysis, would embrace the whole of mathematics – and the aim of several of the new generation went thus far and no further. But others saw a different potential in the machines that were taking shape, and launched a project that had not been there (as anything like a practical proposition) before.

In this chapter and the next I shall look at the new developments as bringing Babbage's old plans for a calculator to fruition; in the one following, I shall turn to what was new.

The Interregnum

The hiatus between Babbage's plans of the 1840s and their realization, at least in part, in the 1930s has of course attracted comment. It has been suggested, for example, that after Babbage there was no-one with the talent necessary to prosecute his plans. But though certainly they may have 'frightened' the commission appointed to consider their feasibility in 1879, as Hyman suggests,[1] there were brains enough, working towards the end of the century, without a shadow of a doubt: the fact is only, surely, that they chose to work in other directions. Besides, the really crucial work had been done. Babbage had articulated the idea: the remaining task of putting it into some material form or other was of a different order – like the task accepted by Scheutz, that of finding a way of building the Difference Engine he had read about in the *Edinburgh Review*.

The Scheutz case is also relevant to another claim that is put forward, namely that the Analytical Engine as Babbage envisaged it called for metallurgical and engineering techniques that went beyond those available in the latter part of the nineteenth century.[2] For Scheutz's way of building a Difference Engine was quite different from Babbage's. Babbage was an engineer of genius, driven relentlessly by the imperative to find the best possible way of doing what might be done in any number of less than optimal ways. If the detail of Babbage's plans demanded too much of contemporary resources (which has not been demonstrated), other less taxing ways of achieving the same ends may well have been feasible.

Nevertheless, one feature of the 1930s' machines stands out: in one role or another, all of them called on *electricity*. Later the role was to become absolutely central, but to begin with, the contribution it made was to eliminate a whole level of complication in the problem of design. An automatic calculator had to have a number of components among which numbers and instructions had to be moved about. Mechanically, this meant linkages of metal rods, trains of cogs and the like, all arranged and maintained very precisely in space. Electricity, even in its earliest applications, meant that mechanical linkages of daunting (and limiting) complexity could be replaced by lengths of flexible wire that connected switches in one part of the apparatus with electromagnets in another.

In one way, therefore, there is something in the claim that twentieth-century technology made the Analytical Engine an easier practical proposition than it had been in the mid-nineteenth. But, on the other hand, it would be wrong to suggest that electricity provided a solution in this respect to a problem that had been engaging active and urgent interest. The truth is rather that for a long while after Babbage's proposals the need for automatic calculating machines was not felt with any acuteness.

This was partly because of the nature of the scientific work being done. Little of the physics of the second half of the nineteenth century was dependent on extensive programmes of calculation; nor was the work which overthrew the Newtonian perspective in the early part of the next century. But this was not the whole of the story, since there certainly were scientific projects in this period that would have benefited if such a machine had been available. Work in astronomy[3] in particular continued to test the endurance and dedication of human computers throughout the century, as indeed it had always done.[4] For these and other scientific purposes, the desk calculator, available in reliable form since about the middle of the century, was there to be pressed into use; but it was almost totally neglected by science until 1928, when L.J. Comrie of the Royal Naval College used office machinery to produce astronomical tabulations. (He later set up a small independent bureau, undertaking calculations for scientific purposes, using a range of commercial machines.)[5] As late as 1941, those who took the trouble to explore what was available in the way of calculation aids were shocked to find facilities of great potential value to the scientist and engineer just not being called on.[6]

Certainly in the period between Babbage and the 1920s, then, the stimulus for scientists to search beyond their own world for greater resources was lacking, and the divide between them and the world of commerce rarely crossed.

I have said that when the new automatic calculating machines of the thirties emerged, they used electricity in one way or another because it simplified the engineering task. But electricity played a more fundamental role than this.

The end of the nineteenth century saw a tremendous growth, in the industrialized world, in the size of organizations – commercial organizations like insurance companies, cultural organizations like school systems, and political organizations of which, of course, the modern state itself is the best example. The maintenance and nourishment of such structures required elaborate communication networks, responsible for the efficient circulation of people and goods, information and energy. Electricity was used as the basis for many of these.

It was in developing the technology of electrically-based communication systems – particularly telegraph and telephone systems and power supply grids – that the demand for enhanced calculational aids finally became insistent. Work of this kind – handling voltages and currents in complicated networks of conductors – depended on the manipulation of differential equations of the first and second order, and it was for this that some kind of aid became highly desirable. The sections that follow explain something of the nature of this particular role, and of how antecedent roles had been filled prior to the 1930s.

Planimeters and Integrators

Differential equations were easily thought of in terms of the type of physical relationship they were devised to describe – rates of change in a quantity where that rate depends on the value of the quantity itself at the given time. For example, the rate of change of current in a circuit to which a given voltage is applied depends, if the circuit contains both inductance and impedance, on what the current is at the time.[7] One approach to the devising of a mechanical aid for solving these equations was, therefore, to set up a physical system with relationships of the exact kind described in the equation to be solved, to set it in motion and to read off what happened to the quantity whose value was being sought.

Mechanical aids of this 'analogue' kind had been used in the course of the extensive programme of road and permanent way building pursued by the industrializing world during the early part of the eighteenth century. Rational choice of route for a new way depended on comparing, for the different options, the total quantity of infill required for embankments and the total amount of earth removal implied by the necessary cuttings. At the root of such estimation was the calculation of areas enclosed by curves – for example, the area between the straight line of a proposed level road and the undulating surface of the ground over which it might be built.

Such a calculation could be done graphically by drawing the two lines on squared paper and counting the squares enclosed: but mechanical devices were invented to do the job more conveniently. They were called 'planimeters'. One of the first was invented by an engineer called J. H. Hermann in 1814,[8] and one of the most widely used by Jacob Amsler in 1854.[9]

Measuring the area under a curve is the graphical equivalent of integration, and had application far beyond surveying. For example, integration is necessary for the procedure known as 'harmonic analysis', whereby a complicated waveform is split up into the several simple waveforms of which it may be thought to be composed. This has an application in the prediction of tides, which may be thought of as the net effect of several jointly operating simple wave disturbances, and a mechanical integrator was engineered for this purpose by James Thomson between 1861 and 1864.

What was wanted was a continuously variable gear, seen perhaps most easily in the 'Wheel and Disc Integrator', which was not quite Thomson's device but one which grew out of his.[10] Here a turntable is used to drive round a small index wheel that is arranged to bear on the turntable at right angles, as though it were the stylus on a record player (see Figure 10.1). The gearage between index wheel and disc can then be varied by moving the wheel towards or away from the centre of the revolving turntable. Thomson's own arrangement was to have the motion of a disc transmitted to a cylinder, via the intermediary of a sphere. The gearing ratio was then changed as the point of contact between sphere and disc varied relative to the centre of rotation of the disc.

James engineered a suitable integrator, but it was his brother William, Lord Kelvin, who built a tidal harmonic analyser and tide predictor out of it (using several integrators, in fact).[11]

Kelvin also explained how integrators may be combined to form a machine that would be capable of solving differential equations.[12] As I

Differential Analyser devised by Vannevar Bush, operational in 1931

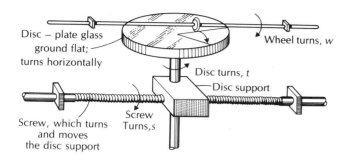

Wheel - steel hub and steel edge, elsewhere magnesium;
0.002 inch wide at edge; turns vertically in
contact with the disc

Disc – plate glass
ground flat;
turns horizontally

Wheel turns, w

Disc turns, t

Disc support

Screw, which turns
and moves
the disc support

Screw
Turns, s

Figure 10.1 Principle of the Wheel and Disc Integrator

Source: E. C. Berkeley, *Giant Brains* (Wiley, New York, 1949) p. 79

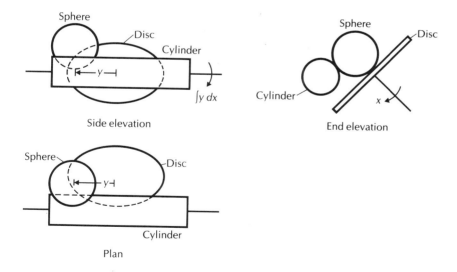

Sphere

Disc

Cylinder

$\int y \, dx$

y

Side elevation

Sphere

Disc

Cylinder

x

End elevation

Sphere

Disc

y

Cylinder

Plan

Figure 10.2 Principle of Thomson's disc, globe and cylinder integrator

Source: Hartree, *Calculating Instruments* (see note 7) p. 6

Differential Analyser built in Meccano by Douglas Hartree

pointed out above, a differential equation describes relationships in a system in which one of the things that governs the rate of change in a certain quantity is the instantaneous value of that quantity itself. In our example of a circuit containing both inductance and resistance, the rate of change of current at any time depends on what the current itself is. Solving such an equation – in this case determining what the current would be at a given time – is a matter of conducting a series of integrations, each one giving the current after an infinitesimally small time lapse, but each one taking as its figure for the existing current the result of the integration just completed. The first gives the current after an infinitesimally small period has elapsed since the voltage was applied. The second calculates what happens to the current at the end of a second infinitesimally small time period; and it has to include as its data the figure for the current obtained by the first integration. Thus begins a whole series of integrations, each moving the evaluation a step further towards the time for which a figure for the current is actually sought, and each taking as its figure for the current the result of the last one. In mechanical terms, therefore, what is required is that the result of an initial integration be fed into the integrator as part of the input for the next integration.

The Differential Analyser

Though Kelvin had shown the way, work on practical machines capable of solving differential equations did not begin to gather momentum until the 1920s, and then apparently as a new initiative owing nothing to Kelvin's 1876 papers. Its culmination was the differential analyser designed by Vannevar Bush at MIT, announced in 1931.[13]

Quantities are represented in the analyser by degrees of rotation of steel shafts, a number of which lie parallel to each other along a long bench. The shafts may be interconnected through gearing in a variety of ways, and it is possible to take off any of the quantities and feed them into integrators, which are ranged alongside the bench in a bank. For any particular equation the operator has to work out which sequence of integrations, additions, etc., and of which quantities, will generate the result, and design a pattern of interconnections accordingly. Some of the components of more recalcitrant equations have to be fed into the analyser via 'input tables', with operatives physically moving pointers along graphs of the required functions. Figure 10.3 shows the pattern of interconnections for the equation shown.[14]

The differential analyser was the most general of the machines that proliferated in the thirties in response to the calculational needs of electrical engineering, and it was they that provided the context within which experimentation with digital approaches to the same challenge arose.

The digital approach itself had no flourishing tradition within science to draw on. Scientists had not seen the point of taking further the initiatives so passionately prosecuted by Babbage in the mid-nineteenth century. But

Hollerith Electric Tabulating System: machines used in the Austrian census of 1890

people in other institutions had. The desk calculators experimented with throughout the eighteenth century always had great potential for those who had to manipulate figures on a small-scale, routine, day-to-day basis: a category which, as trade and particularly money business like insurance grew, came to represent a substantial market. And as they grew, the framework itself began to shift. For evolving towards the close of the nineteenth century there came the giant organization, which looked to regimented number-handling on an unprecedented scale to help maintain cohesion and control.

Office Machinery

Among the most significant large organizations to take shape was the bureaucratic state itself, and it was in connection with the steadily enlarging scale of the national census in Europe and North America that the need for a different order of 'data' manipulation arose most powerfully. An observer of the 1880 census in the USA, an assistant to an academic consultant,

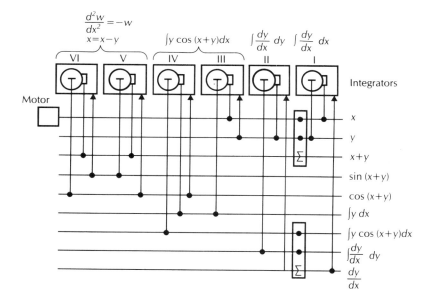

Figure 10.3 Schematic set-up of Differential Analyser for equation:

$$\frac{d^2y}{dx^2} - y\cos(x+y) + \left(\frac{dy}{dx}\right)^2 = 0, \text{ or } \frac{dy}{dx} = \int y\cos(x+y)dx - \int \frac{dy}{dx}dy$$

(Scale factors and signs omitted.)

Source: Hartree, *Calculating Instruments* (see note 7) p. 19

The IBM Automatic Sequence Controlled Calculator (Mark I). Calculator completed 1944.

calculated that the next census might involve the repeated handling of five hundred miles of paper: or, if it were done using simple cards instead, a stack over ten miles high.[15] On that prospect he founded the suggestion 'that the work be done so far as possible by mechanical means,'[16] and went on to work up the idea of coding the information on punched cards and sorting them electromechanically.

The observer's name was Herman Hollerith, and his proposals, submitted for a PhD and for a patent, were the basis for equipment readied for the subsequent census in 1890. The approach proved extremely successful. Hollerith's name still attaches to the dollar-bill-sized cards he introduced, and which have yet to be entirely displaced, and his initial, at least, stands enshrined in the Hollerith string of FORTRAN code. Doubtless even more enduring, the company he founded formed a major tributary to the mighty IBM.[17]

The use of patterns of perforations to carry data was, of course, not new. Jacquard's loom had used it, and so had Babbage. Hollerith was able to call electricity to aid, however, and had the material carrying the perforations (continuous paper in the earliest proposal, then cards) interposed between a series of pairs of electrical contacts. At those points at which the material was perforated, contact was not prevented, and a circuit was completed. There was a pair of contacts, and thus a circuit, for each possible perforation position, and each circuit incorporated an electromagnet. When a circuit was closed, its electromagnet was activated, and this was arranged to advance a mechanical counter by one. A bank of counters thus kept track of how many times a particular feature, coded by the position of a hole on a card or paper, occurred in the records as whole.

This early formulation left much in the hands of the operator. Subsequent developments extended the number of operations mechanized, and also the mechanism's repertoire. Application of the basic idea to the accounting problems of commercial organizations, now becoming very large, led before the end of the century to Hollerith giving his system the power to add as well as count, for which he developed what might be regarded as an electronic version of the Leibniz stepped cylinder.[18]

The Hollerith system used electricity, but electricity played no essential role. As late as 1933, Louis Couffignal describes an alternative system, devised by James Powers, which relied on sets of needles (like the rods of Babbage and Jacquard) instead of electrical contacts to 'read' the hole-coded data. Clearly, the mechanical approach retained superiority in some applications.[19]

By 1933, however, there were also available what Couffignal calls 'synchronized' machines, and in these electricity was essential. They consisted of machines with different functions harnessed together so as to come under the efficient control of a single operator. A tabulator, for example, could be much enhanced if linked to a calculating machine capable of multiplication and division, so that these operations could be applied to figures in a projected tabulation, and the results included also. The necessary interfacing was too complicated to be done mechanically, so that in these clusters electricity, powering relays that actuated remote electro-magnetically operated levers, now played a necessary role.[20] They represented, in Couffignal's words of 1933, the capacity to perform 'very diverse and often very complicated accounting operations with great ease.'[21]

When the practical importance of developing powerful calculational aids, led by electrical engineering, began to assert itself in the 1920s and 1930s, Bush's response in building the differential analyser was, therefore, not the only one available. Another, urged by L. J. Comrie, was to point to the unexploited potential of the best commercial desk-top calculators – machines like the Brunsviga and the Universal. Yet another was to turn to the sophisticated statistical machines of the Hollerith tradition, and to argue that automation of complex or extended calculating could be achieved by linking a number of them into a network, and arranging for numbers to be passed around and operated upon in a pre-set sequence. This was the proposal of Howard Aiken, made in 1937, and realized in 1944. And it was this machine, the Automatic Sequence Controlled Calculator or Harvard Mark I, that Comrie hailed as 'Babbage's dream come true'.[22]

Networking Statistical Machines

Aiken's 52–feet by 8–feet giant was, in terms of structure, very little like the Analytical Engine as Babbage had detailed it. The various operations took place not in a single mill but in the appropriate participant machines. Numbers were represented sometimes by the partial rotation of wheels, but sometimes by the duration of currents of electricity moving about the machine. Translations between these two representations was achieved with electromagnetic clutches. Power was supplied by a single rotating main shaft, running the length of the machine, and a clutch transmitted movement from the shaft to a counter only while the clutch was 'turned on' by a current. Thus, varying the duration of the current varied the degree of rotation imparted to the counter. The net effect was that the number represented by current duration was passed to the counter, where it was represented, classically as it were, by the degree of rotation of a wheel.

This use of electricity involves switches, and for this purpose Aiken took over the relay. A circuit switched by a relay, in its simplest form, is one which is routed through a strip of metal, one end of which is spring-loaded against a stud. An electromagnet is located behind the strip, so that when activated it pulls the strip away from the stud, and the circuit is broken. Should the electromagnet then be deactivated, the strip of metal springs back and its circuit is restored.

Switching circuits on and off rapidly and reliably was a requirement of using electricity for communication, one of its first great applications, and it was in the context of telegraph networks that the relay was introduced and

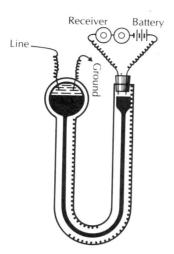

Figure 10.4 Wheatstone's electric relay, 1837

Source: Daumas *History of Technology* (see note 24, p. 60 above), p. 382

refined (in the 1830s, just as Babbage was beginning to work out the details of the mechanical Analytical Engine).[23] Later, relays were to be used as the very basis of sophisticated calculators, but in Aiken's Mark I they played a subsidiary role: they did not carry out arithmetic processes, but moved the numbers about.

Perforated paper tape, read by a series of contact brushes which established circuits only where no paper intervened (in the manner pioneered by Hollerith), was the means by which the machine was given a sequence of operations to perform. Each line of the paper could carry a maximum of 24 holes. The first eight locations coded for the counter out of which a number was to be taken. The second eight coded for the counter holding a second number, and the third eight told the machine which

Table 2 Harvard Mark I operations and their execution times

Operation	Execution time (seconds)
Addition	0.3
Subtraction	0.3
Multiplication	6.0
Division	11.4
$Log_{10}x$	72.6
10^x	61.2
Sin x	60.0

Source: Fernbach & Taub, *Computers and their Role in the Physical Sciences* (see Fig 8.1 p. 117 above) p. 48

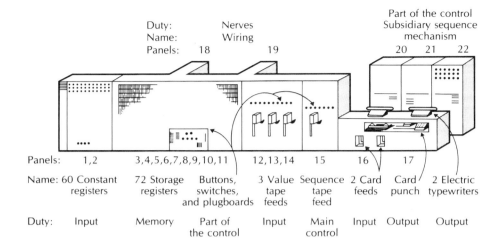

Figure 10.5 Scheme of Harvard Mark I

Source: Berkeley *Giant Brains* (see Fig 10.1 p. 141 above) p. 90

operation was to be undertaken with them. Different patterns of holes activated different patterns of relays, which established the circuits necessary for the specified operation to take place.[24]

In its original form, the ASCC did not quite match the specification for his own machine that Babbage had laid down. It lacked a full capacity to use intermediate results to select among alternative sequences of operations – the capacity for conditional branching which Babbage had planned to realize by exploiting the potential of the wheel carrying the 'sign' of a number in his machine.[25] This was a significant weakness from the point of view of the machine's powers, but its other features – its capacity (72 registers capable of conducting additions as well as storage, 60 registers for storing constants, a normal accuracy of 23 significant digits) and above all its power to perform automatically on receipt of a single input of a set of ordered instructions – went a long way towards justifying Comrie's welcome for it as Babbage's Analytical Engine come to pass.

Notes

1 Hyman, *Babbage*, p. 254.
2 See, for example, Konrad Z use, 'The Outline of a Computer Development from Mechanics to Electronics', reprinted in Randell, *Origins*, pp. 171, 172.
3 One of the great architects of the modern computer, Wallace J. Eckert, came to articulate the need for more powerful computing machinery against the background of distinguished work in astronomy – and as the inspiration of the Astronomical

Computing Bureau established in 1937. See Goldstine, *Computer from Pascal*, pp. 27 ff, 108, 109.

4 But once the problem of longitude had been solved effectively (with the successful trials of marine chronometers by Le Roy and Harrison in the middle of the eighteenth century) the practical relevance of astronomy's advance lessened, and its command of resources correspondingly weakened. See Usher, *Mechanical Inventions*, pp. 326–8.

5 L. J. Comrie, 'On the Construction of Tables by Interpolation', *Royal Astronomical Society Monthly Notices*, 88 (1928), pp. 506–623.

6 E. V. Crew, 'Calculating Machines', *The Engineer*, 172 (1941), p. 441.

7 D. R. Hartree's example: Hartree, *Calculating Instruments and Machines* (Urbana, Ill., 1949), pp. 4, 5.

8 George Stibitz, 'Mathematical Instruments', in *Encyclopaedia Britannica*, Fourteenth Edition (1973).

9 Daumas, *History of Technology*, Vol. II, p. 241.

10 W. D. Niven (ed.), *The Scientific Papers of James Clerk Maxwell* (Dover, New York, 1955), pp. 230–2.

11 Lord Kelvin, *Mathematical and Physical Papers* (Cambridge, 1882–1911), Vol. VI, pp. 272ff.

12 W. Thomson (Lord Kelvin), 'Mechanical Integration', *Proceedings of the Royal Society*, 24 (1876) pp. 269–75.

13 Vannevar Bush, 'The Differential Analyzer', *Journal of the Franklin Institute*, 212 (1931), pp. 447–88.

14 Hartree gives a clear account. See *Calculating Instruments*, ch. 2.

15 Herman Hollerith, 'An Electric Tabulating System', in Randell, *Origins*, p. 129.

16 Hollerith, 'Electric Tabulating System', in Randell, *Origins*, p. 129.

17 Randell, *Origins*, p. 126.

18 Randell, *Origins*, p. 126. The reference is to an anonymous contribution in *American Machinist*, 25 (1902), pp. 1073–5, under the title 'The Electrical Tabulating Machine Applied to Cost Accounting'.

19 Couffignal, 'Calculating Machines: Their Principles and Evolution', in Randell, *Origins*, pp. 146–8.

20 For a brief survey see Couffignal, 'Calculating Machines', in Randell, *Origins*, 149, 150.

21 Couffignal, 'Calculating Machines', in Randell, *Origins*, p. 150.

22 Randell, *Origins*, p. 17.

23 Daumas, *History of Technology*, pp. 380–2; cf. Hartree, *Calculating Instruments*, p. 55.

24 An authoritative account of the ASCC is found in the articles by Howard Aiken and Grace Hopper reprinted in Randell, *Origins*, pp. 199–218. Hartree gives a brief and lucid account in *Calculating Instruments*.

25 Hartree, *Calculating Instruments*, p. 79.

11 Giant Calculators

In the laboratories of the Bell Telephone Company, the attractiveness of automatic computing machinery was felt when the need arose to do a good deal of calculation with complex numbers. (Complex numbers are numbers that consist of the sum of an ordinary number, positive or negative, and the product of an ordinary number and whatever '$\sqrt{-1}$' represents. Numbers of this type were invoked because their two elements could be used to represent the two key types of circuit element in telephone network design.) Human computers were perfectly capable of handling complex numbers, which are subject to simple rules: only the work took time, and errors were made. Mechanization was attractive on both scores, and in 1937, George Stibitz, a mathematician at Bell, began to think how this might be realized.

It was not surprising, perhaps, that within the particular context of designing telephone equipment, that equipment itself should have been fixed on as providing the basis for the desired machine. That is to say, the use of relays was taken over from the telephone system to the automatic computer – not, as in the Harvard Mark I, for linking mechanical elements, but instead of them. In place of a counter wheel, which represented a count of ten by a complete revolution and was capable of representing the numbers from one to nine by means of partial rotation, the Bell computer put the relay, capable of only two states (essentially: closed and open).

Counting with Switches

How might a relay, or set of relays, represent a number? One simple way would be to have a set of ten relays for each digit and to let the number of relays switched on in each of these sets represent the required digit. (See table 3.)

Such a scheme would be less economical in use of relays, however, particularly when it came to designing circuits for the addition of numbers represented in this manner, than one which could be devised if the counting did not have to be done in tens. For the use of the relay, with its two states, lends itself to counting not in tens but in twos – the binary system. A

Bell Laboratories "complex number" relay calculator, completed 1939

Table 3 Representation of a
three-digit number using
sets of ten relays

First digit	Second digit	Third digit
On	On	On
On	On	Off
On	On	Off
Off	On	Off
Off	Off	Off
Off	Off	Off
Off	Off	Off
Off	Off	Off
Off	Off	Off
Off	Off	Off

3 4 1

number expressed in binary, such as 1010, can be represented straightforwardly by a set of relays, one for each digit. Just as each digit is capable of
just two forms, 0 and 1, so each relay is capable of just two states, on or off.
1010 might then be represented by a set of four relays, the first and third of
which were on, the second and fourth off.

Addition of numbers expressed in binary form can, of course, be reduced
to simple rules of thumb, just as addition with base ten numbers can. They
are these:

$$0 + 0 = 0$$
$$0 + 1 = 1$$
$$1 + 0 = 1$$
$$1 + 1 = 10$$

The machine needs three sets of relays, therefore: one to represent the first
number, another to represent the number to be added to the first, and a
third to represent the result of the addition. The relays of each set that are

Table 4 Representation of Binary number
using a bank of relays

Number		1	0	1	0
Set of relays:		On	Off	On	Off

Table 5 Binary addition

Carry

0	+	0	=	0	0
0	+	1	=	0 ·	1
1	+	0	=	0	1
1	+	1	=	1	0

furthest to the right represent the digits of each of the three numbers that are furthest to the right. These relays must be connected so that if the first two are both off, the one representing the result goes off; if the first two are both on, the third goes off but a carry is passed on; and if one is on and the other is off, the result relay goes on. The same rules apply to the digits next on the left on each of the three numbers, with one complication: if a carry has been registered (that is, a special relay has been switched on) 1 has to be added to the sum of the digits as they stand, and if that sum is 10 (binary), the result, 11 (binary), has to be represented as the result relay going on and a carry going forward.

Addition thus becomes a matter of connecting sets of relays in the appropriate way, and since the other operations of arithmetic can be built out of additions (and were in the first Bell Laboratories machine) we have a new approach to the basics of calculator construction.

Relays were also to be the basis of the machine for which Konrad Zuse sought a patent in Germany in 1936. His motivation was apparently the intelligible desire to ease the labour of calculations set him as an engineering student;[1] and even in 1939 when his collaborator Helmut Schreyer wrote to urge the importance of Zuse's work, he gave most stress to the general utility Zuse's machine would have in the engineering or scientific laboratory.[2] But

Table 6 Representation of Binary addition using relays

Carry

Off	Off	→	Off	Off
Off	On	→	Off	On
On	Off	→	Off	On
On	On	→	On	Off

he also saw its application to gunnery, to weather forecasting, and to control engineering.

Zuse's designs had in fact begun with a purely mechanical device, completed in 1938. Unfortunately, little record of this machine survived the Second World War, but it would seem to have a rather better claim as the realization of Babbage's 'dream' than does the Harvard Mark I. Like the latter it lacked conditional branching. But, following Babbage rather than paralleling Aiken, it was based on the idea of a central 'processor', analogous with Babbage's mill, into which numbers were summoned from store and from which the results were despatched.

The patent application of 1936 proposed an (electromechanical) relay-based device which, again, in overall conception recalled that of Babbage very strongly – almost uncannily, one might say, in view of Zuse's record that he had encountered the work of Babbage only after the application had been submitted.[3] There was to be a 'memory' or store, holding constants and intermediate results, and a central arithmetic unit; and the sequence of operations was to be given to the machine by means of a paper tape carrying perforations. Each set of perforations (that is, each instruction) was to specify an operation together with three 'addresses', or codes for the locations in the machine where numbers were stored: one for each of two operands, and one for where the result was to be sent. The advantages of binary arithmetic for two-state relays, noted by Stibitz at the Bell Laboratories, were not lost on Zuse, and this is one of the features that Schreyer picked out in 1939 as characteristic of Zuse's design.[4] The other, of course, was its capacity to work automatically.[5]

As the Second World War gathered pace, developments were of course heavily shaped by military pressures. Zuse's plans for a 1,500–valve[6] computer were, indeed, rejected by the German government; but on the Allied side, public funds for computer-type projects became readily available the moment immediate military applications were identified. Deciphering enemy radio traffic was one of these, and led in Britain to the series of machines associated with Bletchley Park, still, inexplicably, shrouded in Great British secrecy. Another was the calculation of firing tables for artillery, which led in the USA to the development of ENIAC. A third was the American effort to build an atom bomb, the Los Alamos project, which culminated in the raids on Nagasaki and Hiroshima in 1945, and demanded along the way an enormous calculational effort.

Electronic Logic

The direction taken in Britain was determined by the skills of the British Special Intelligence Services. In collaboration with the Foreign Office and service departments, they established a centre at Bletchley Park in Buckinghamshire for working up 'intelligence' of enemy actions and intentions. A special – and key – project was the deciphering of messages being passed by radio among German units, picked up by listening posts in Britain and elsewhere. The Intelligence Services had to assemble for this special task a team of very special talent, which later turned out to have included most of those who were to make British contributions to computer development after the war, and also, in the person of Turing, one of the most powerful thinkers in the field (or indeed in any).

Simple ciphers map the alphabet onto an alternative set of symbols, or perhaps onto a differently ordered set of the same ones. The Axis forces used electromechanical scrambling devices called ENIGMA machines to introduce, as they hoped, impenetrable complexity by establishing a new mapping for each successive letter of a message. The machines were determinate, in the sense that with any particular setting, typing a particular letter determined which letter was generated at the other end. But the

An ENIGMA machine, Second World War

electronic paths connecting the two were thoroughly scrambled, and changed with every new letter of the message. The person receiving had to have an identical machine, with an identical setting, which would decipher the message automatically. The settings were changed according to a pre-set schedule once a day – and later during the war, once every eight hours.

These precautions were enough to make the task of the eavesdropper who was trying to solve the cipher by having people – even large numbers of people – working systematically through all the possibilities very much too big to be in the least feasible. The possibility of automating the matching of possible interpretations with stretches of ciphered message was recognized, but those who relied on ENIGMA were still confident (with complete justification) that even so, the sort of speed necessary to work through the possibilities was entirely out of the question.

The breakthrough made by the cryptographers at Bletchley Park was to reduce the possible permutations to manageable proportions, by exploiting carelessness on the part of enemy operators to make intelligent guesses about words that might be present in a particular message. If these guesses were good, huge swathes of possibilities were eliminable, and the task of working through the remaining ones much reduced. At this point, machines could be used. The early ones were called 'bombes' (after the Polish 'bomba', their prototypes) and they made possible the regular and reasonably prompt

COLOSSUS, operational from 1943

deciphering of an enormous quantity of Axis radio traffic throughout the war, providing a stream of excellent intelligence which perhaps helped the Allies towards victory and certainly rendered some of their errors inexcusable.

Just which machines were available to the cryptographers is still not absolutely clear, but we know that one of the more sophisticated series bore the name COLOSSUS.[7] The function of a COLOSSUS was to take in data, supplied on a paper tape, and compare a set pattern with successive stretches of the data. Any Boolean function could be selected and used to relate data and pattern, and the results could be counted. Almost all the switching functions were performed by valves, of which there were roughly 2,000 altogether.[8] Operating from 1943 on, these machines were therefore pioneers in the extensive use of electronic components for logical and calculational purposes.[9]

In the USA, the move to electronic switches for calculators came via the work of John V. Atanasoff, an applied mathematician at what was then Iowa State College. He recognized in the early 1930s the very general usefulness there would be in a machine that was capable of solving large systems of linear algebraic equations. He considered the analogue approaches, and then the possibility of adapting commercially available accounting machines, before concluding that to obtain the necessary speed and simplicity of construction the binary number system would have to be employed in a digital machine. This led, he tells us,[10] to the search for a suitable two-state physical device that could serve as the machine's basic number-representing element; and eventually to the use of small electrical condensers. (A condenser stores an electric charge across two plates, separated by insulation. The binary digit 0 was represented by Plate A being positive and Plate B negative; and 1 by the reverse.)

At the heart of this machine were two sets of these condensers or capacitors, one for each of the two numbers to be operated upon. He made no provision for a third – to hold the result – since he found it satisfactory to treat one as an accumulator, having numbers added into (or subtracted from) it cumulatively. Linking the two was his device for conducting the arithmetic operation, which takes the form of a network of valves.

The simplest sort of valve, the diode, had been invented in 1904 by J. A. Fleming, as a device to allow current to pass in one direction only. In 1906, Lee de Forest added a third electrode in between the two of the diode, and so invented the triode. By altering the voltage on the sandwiched electrode (the grid), the current passing through the valve could be adjusted; and because a slight alteration of the grid voltage brought about a larger alteration in the voltage between anode and cathode, the device acted as an amplifier. This was its chief application in radio, and what de Forest had in mind. But by altering the voltage on the grid sufficiently, any current passing through the valve could in fact be stopped completely, so that the triode could also be used as a switch: a switch which, because electronic, could be opened or closed very much more quickly than anything with mechanical parts. The triode could thus be used as an electrical version of the relay.

In the Bell Laboratories machine, as I have explained above, relays were networked in such a way that for a given pattern of input, the output was determined by the same laws that governed binary arithmetic. Atanasoff networked triodes to achieve the same effect.

There were three inputs: a digit from the first operand, a digit from the second operand, and information on whether a carry from any previous operation was to be taken into account. Each of these data was represented by a voltage, and what mattered was not how big the voltage was but whether it was positive or negative. A positive charge represented the binary digit 0 and a negative charge the binary digit 1 and as regards the carry an input of a positive voltage represented the fact that there was no carry to be

Fleming's valve, 1904

Filament   Grid   Plate

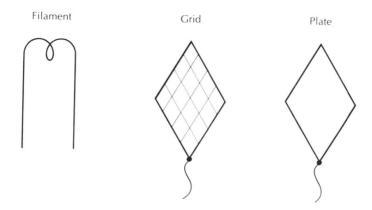

Figure 11.1 Scheme of an electronic valve: flow of current from the plate is determined by voltage on the grid

Source: Randell, *Origins* (see note 26, p. 112 above) p. 224

taken account of, and a negative voltage represented the fact that there was a carry.

These three input voltages were placed on the grids of three triodes. From the anodes of two others, the two output signals were taken: a positive voltage representing binary 0 and a negative voltage binary 1. One of these outputs represented the binary digit to be returned to the accumulator, and the other the new datum to be stored as a carry, ready for the subsequent operation.

Connecting input grids and output anodes was a network of valves, resistors and condensers, whose function was to generate, for any given pattern of input, an output pattern that adhered to the same laws that were followed in binary arithmetic. (Atanasoff constructed all other arithmetic operations out of addition, so in fact the rules for binary addition were the only ones the network had to embody.) The circuit that Atanasoff actually devised is shown in figure 11.2.

In some ways Atanasoff's device was eccentrically designed, off the main line of computer evolution. For example, its only method of storing intermediate results was to burn holes coding for numbers in cards. But it used electronic switches (that is, triodes) for its crucial processing, and for this reason Atanosoff's plans were pioneering. Others, however, were on the same trail. Zuse's collaborator Helmut Schreyer, for example, had by 1942 quite independently built an electronic arithmetic unit for a project which then failed through lack of governmental support; and, as I have indicated, British code-breakers at Bletchley Park turned to electronics for their war work at very much the same time.[15] Even though large relay machines

Table 7 Atanasoff's machine: rules relating input to output

Input representing digit of first operand	Input representing digit of second operand	Input specifying whether there is a carry to take account of	With input specified network generates	Output specifying whether there is a carry forward	Output representing digit of result
+	+	+	→	+	+
+	+	−	→	+	−
+	−	+	→	+	−
+	−	−	→	−	+
−	+	+	→	+	−
−	+	−	→	−	+
−	−	+	→	−	+
−	−	−	→	−	−

continued to be built throughout the 1940s, it was with the electronic approach of these machines – because of its enormous speed advantage – that the future lay.

The Electronic Numerical Integrator and Computer

The most significant Second World War American project to turn to electronics for help with calculating was based at the Moore School of Engineering, in Pennsylvania, where a differential analyser[12] had by 1942 been pressed into service assisting with the calculations required to produce ballistics tables. Knowing of Stibitz' work for Bell Laboratories and also of Atanasoff, one of those involved in the Moore School project, John Mauchly, proposed in 1942 that an electronic digital machine would offer great advantages over the analogue analyser. It would be faster: and in addition, he argued, it could be made to deliver any desired degree of accuracy, and would be capable of supporting systematic error-checking and easy fault-finding, more easily set up for a particular problem, and less labour intensive.[13] This led to the design and construction of a large electronic machine, specifically for the preparation of firing tables, and financed by the US Ordnance Department,[14] but with the facility to act as a general-purpose machine built in.

The ENIAC was neither binary, unlike most of the pioneer electronic machines, nor was it organized around the 'central mill' principle of Babbage and Zuse. It consisted, like the Harvard Mark I – though apparently designed in ignorance of that machine – of a battery of units

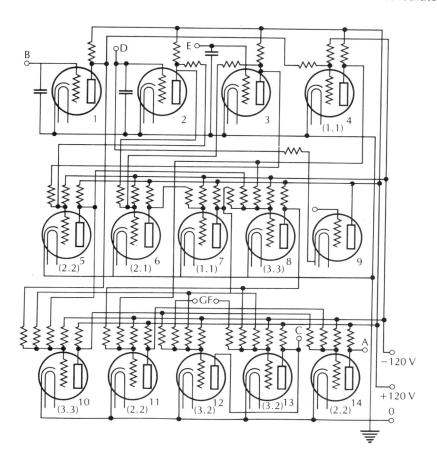

Figure 11.2 Atanasoff's machine: network of triodes

Source: Randell, *Origins* (see note 26, p. 112 above) p. 224

linked together, each offering a particular arithmetic facility. A central electronic 'master programmer' unit organized the sequence of operations and the routing of numbers round the machine.

The basic component from which the various processing units were built was the traditional counter, though in the ENIAC it was built out of triodes. In the Atanasoff machine, the triode was used as a simple switch – a switch that could only be kept open by maintaining a negative voltage on the grid. The ENIAC made use of a slightly more sophisticated device, consisting of a pair of triodes connected together in such a way as to allow one of them, and

The ENIAC, completed 1946

only one of them, to pass current at any particular moment. A voltage arriving on one of the two input lines put the pair in one of its two stable states, and one arriving on the other switched the pair over to its alternative stable state. W. H. Eccles and F. W. Jordan, who invented the circuit in 1919, called it a 'one-stroke relay',[15] but it later came to be referred to more colourfully as a 'flip-flop'.

A 'ring counter' was constructed by connecting ten flip-flops in a circle in such a way that at any one moment only one of them was in state A, with the remainder in state B. A voltage pulse arriving at the ring had the effect of switching the flip-flop in state A to state B, and the flip-flop immediately following in the ring to state A. If we think of a flip-flop as 'lighting up' only when in state A, the arrival of four pulses would have the effect of moving the 'light' round by four places. The device represented a digit, therefore, by the position in the ring of the flip-flop in state A. A ring counter of this kind was provided for each digit of the number to be handled (a total of ten), and each was linked to the counter representing the next highest order of digit to accommodate carries. There was an additional special counter to hold the number's sign.

It was these sets of counters that performed the elementary operations at the heart of the machine's functioning. Numbers were conveyed to and from them in the form of voltage pulses, a separate channel being provided for each digit. Thus there were eleven channels (carrying a ten-place number and its sign): and, for example, four pulses carried by the channel corresponding to the first digit represented a first digit of 4.[16]

The ENIAC had about 18,000 valves, and it worked. Once a problem had

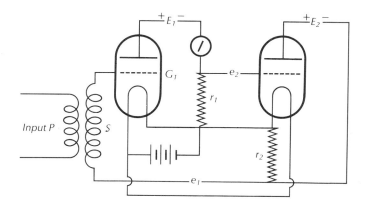

Figure 11.3 Original flip-flop circuit

Source: Eccles & Jordan, 'A Trigger Relay' (see note 15) p. 145

been set up on it, it calculated more quickly than any other contemporary machine. But the process of setting up was complicated and time-consuming. Each of the sub-units that was to play a part in a given calculation had to be configured using banks of switches dispersed throughout the machine; connections between the different sub-units had to be organized (using plug and adaptors); the master programmer unit had to be set, and the necessary constants entered using either switches or a card-reading unit. The result was that, as originally designed at any rate, it was only worthwhile to use the machine for very large calculations. Later, as intense interest was focused on it by European as well as American scientists, modifications were introduced to address this weakness.

The most important response, however, was not to modify the ENIAC in any particular way, but to meet its limitations by building again from scratch. Well before the ENIAC became operational, planning had begun for its replacement. The Moore School team was augmented in 1944 by the secondment to the project, on a consultancy basis, of the outstanding mathematician John von Neumann. Von Neumann had many interests, but had become seized of the potential of automatic calculating machines the year before, in connection with the application of the theory of hydrodynamics to the Los Alamos bomb project. After some months with the team, it was von Neumann who undertook to draw together their ideas for the next

John von Neumann, 1903–57

development in a kind of prospectus for a new machine, to be called the EDVAC (Electronic Discrete Variable Computer).[17]

In that report, the first published mention was made (at least in the context of twentieth-century work) of a concept that was to become fundamental to the subsequent developement of computing: that of the 'stored program'.

The Stored Program

As I have said, the ENIAC's outstanding shortcoming from the point of view of interest in a general-purpose machine was the time-consuming difficulty of setting it up for a particular calculation. The use of plugboards, banks of switches, cable reroutings and so on was not only slow: it also placed limitations on the complexity of the problems that could be accommodated. What was needed, von Neumann saw, was a control mechanism that could accept and effect any sequence of instructions that an operator might choose to feed in. Such an arrangement was not, of course, new. In the Harvard Mark I, for example, the operator set the sequence of operations by feeding into the machine a prepared paper tape; and the ENIAC itself employed a punched card reader for the supply of constants. The difficulty was, however, that card or paper tape readers could not begin to keep up with the electronic processes that were providing such immense advantages of speed in the new machines. There was a clear need for the sequence of instructions, however input into the machine in the first place to be stored electronically. They would then be accessible at electronic speeds, and the full speed advantage of electronic processing would be realized.

This was the proposal in von Neumann's 1945 report, put without rationale or discussion: 'The instructions which govern a complicated problem may constitute a considerable material [...] This material must be remembered.'[18] There is no hint here of the enormous potential that would thus be unleashed, and therefore little to distinguish von Neumann's formulation of the proposal from earlier statements by Eckert and others. The resentment felt by von Neumann's collaborators at the Moore School when he was acclaimed as having originated the 'stored program' concept was therefore understandable.[19]

The introduction of storing the instruction sequence internally (whatever the original reason for doing so) was later recognized as revolutionary because it made it possible for the machine to change, during the running of a phase of a program, the very instructions it was to follow in a subsequent phase. Much later[20] it was shown that being able to modify the address part of an instruction during the running of a program was necessary in order to complete the repertoire of the computing machine, as set out by Turing:[21] without this facility, some theoretically computable formulae were incapable of computation.[22] But the immediate practical exploitation of internal program storage was in the introduction of 'sub-routines'.

Institute of Advanced Study (Princeton) machine, inspired by von Neumann, completed 1952

Where a discrete sequence of instructions (for example, a sub-sequence to calculate a number's squareroot) was required repeatedly at different points in a calculation, it could, with internal program storage, be entered just once and the address of the number to be operated upon changed as appropriate to different stages of the calculation.[23] It was recognized that internal storage thus made it possible for the machine to take some of the drudgery and difficulty out of writing programs for it, and assemblers, compilers and operating systems were introduced to this end.

Although the idea of storing the program internally occurred in von Neumann's draft report of 1945, which looked towards the building of a successor to the ENIAC at the Moore School, machines embodying the idea were actually first built elsewhere. Perhaps the very first, at least among electronic machines,[24] was the experimental device designed by a team led by M. H. A. Newman at Manchester University in Britain, and first running in 1948.[25] Members of Newman's team, including Newman himself, had had some contact with workers at the Moore School, so it is possible that the idea of the stored program originated solely with the School. On the other hand, Newman and several others who went to Manchester had been at the heart of whatever had gone on in Bletchley Park; and so had Turing, whose theoretical discussion of the limits of computation certainly included the idea of a machine capable of altering the list of instructions it was about to follow. The Manchester machine (MADM: Manchester Automatic Digital Machine) may thus have owed as much to Bletchley Park as it did to Pennsylvania; and there is also the possibility that during Turing's contact with von Neumann either before the war or during its early stages, it was von Neumann who benefited from discussing with Turing the conception of a stored program machine which appeared in the latter's 1936 paper.[26]

If the Manchester MADM was the first electronic machine of any sort to embody the stored program concept, the first practical computer to do so (since the MADM had been designed as a test-bed for a new storage device, not actually to conduct computations) was another British effort, the EDSAC, built by Maurice Wilkes and his team in Cambridge, UK. Wilkes had visited the Moore School in 1946, and it is not contested that therein lay the EDSAC's inspiration. It ran its first (stored) program in 1949.

'The Modern Computer'

With the explicit (if undeveloped) mention of the stored program idea in the draft report of 1945, the component concepts of the type of machine that was to support the development of AI from the 1950s on were all in circulation.

First, the stored program idea itself, significant because once stored internally, a program was capable of self-structuring. This made feasible the highly complex programming upon which AI is dependent.

Second, the idea of, and technological foundations for, a large electronic

Manchester Automatic Digital Machine (MADM), operational 1948

memory. This was necessary to accommodate large programs and large quantities of data, both capable of being accessed at electronic speeds.

Third, electronic speed. A corollary of AI's dependence on large programs and, often, large amounts of data is that a machine must be fast enough to run the programs in times which relate acceptably to human time scales.[27] The move from electromechanical to electronic devices was revolutionary in this respect.

Fourth, the advantages of binary. Though the ENIAC was electronic without being binary (a clumsiness due to the wartime imperative that off-the-shelf devices and techniques should be utilized wherever possible), the advantages of binary, in conjunction with electronic components, had been clearly recognized – not only in the von Neumann 'Draft Report' but in the machines of Atanasoff and Zuse.

Fifth, again with Atanasoff, the idea of basing a machine's operations not on counters but on Boolean logic elements. (The 'Draft Report', incidentally, rejected this idea.)

And finally the idea, rejected in the Harvard Mark I and in the ENIAC but embraced by Atanasoff and Zuse, that the core arithmetic operations should be carried out centrally in a single unit rather than dispersed in several locations throughout the machine.

Not all the machines built in the wake of the ENIAC embodied the same design decisions on these fundamental points. Machines based on electromechanical relays, for example, continued to be built.[28] But it was the thinking and development work that went on around von Neumann, who moved after the war to Princeton's Institute for Advanced Studies, that had all the influence on subsequent computer evolution. The machine he built there, the IAS machine (or JOHNNIAC, as it was more disarmingly known),[29] acted almost as a prototype for the great bulk of machines built since.

The IAS machine was of course electronic, and binary. Its internal memory was undifferentiated, storing data and program alike. (It consisted partly of a series of cathode ray tubes. A binary digit was represented by whether a particular location on a screen was charged, illuminated, or not, this method of storage having been invented by F. C. Williams. Additional storage was provided by a magnetic drum device.)[30] And the machine was based on the idea of a single arithmetic processor, as opposed to dispersed processing and possibly 'parallel' operation.

Von Neumann presented the arguments for the decision to use a single processor – a sharp break with the logical structure of the ENIAC – in his 1945 'Draft Report'. He pointed out that carrying out component parts of a calculation 'in parallel' increased the speed of a device at the expense of complexity. Yet complexity was the limiting factor in electronic machines of the time, not speed: the difficulty then lay in making and keeping operational networks of components, the engineering knowledge of which was still nascent. In these circumstances it was more important to minimize complexity than to maximize speed, and the recommendation was for a single central arithmetic unit, with the implication that all operations would be conducted by it in a single sequence one at a time. In spite of the immeasurably richer engineering experience of later years, this 'serial' principle became very deeply entrenched. It is only relatively recently that serious consideration has been given to parallel processing resulting in commercial products.[31]

Technological improvements, often dramatic, continued to be made after the IAS machine had become operational in 1952. The massive WHIRL-WIND computer project at MIT developed a superior system of high speed storage, based on the reversal in the direction of magnetization of ferrite core materials, and this displaced the Williams tube used in the IAS machine.[32] Magnetic tape was adopted as an 'external' (or 'peripheral') storage medium, displacing paper; and towards the end of the 1950s transistors replaced triodes.

Nevertheless the von Neumann machine continued to serve as the prototype as far as logical organization was concerned, and went on doing so through the next wave of technological advance.

Notes

1 Zuse, *Der Computer – Mein Lebenswerk*, (Verlag Moderne Industrie, Munich, 1970) is autobiographical; briefer is his paper 'Some Remarks on the History of Computing in Germany', in N. Metropolis, J. Howlett, and G. C. Rota (eds), *A History of Computing in the Twentieth Century* (Academic Press, New York, 1980), pp. 611–28.
2 Helmut Schreyer, 'Technical Computing Machines', in Randell *Origins*, p. 168, 9.
3 Randell, *Origins*, p. 156.
4 Schreyer, 'Technical Computing Machines', in Randell, *Origins*, p. 167.
5 Zuse's Z3 computer did not quite fit the specification given here (it had a single address code, for example, and a keyboard for input), though it must have been very similar. It can, however, be claimed as the world's first program-controlled general-purpose calculator, since it became operational, according to Zuse, in 1941. It was destroyed in an air-raid in 1944. See Zuse, 'Outline of a Computer Development', in Randell, *Origins*, p. 179.
6 On valves, see below, pp. 159 ff.
7 There may have been an even more sophisticated machine, according to the researches of Randell. See Randell, 'On Alan Turing and the Origins of Digital Computers', in B. Melzer and D. Michie (eds), *Machine Intelligence 7* (Edinburgh UP, Edinburgh, 1972), p. 17.
8 Randell, 'On Alan Turing', in Melzer and Michie, *Machine Intelligence 7*, p. 12.
9 Andrew Hodges has a powerful discussion of the Bletchley Park operation, in *Alan Turing: The Enigma of Intelligence* (Unwin, London, 1983), ch. 4.
10 John V. Atanasoff 'Computing Machines for the Solution of Large Systems of Linear Algebraic Equations', in Randell, *Origins*, p. 308.
11 Hodges, *Alan Turing*, p. 225.
12 See above, pp. 143–5.
13 Mauchley, 'The Use of High Speed Vacuum Tube Devices for Calculating', in Randell, *Origins*, p. 329.

14 Goldstine, *Computer from Pascal*, p. 149.

15 W. H. Eccles and F. W. Jordan, 'A Trigger Relay Utilising Three-Electrode Thermionic Vacuum Tubes, *The Radio Review*, 1 (1919), p. 144.

16 A full account of the ENIAC's workings is provided by H. H. and A. Goldstine, 'The ENIAC', in Randell, *Origins*, pp. 333–47.

17 The 'First Draft of a Report on the EDVAC' (in Randell, *Origins*, pp. 355–64, prepared in June of 1945, was never cast into final form, but it was widely circulated and very influential. Von Neumann used it later to claim patents, much to the disgust of other members of the team, who claimed von Neumann was simply 'writing up' their contributions. There is a discussion in N. Stern, *From ENIAC to UNIVAC* (Digital, Bedford, Mass., 1981).

18 von Neumann, 'Draft Report', in Randell, *Origins*, p. 356.

19 Stern, *From ENIAC to UNIVAC*, pp. 74, 75.

20 In 1964, by C. Elgot and A. Robinson, 'Random-Access Stored-Program Machines', *Journal of the Association for Computing Machinery*, 2 (1964), pp. 365–99.

21 See below, pp. 187, 8.

22 Goldstine, *Computer from Pascal*, p. 266.

23 Goldstine, *Computer from Pascal*, p. 265.

24 The IBM SSEC, commissioned in 1947 but not electronic, could modify stored instructions. See Randell, *Origins*, p. 352.

25 Randell, 'On Alan Turing', in Meltzer and Michie, *Machine Intelligence 7*, p. 16.

26 Hodges, *Alan Turing*, chs. 5, 6; Randell, 'On Alan Turing', in Meltzer and Michie, *Machine Intelligence 7*, pp. 3–20.

27 Turing, 'Computing Machinery and Intelligence', *Mind*, 59 (1950), reprinted in E. A. Feigenbaum and J. Feldman, *Computers and Thought* (McGraw-Hill, New York, 1963), p. 16.

28 Randell, *Origins*, p. 239.

29 Not to be confused with the Rand machine used by the Newell team (see below, p. 214) which was also nicknamed JOHNNIAC'. See Pamela McCorduck, *Machines Who Think* (Freeman, San Francisco, 1979), p. 116.

30 Goldstine, *Computer from Pascal*, p. 314.

31 The machine eventually completed at the Moore School as a successor to the ENIAC, the EDVAC, took the serial principle to the limit: its central arithmetic unit dealt with each binary digit of a number in series (a consequence of the intrinsically serial storage device it employed). The machine von Neumann himself masterminded, the IAS machine, handled all the digits of a number at once. For this reason it is sometimes (confusingly) called a 'parallel' machine.

32 K. C. Redmond and T. M. Smith, *Project Whirlwind* (Digital Press, Bedford, Mass., 1980).

Part III

Turing's Project

12   The Universal Machine

In the face of the enormous development effort that has engaged some of the best minds, some of the most sophisticated techniques and some of the biggest money from the 1940s on, we need to remind ourselves of the awesomely simple root object of it all: to add, subtract, multiply, and divide, more quickly.

It is not on the divising of some esoteric and sophisticated means of getting these operations conducted that all the effort has been spent. After the counting wheel, those developing the computer settled for nothing more complicated than the two-way switch – a device capable of two states, on or off, open or closed: first the electromechanical relay, then the triode, the flip-flop, the discrete transistor, and finally, increasing numbers of transistors incorporated into integrated circuits: The aim has been to find faster and faster switches, and to connect them up in ways that reflect the laws of elementary arithmetic.[1] Part of the fascination of the modern machine is the utter simplicity of its basic principles seen against the background of its tremendous powers.

But what exactly are those powers? In the minds of most of those who were actually building the practical machines of the 1930s, their project was not conceptually pioneering in the way that the Analytical Engine had been for Babbage and Lovelace. They had glimpsed something of the reach of such a machine beyond mathematics, but this thought was not what inspired the builders of the thirties. They thought that what they were building were giant arithmetic calculators.

This in itself, however, by then meant a very great deal. For one of the most spectacular achievements of the nineteenth century was what is known as 'numerical analysis',[2] which demonstrated that there were indeed arithmetic ways of effectively solving the great bulk of soluble mathematical problems. Often such methods called for calculation on a vast scale, but this is exactly where the new machines were seen to have a crucial role. There is no doubt that the enormous usefulness of a powerful calculator, seen simply as such, was easily appreciated.[3]

Nevertheless, as we now understand, to see this is only to see half of it.

The potential of the 'arithmetic calculator' goes beyond arithmetic and beyond the wider mathematics that numerical analysis gives access to. Only a few saw this from the beginning: Alan Turing was one of them. In 1936 he had established in theoretical terms the logical omnipotence of a simple calculator-type machine. Ten years later he was proposing in sober terms to exploit this discovery in the building of a brain.[4]

The Background to the Project

It was of course the sobriety of Turing's project and not its thinkability that was new. The term 'robot' had come into English two decades earlier (when Karel Capek's play, *Rossum's Universal Robots*, was translated from the Czech in 1923); and Fritz Lang's *Metropolis*, with its robot that is indistinguishable from a woman, had appeared in 1926. Nevertheless, the building of a brain had not always seemed conceivable. Not so long before, Lovelace, in the midst of all her enthusiams for the Analytical Engine, had not felt able to go that far, drawing the line at the human brain's capacity for original thought; and this was a point Menabrea had also felt to be clear: 'Thus although it [the Engine] is not itself the being that reflects, it may yet be considered as the being that executes the conceptions of intelligence.'[5]

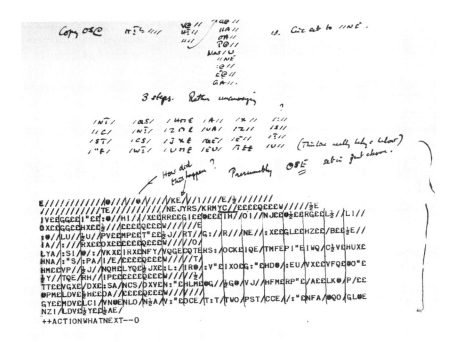

Printout from MADM, with Turing's debugging annotations

Turing's project was borne on the confluence of two strongly running waters, both of which had been flowing since before the beginning of the nineteenth century, when they were invigorated by the drive to extend the regimen of physics and chemistry. The first was the sustained attempt to extend experimentation as the touchstone of authoritative knowledge, and the second the imperative of formalization – that is, the distinguishing in any field of form from content, and the emphasizing of the significance of the former at the expense of the latter.

Experimentalism – taking things apart, subjecting them to tests, recognizing knowledge based on active interventions rather than on passive observation – is linked to a mechanistic view of the objects under study, since it is mechanisms that are likely to yield such secrets as they have when subjected to its disciplines. A form of mechanism as applied to animals is discernible among a small minority of writers in the eighteenth century, when the agenda followed by the leading spirits was not the analysis of mechanisms but the discovery and laying out of the order of nature. But the mechanistic view began to attract majority interest towards the middle of the nineteenth century. Physiology was its first vehicle, beginning with Hermann von Helmholtz; then moving on with François Magendie, Claude Bernard

The London production of Capek's play 'RUR' in 1923 introduced the word "robot" into English

and Julius Sachs in the later part of the century; then spreading to embryology with Wilhelm Roux as the nineteenth century ends.[6]

In the twentieth century, the view of the animal or plant as a simple mechanism gave way to a more sophisticated concept of the organism, as the suggestions for a new direction sketched by Bernard were taken up by L. J. Henderson, C. S. Sherrington and Walter Cannon. What resulted was the conception of the organism as a multilevel system of elaborate complexity, buffered in several dimensions so as to maintain its metabolic stability in the face of changes in its environment, and equipped with a repertoire of behaviours to ensure necessary intake of energy, materials, etc. All this implies sophisticated systems of control, and emphasizes a control role for the brain, as the top-level co-ordinator of it all.

Experimentalism, then, in gaining knowledge of living things prepared the ground for the brain project. At the same time, it gave rise to a psychology sympathetic to its concepts, for it brought to an end, as far as 'scientific' psychology was concerned, any attempt to take account of the 'subjective' in human experience. In 1914, inspired by the experimentalist conviction that only the objectively observable could serve as the basis for science, J. B. Watson published *Behaviour*, which called for psychology to restrict its attention exclusively to that phenomenon.[7] In 1938 B. F. Skinner confirmed the necessity and wisdom of this approach, and the course of psychology for decades to come was set.[8] When, in 1950, Turing proposed to interpret the question 'Can machines think?' without regard to anything that might be going on in their 'minds', he was only reflecting psychological orthodoxy.[9]

So much for the expansion of experimentalism, in biology and in psychology, which prepared the way for the brain project. The other movement was formalization, again flowing through the nineteenth century and into the twentieth. This time, Turing himself made a seminal contribution, in showing (though he was not the only one to do so) that a digital computing machine after the von Neumann pattern was logically omnipotent – that is, could do everything in logic that any other machine could do. It was an idea that arose in a somewhat surprising context, that of the attempt to dig out the foundations of mathematics – or, as some saw it, to construct some for it.

The Introduction of Predicate Logic

In reaction to its 'heroic' period, when mathematicians built high on unproven foundations, the nineteenth century saw a sustained attempt, started by the English algebraists, to restructure mathematics along systematic lines: setting the subject out as a deductive system and in the end presenting an axiomatization. This was attempted, notably, by Georg Cantor, Richard Dedekind and Guiseppe Peano in the last decades of the nineteenth century; and by Frege, who took further than any of the others the project of identifying for mathematics a set of axioms of a purely logical character. His proposals were not adequate as they stood, however. Frege had to come to terms with this disappointment, which, as a result of a celebrated intervention, must have been intense indeed; for at the very moment of completion of his great project, one of his axioms was shown by Russell to yield an inconsistency.[10] Nonetheless, further attempts to identify a set of theorems in logic that would serve as an axiom set for mathematics were made. Ernst Zermelo produced one in 1908, for example; Russell himself in collaboration with A. N. Whitehead formulated another in 1910–13.[11]

In these attempts to establish an axiomatization of mathematics, the resources of the traditional – that is, syllogistic – logic were never seen to have much potential. Despite the enormous attention syllogistic reasoning has attracted down the centuries from logicians, a great deal of the reasoning employed in practical affairs clearly escapes its formulations – Russell claimed, wryly, to have come across useful syllogistic reasoning 'in real life' just once.[12] The fate of Jevons' logic machine, for example,[13] tends to confirm this evaluation: devised to do for logic what Babbage's Analytical Engine had done (in principle) for arithmetic and algebra, it actually remained a curiosity, a tool maybe for teaching logic, but not for helping with anything practical.

It should not be surprising, therefore, that when attempts at the axiomatization of arithmetic came to be made, reasoning of kinds not

Gottlob Frege, 1848–1925

covered by the syllogistic had to be invoked. Frege's work was the most influential, and he, rather than attempt any kind of extension of the logic of terms, in effect built logic again from scratch. Later, the logic of the syllogism was shown to amount to a special case of the general or predicate logic Frege devised; but in building the latter, the syllogistic provided very little in the way of a platform or a scaffold. His starting point in his 'Begriffsschrift' of 1879 was to challenge the analysis, fundamental to the traditional logic, of a judgement into *terms* (subject and predicate) joined by a *copula* (either '... is ...' or '... is not ...'). Instead, he looked to a mathematical model.

In mathematics, one quantity is a 'function' of another if it can be generated from the other by applying a fixed procedure. If we consider the equation

$$x = y^2$$

then we should say that x is a function of y, since x is calculable by taking y and squaring it. We could write

$$x = f(y)$$

to show that there was some definite procedure, symbolized by 'f( )', which, when applied to y, produced x. y would then be called the 'argument' of the function.

Frege suggested that a judgement could be similarly construed as made up of an argument acted upon by a function. Together, these comprised a 'sense-content' or 'proposition'. A proposition was turned into a judgement proper when subjected to an 'operator'. Take, for example, the judgement, 'Odysseus excelled'. First, Frege would say this judgement is distinguished from its denial, 'Odysseus did not excel', by the fact that different operators (assertion in the first place, denial in the second) are being applied to one and the same sense-content, which might be expressed perhaps as 'Odysseus excelling'. Second, this sense-content is to be analysed into function and argument. '... excelling' would be the function, 'Odysseus' the argument. Conditional judgements, like 'If such-and-such then so-and-so', are construed as made up of two propositions linked by the operator 'if ... then ...'. '... and ....' is identified as another operator, and so is '... or ...'.[13]

One thing that Frege did, then, was to take as central for logic relations between propositions, rather than relations between classes as did the syllogistic. He thus made provision for the symbolization of such arguments as:

Tom has a temperature, and since if he has a temperature he must be ill, he must be ill.

The notation that Frege introduced – his 'concept-script' – was not taken up by those who admired and promulgated the substance of his analysis, so I give here the representation of the form of this argument as it would appear using the hook sign for implication, introduced by the much more influential notation of Russell and Whitehead (itself based on Peano's).

$$\vdash : p . \, p \supset q \supset q$$

This might be read:

If both p and p-implies-q, then q

and we could substitute

for p	:	Tom has a temperature
for q	:	Tom must be ill
for p $\supset$ q:		If Tom has a temperature, then he must be ill

to get our particular statement.

But this alternative casting for the proposition was by no means new in itself, as I pointed out earlier. The Stoics had taken it seriously, and so had important medieval logicians. It was also pursued in the nineteenth century by writers besides Frege, although they mostly tried to accommodate it as an extension to the logic of terms. (This is the treatment to be found in Richard Whately, Augustus de Morgan, Boole, Jevons, and Charles Sanders Peirce.)[14] Hugh McColl is credited with developing the first propositional calculus.[15] Frege's distinctive contribution lay in the fact that the system he devised, which allowed for the analysis of proposition into function and argument, made possible the symbolization of degrees of generality.

Up to a point, the traditional logic of terms had already tried to systematize the workings of different degrees of generality in arguments. For example, the argument:

Some cats are wild and all wild animals are a health risk. Therefore, some cats are a danger to health

hangs on the occurrence of 'all' and 'some', and it is 'different degrees of generality' that these express. In the logic of terms, such an argument is seen as a matter of asserting how classes of things, defined by different degrees of generality, are related to each other. But for many arguments in which degrees of generality play a crucial role, those degrees occur within the propositions that appear to be logically related: for example, 'if every number has a successor, then there is no number such that it is larger than every other number'. The logic of terms cannot express these arguments, because, as I have described them, they hang on logical relations between propositions, not classes of things. But neither can the propositional calculus, since such a calculus makes no provision for the *internal structure* of a proposition to be expressed. (It treats a proposition as 'atomic'.)

The mathematical model of functions that Frege drew on for his analysis of proposition into function and argument suggested an analysis of generality as a *second-order* function. We have seen he suggested that a judgement such as 'Odysseus excelled' should be seen as consisting of an operator (assertion) applied to a sense-content (written perhaps 'Odysseus excelling') which in turn should be seen as consisting of a function ('... excelling') applied to an argument ('Odysseus'). We might rewrite this as 'x excelling' if we used 'x' as a variable holding a place for the name of an individual.

Take now an example of a judgement which makes reference to a degree of generality – say, 'Everything whatever takes up space'. Again, we can see this as the assertion of a sense-content; and we can see the sense-content as involving a function, 'x taking up space'. The sense-content 'everything taking up space' can then be seen as meaning that this function takes every individual name as its argument. This is expressed by writing

> For all x, x takes up space

What we have here, Frege suggests, is a new function: a function which takes another function as its argument. It is a second order function in the way in which a differential is a second-order function: for example, acceleration is a function of speed, which is itself a function of distance covered.

Frege was thus able to treat propositions that differed only in degree of generality as produced by different second-order functions. Thus 'Everything burns' and 'Some things burn' would be construed as the two results when one and the same function, 'x burns', is treated as the argument, by (in the first case) the 'universal quantifier', and (in the second case) the 'particular quantifier' (terms suggested later by Peirce). One way of writing this analysis is to put

> Πx   for the universal quantifier,

and

> Ex   for the particular quantifier.

If we use 'ϕx' to mean 'x burns', we can then write:

> Πx ϕx   to mean 'Everything burns'

> (read: 'For all x, x burns'),

and

  Ex φx   to mean 'Some things burn'
  (read: 'For some x, x burns').

This construal of generality proved extremely helpful, allowing for the first time the systematization of arguments hanging on relations between propositions in which different degrees of generality play a crucial role. And these were the kind of arguments that needed to be systematized if the axiomatization of mathematics in logical terms was to be achieved.[16]

In fact, most categories of arguments that we acknowledge as logically valid prove susceptible to the type of analysis Frege articulated, and those that have yet to yield (such as those that depend on tense differences) may well do so eventually.[17] The capacity to systematize our reasoning processes is, of course, a necessary condition of mechanizing them: so that it is to Frege that the machine owes its pregnant power to give us serious help with out everyday reasoning as well as with our sums.[18]

The Brain Project

In assessing any proposed axiomatization, two questions have to be asked. The first is the test of consistency, failed by the set of axioms proposed by Frege: do they allow the derivation of a contradiction? The second asks about completeness: are the proposed axioms sufficient, when taken conjointly, to yield every valid mathematical proposition that is capable of formulation?

With the beginning of the twentieth century it appeared that if a set of propositions could be set out which passed both these tests, a line of enquiry stretching back to the beginnings of formality in mathematics (that is, to Ancient geometry), and gaining particular momentum throughout the nineteenth century, would have reached a highly satisfactory, not to say quite thrilling, conclusion. The vast eleboration of mathematics in all its branches would have been shown to be deducible from a tiny handful of simple propositions. In the years prior to the 1936 denouement, this was the prize for which many mathematicians laboured, with David Hilbert at the head. For Hilbert, this search was an expression of his 'formalist' theory of the nature of mathematics: that mathematics was nothing other than a formal system, a set of axioms and inference rules and the theorems they supported.

In 1931, Kurt Gödel showed that no axiomatized system rich enough to express arithmetic could be complete: there would always be, within such a system, at least one theorem which was valid but which could not be proved to be valid.[19] This was damaging, of course, not only to the particular axiomatizations for mathematics that had been proposed but to the formalist conception of mathematics that Hilbert was championing.

Turing's endeavour, in response to M. H. A. Newman's 1935 lectures on 'Foundations of Mathematics', was to seek to settle what question remained in the wake of Gödel's demonstration. The formalist thesis conceived a mathematically valid statement to be construable purely as a formula that was: (a) constructed according to a symbol-system's formation rules (i.e. was a well-formed formula for that system); and (b) deducible, again according to rules belonging to the system, from the system's axioms. If this were so, it should be possible to find a definite procedure that would with certainty test whether a given proposition was valid. It was the task of demonstrating whether such a procedure existed that Hilbert called the 'Entscheidungsproblem' ('decision problem'): he saw it in his time as the fundamental problem of mathematical logic. Turing managed to prove that such a procedure could not exist.[20]

David Hilbert, 1862–1943 (left) and Kurt Gödel, 1906–78 (right)

His proof grew out of taking seriously the idiom in which the issue had been presented by Newman. Is there, Newman had asked, a 'mechanical' process by which provable propositions might be identified? Turing gave first a rigorous articulation of this notion of a mechanical (or 'definite') procedure, and then showed that it was impossible to prove that such a procedure would always yield a verdict on whether a specified proposition were deducible or not.

For our purposes, the means by which he arrived at his conclusion are more important than the conclusion itself. In order to confer rigour on the notion of a 'definite procedure', he articulated the idea of a machine capable of a finite number of different states. A definite procedure could be understood as any sequence of steps such a machine was capable of. A discrete-state machine was thus, he made clear, the embodiment of a definite procedure. (And he then showed that no proof could possibly be given that such a machine would necessarily identify any deducible proposition put before it.)

He also showed, however, that a discrete-state machine possessed of a very limited repertoire of actions would be capable of embodying *any* definite procedure. Thus he launched the notion of a 'universal machine'.

The elementary but omnipotent machine described by Turing for these analytical purposes may be thought of – probably was thought of, Turing's biographer Andrew Hodges points out[21] – as something like a simple kind of automatic typewriter, with a head capable of reading as well as writing in place of the typing head, and an infinitely long tape in place of the sheet of paper. The tape is thought of as divided up into cells, and each cell is capable of having just one symbol written in it. The head can move one cell at a time, either forwards or backwards; and when it arrives at a cell, it reads the symbol. It may then either erase the symbol, replace it with another one, or leave it as it is.

The construction of the machine determines which of these various alternatives are realized. But Turing conceived of it as having some complexity of construction, so that it is capable of being put into a plurality of different configurations. The action it takes on encountering a given symbol is then thought of as determined by two factors: the symbol, and the configuration the machine finds itself in at the time. Finally, the machine's configuration is thought of as subject to change at each move of the head, in a manner that is governed by the two factors of the existing configuration and the identity of the symbol encountered.

The behaviour of a machine such as this is expressible by drawing up a table, which would set out what the machine would do in each possible combination of internal configuration and scanned symbol. Such a table would represent a complete description of the machine, defining exactly its response to any possible circumstances. Then one could conceive of machines built so as to possess a different range of configurations, and a different pattern of responses to scanned symbols. Each would behave

Last State

		q_1	q_2	q_3
Input	i_0	q_2	q_3	q_1
	i_1	q_1	q_2	q_3

State	q_1	q_2	q_3
Output	o_0	o_0	o_1

Figure 12.1 Table for a universal machine, from Turing's 1950 paper

Source: Turing, 'Computing Machinery' (see note 27, p. 173 above) p. 16

differently, but each would be capable of having its behaviour defined in terms of the kind of table I have just described.

Any symbol-manipulation that could be analysed into a sequence of definite steps could be carried out on a machine of this type, given that it had been constructed so as to embody the appropriate table. But Turing then pointed out that following the rules expressed in any table is itself a definite procedure, which could be expressed in a table of its own. A machine built according to that table would thus be capable of carrying out any definite procedure whatever: it would be, as Turing dubbed it, a universal machine, and he was able to draw up its table.[22]

When, in the thirties, Turing and others began to discuss the possibility of building brains, or of machines 'thinking', these developments in mathematical logic formed part of the background. Indeed, in Turing's case, they were the route by which he arrived at them. His own logical work had led him to develop a clear account of what a mechancial procedure was, and it had yielded the corollary that all discrete-state machines (so long as they possessed a basic repertoire of simple actions) were logically equivalent. Given the dominant conception of the organism as a complex system with a range of appropriate behaviours, it was possible to conceive of the brain as a discrete-state machine performing the function of controlling behaviour. It therefore did not seem absurd to entertain the possibility of one day building a mechanical or electronic equivalent.

Notes

1 Or logic, which amounts to the same thing.
2 E. E. Kramer, *The Nature and Growth of Modern Mathematics* (Hawthorne Books, New York, 1970), pp. 528–49.
3 Aiken and Hopper, 'The Automatic Sequence Controlled Calculator', in Randell, *Origins*, p. 201; Goldstine, *Computer from Pascal*, pp. 286–9.

4 Hodges, *Alan Turing* p. 290.
5 Lovelace, notes to Menabrea, 'Sketch', in P. and E. Morrison, *Calculating Engines*, p. 284 (for the Lovelace reference); p. 243 (for Menabrea's comment).
6 See, for example, Garland Allen, *Life Science in the Twentieth Century* (CUP, Cambridge, 1978).
7 Watson, *Behaviour: An Introduction to Comparative Psychology* (Holt, Rinehart, Winston, New York, 1914).
8 Skinner, *The Behaviour of Organisms* (Appleton-Century-Crofts, New York, 1938).
9 Turing, 'Computing Machinery', in Feigenbaum and Feldman, *Computers and Thought*.
10 Axiom (v) was shown to yield the theorem that if a set were a member of itself, it was not a member of itself. See, for example, W. and M. Kneale, *Development of Logic*, pp. 652–7.
11 The extent to which these attempts to show that mathematical reasoning is a kind of logical reasoning have been successful is controversial, but this controversy is not in the centre of our stage. Computers are capable of arithmetic and the development of numerical analysis satisfies us that arithmetic machines can determine any acceptable approximation to any mathematical function. Since it is capable of maths as well as logic, the derivability of mathematics from logic does not affect the question of the computer's powers.
12 Russell, *An Outline of Philosophy* (Allen & Unwin, London, 1927), p. 82.
13 See above, pp. 130–3.
14 Prior, *Formal Logic*, p. 107.
15 Church, *Mathematical Logic*, p. 156; McColl, 'Calculus of Equivalent Statements', *Proceedings of the London Mathematial Society*, 9 (1877, 8), pp. 9–20.
16 For expositions of this aspect of Frege, see, for example, W. and M. Kneale, *Development of Logic*, chs VII and VIII; G. P. Baker and P. M. S. Hacker, *Language, Sense and Nonsense* (Blackwell, Oxford, 1984), pp. 30–9.
17 Samuel Guttenplan, *The Languages of Logic* (Blackwell, Oxford, 1986), pp. 277–306.
18 W. and M. Kneale, *Development of Logic*, pp. 510, 512.
19 Godel, 'On Formally Undecidable Propositions of *Principia Mathematica* and Related Systems I', *Monatshefte fur Mathematik und Physik*, 38 (1931), pp. 173–98, reprinted in Martin Davis (ed.), *The Undecidable* (Raven Press, Hewlett, New York, 1965), pp. 5–38.
20 Davis, *The Undecidable*, p. 108.
21 Hodge, *Alan Turing*, p. 96.
22 Turing, 'Computing Machinery', in Feigenbaum and Feldman, *Computers and Thought*, pp. 17–19.

13 Cybernetics

Turing's discovery about the power of machines grew out of his interest, as a mathematician, in mathematics. But he then applied it to psychology (his paper of 1950 was addressed to the question 'Can machines think?'), drawing the conclusion that every human thought, provided it could be expressed in language, could be mimicked by his universal machine if it was suitably programmed. His thought was, presumably,[1] that since the brain was a sophisticated device for controlling the organism's functioning, including its behaviour, and since his universal machine was the logical equivalent of any discrete-state machine, it was, in particular, the logical equivalent of a brain and could therefore be programmed to mimic the brain's functioning.[2]

Such a movement of thought relies on a conception of the relationship between an organism's brain and its functioning (and indeed on the very concept of 'functioning') that was part of the intellectual furniture of the thirties. By then it had become 'obvious' that the human being is an 'organism', and that an organism is a physicochemical system that needs to be maintained in a steady state physiologically, and therefore to direct itself in the deployment of a repertoire of behaviours that ensure its metabolic needs are continuously met. It is this picture in which the brain is seen as essentially the directive centre – the topmost element of an elaborate control hierarchy.

This conception was not sponsored by psychology, though it was at least consistent with the concentration of psychology (at the time at which the brain project was being thought through) on behaviour as distinct from 'mental' process. Instead, it came from those working from the biological perspective. In the early decades of the twentieth century there was serious work done on the nervous system, including the brain, as a control device, and in the thirties this work became funnelled into what became known as 'cybernetics'. It is the intellectual origins and concerns of this movement, therefore, that I shall outline, to develop that side of the context in which the brain project was pursued. There is an additional reason for dwelling on cybernetics: it was this movement that gave the electronic stored-program machines that had emerged from the war their most intellectually resourceful reception.

It was mathematicians who, by and large, understood the machines, and they were interested in the contribution they might make to mathematics. Many of those who might have seen non-mathematical applications for the machines did not have the necessary understanding of their principles.

To this general rule there were perhaps three exceptions. First, there were engineers who knew all about the machines and could think imaginatively about their potential. An exceedingly ambitious early project was to use a (purpose-built) machine of the new type to control a flight simulator – Project WHIRLWIND, launched in 1944 under the inspiration of Jay Forrester, and laying the foundations in MIT for one of the two great centres of research in the post-war period (the other being the Carnegie Institute of Technology).[3] Missile guidance systems were developed after the war involving an application of the same general kind.

The second type of people who felt easy with the new machines straightaway were those administration and business users who had supported the introduction of automatic data-handling since Hollerith developed his punched-card system towards the end of the nineteenth century. It was IBM, to which Hollerith's company formed a tributory, that made most of the machines used for non-mathematical research applications in the post-war years, beginning in 1952 with the IBM 701 (a series modelled

Norbert Wiener playing the chess automaton (designed by Torres y Quevedo) at the 1951 Cybernetics Conference in Paris

on von Neumann's IAS machine);[4] though it is true that one of the first applications in this field used a UNIVAC machine, built by the commercial company set up by Eckert and Mauchly,[5] to help with the work of the US Bureau of the Census. A second major military application also belonged to this category: very large computing facilities were developed to collect and marshal data for the purpose of controlling the deployment and action of the US Strategic Air Command (SAC).

Cybernetics represented the third activity involving people equipped to understand something of the powers of the new machines, and this time one that had a major interest in exploiting them for pioneering intellectual purposes. Cybernetics was essentially a network of researchers, with mathematics and engineering strongly represented in their collective background, whose programmes were drawn together under the inspiration of Norbert Weiner in the 1940s.

Wiener's own background was in mathematics and mathematical logic (he had been a pupil of Russell's), and his major contributions had been in statistical mechanics: but the two fields he brought together in the formation of cybernetics were fiercely empirical. The first was the engineering of control mechanisms in complex machinery, and the second the study of control mechanisms in animal functioning and behaviour. Nevertheless, it may have been the power of abstraction inculcated by his mathematical training that brought Wiener to see in the animal physiology of the thirties and forties, and in contemporaneous control engineering, a convergence on the same nexus of problems.

Control in Organism and Machine

Wiener had become familiar with the engineering dimension through his work in the early years of the war, when he was engaged in a project concerned with the improvement of anti-aircraft artillery. With a swiftly moving target such as an aircraft it was, of course, important to have the missile dispatched not at where the target was when the trigger was pulled, but at where it would be by the time the missile reached the same altitude: a problem compounded, and given its real mathematical interest, by the capacity of the pilot to take evasive action. The missiles in question were, at the beginning of World War II, artillery shells and therefore 'guided' only by their mode of dispatch, so that the problem was essentially one of calculating in advance the likely trajectory of the target, and of fixing the aim accordingly. There was no practical question, at that stage, of building into the missile itself a self-steering capacity. Nonetheless, the project put Wiener in touch with state-of-the-art control engineering and in particular with the theory and practice of the 'servo-mechanism'.[6]

In a mechanism of this type, large, perhaps heavy machinery is brought under the control of relatively modest movements – for example, human ones – by arranging for those movements to be amplified. The success of these devices hangs on the precision with which the guiding movement is informed from moment to moment of the effects of its action; that is, on the adequacy of the feedback it receives. For example, if in a power-assisted steering mechanism there is too much delay between moving the steering wheel clockwise and the road wheels turning to the right, there is likely to be an overshoot in one direction, leading to a further overshoot in the opposite direction, and so on, and eventually leading to complete loss of control.[7]

Servo-mechanisms in their established form were not the first devices to employ feedback. The swivel windmill fitted with a back vane, so that any shift in the wind blew the mill round and kept its face to the wind, is often cited as an early machine which used this principle, since one of the effects of the wind acting on the rear vane was to reorient the head so that the force of the wind on the vane was reduced to zero Wiener himself regarded James Clerk Maxwell's discussion of Watt's steam engine governor, published in 1868, as the first significant paper on feedback mechanisms.[8]

Watt's governor

Watt's governor is an arrangement that keeps the speed of the engine steady in spite of variations in load. The engine is made to swing round two arms with weights at their extremities, so that as the speed of rotation increases these weights lift up under the influence of the increasing centrifugal force. This upward movement is used to close down a valve through which the steam must flow to the cylinder. The engine is thus slowed. But as it slows, the weights fall, the valve opens and the engine picks up speed again, and so on. What is effectivley a steady speed – a sort of 'homeostasis'[9] – is thus maintained, by the effect of an action being fed back into the mechanism controlling the action. In this case, the bigger the effect, the more the action is inhibited, so that the feedback is said to be negative.

Wiener's anti-aircraft project involved him directly in the question of control in the organism as well as in the machine, since any practical device had to plan for a gunner to be sitting with the machine and responsible for pressing the trigger: besides which, the target was also a machine under human direction. This was basis enough, apparently, for Weiner to see that feedback mechanisms must play a crucial role in the voluntary movements of human beings, which introduced the physiological dimension into the cybernetic mix.

However, Wiener had already a longstanding rapport with physiology via his association with Arturo Rosenblueth, who was on the Faculty of the Harvard Medical School when they first met in the mid-1930s, in the context of an interdisciplinary discussion group. The value of concentrating on the areas where established sciences overlapped was, Wiener tells us, recognized by the two of them from this early stage – as the interdisciplinary character of the discussion group that brought them together (and was convened by Rosenblueth) testifies. The specific idea that 'control mechanisms in animal and machine' might be the focus for a joint study, drawing on both physiological and engineering perspectives (as well as on statistical mechanics), therefore provided a project they had been looking for.

They put flesh on their initiative by convening a series of interdisciplinary discussions, the first at Princeton in 1944, later ones under the auspices of the Josiah Macy Foundation in New York. They also introduced the word 'cybernetics' in an attempt to give a name to the identity of interest they had discerned (alluding to the Greek '*kybernetike*', 'the art of steersmanship').[10]

What the physiologists brought to those discussions, as I have indicated, was a recently developing concept of the organism. At the turn of the century, interest in the nature of organic processes had focused on embryology. Opinion had become polarized between those who followed Wilhelm Roux in maintaining that the development of the individual was to be explained as a set of component elements each undergoing a predetermined sequence of transformations, and those who supported Hans Driesch in his thesis that the complex organization maintained and developed during ontogeny could only be explained on the assumption that the components were subject to central 'direction'. Driesch regarded his posited central organizing influence as 'immaterial', and his view was regarded as a species of vitalism on that account. Roux, on the other hand, stood for the thesis that life processes were exclusively physicochemical.

The synthesis that emerged out of this polar opposition was a conception of the organism that took the establishment and maintenance of organization among the components very seriously, but sought to explain it in terms of a subtly interacting hierarchy of physicochemical control mechanisms.[11] The new view was principally the outcome of studies conducted in the first two decades of the twentieth century by Lawrence J. Henderson, Charles Scott Sherrington and Walter B. Cannon. Henderson, a leading architect of the new physiology, studied the way in which a number of interlocking mechanisms kept the pH value of the blood at a constant level. Sherrington studied the control of reflex actions, mediated by the spinal chord, and identified a hierarchy of levels of control. The experience of Cannon with World War I shock victims led him to see the importance of regulatory mechanisms in maintaining the body in a steady state, and shock itself as their collapse.[12]

The conception of organic processes which these workers were articulating reached back to the ideas of Claude Bernard, set out in the middle of the previous century.[13] Bernard had spoken of the essential metabolism of an organism as proceeding within a set of conditions which were held steady by a protective envelope of buffering mechanisms. It was, he claimed, the maintenance in a steady state of such an 'internal environment' that made life, as a distinctive phenomenon, possible. Later, Cannon (who was to be a colleague and collaborator of Rosenblueth) coined the term 'homeostasis' to describe the steady state an organism's metabolic environment had to maintain.[14]

The concept of a system maintained in a steady state of dynamic equilibrium by the complex interaction of many regulatory processes thus displaced Roux's brasher conception of the living thing as a piece of extremely complicated molecular clockwork. From moment to moment, according to the new concept, changes in external conditions meant that a battery of compensatory processes had to adjust their operation. The successful functioning of these processes to maintain homeostasis required a very sophisticated means of control, accurately related to prevailing conditions and (for this and other reasons) depending on communication between process and environment, and between process and process. Part of the picture, too, was the notion that the elementary processes of which the regulatory system was built up were co-ordinated *hierarchically*, as I have mentioned. That is to say, they were not subject to the direct instruction of some overall central control, but were organized into subsystems, which were made up of sub-subsystems, and so on. Though overall co-ordination of the highest level of subsystems was certainly required, the co-ordination of the sub-subsystems was achieved at subsystem level, and so on down the hierarchy. This means that not only was communication between processes necessary, but so was communication between levels of co-ordination. One need not add that much of this information flow constituted what the control engineers were calling 'feedback' to make it clear that physiologists and engineers had much to talk to each other about.

The foundational research projects in cybernetics, then, had to do with applying control engineering concepts to the understanding of physiological and neurophysiological processes. Wiener himself, in 1945, collaborated with Rosenblueth on studies of the control of heartbeat and leg-muscle contraction in the cat,[15] and Oliver Selfridge at MIT continued to work on heart flutter in 1948. In the late 1940s, Walter Pitts took the other line begun by Wiener and Rosenblueth and extended the statistical techniques they applied to the study of networks of muscles in the heart to the treatment of networks of neurons. McCulloch and Pitts together worked on visual detection in the frog.[16]

The interest of cybernetics in nerves and communication, of which the work of Wiener and Rosenblueth on heart muscle and its continuation by Pitts was an instance, led to a major preoccupation with the properties of abstractly conceived 'nerve-nets': an expression of the drive towards formalism which I shall return to later.[17]

Nerve-nets

During the 1880s, the Spanish histologist Ramon y Cajal had established through a painstaking series of observations the essential anatomy of the nervous system: that is, it was built up not of communication channels running continuously from sensor or effector to spinal cord or brain, but of a great multiplicity of small cells or neurons which communicated with each other over short gaps (later dubbed by Sherrington 'synapses').[18] Communication was then seen as effected by a stimulus being passed from neuron to neuron. Moreover, it was clear that the neurons were not simply arranged in chains, with each having one link backward. Instead each was seen to have a plurality of connections, and it became clear that whether a given neuron was 'switched on' depended on which of the potential inputs to it were operative.

It was possible, then, to theorize about the properties of systems made up of numbers of neurons, each with specified properties attributed to it, interconnecting in various ways. A pattern of interconnections might be drawn up and an input at a particular point postulated, and the pattern of 'switched on' neurons that would get generated as the initial stimulus was diffused throughout the system could then be worked out.

The cyberneticists' connections and, in several cases, background in biology led them to attach great significance to the capacity of simple and randomly structured nerve-nets to organize themselves, without external direction, into systems with greater complexity and therefore greater powers. For the problem of how simple systems could on their own become more highly organized seemed to them to be at the heart of evolution, and of any post-Drieschian embryology. In both cases, more complexity emerges out of less – multicellular complexes from simple unicells – and if the idea of an immaterial organizer like Driesch's 'entelechy' were discarded, the problem became that of understanding how self-organization occurred.

'Complexity' is by no means as clear a notion as its easy feel suggests – no measure of it like that of the potentially related notion of 'information' has, for instance, ever been devised. The complexity of a randomly connected set of elements could be said, approached from one direction, to be greater than that of a set of elements organized according to some strict logical plan: but to be less complex from a different point of view. The cyberneticists' assumption seems to have been that the degree of organization represented by a system is shown in the degree of the selectiveness of its response. A simple system will react similarly to all stimuli, a complex one differentially. The more complex a system, on this assumption, the more capable it is of discriminating between stimuli. But a system that begins with no discrimination and then proceeds to acquire it can be said to be learning – learning the differences between stimuli. Much of the work on self-organizing nerve-nets was regarded, therefore, as a study of learning.[19]

The exploration of the properties and learning potential of nerve-nets was taken up by a number of workers (notably Ross Ashby, author of an influential paper published in 1948).[20] Some of their work used computers to simulate the behaviour of nerve-nets, as Wiener (and Turing) had anticipated.[21]

Another tool in this enquiry was Boolean algebra, applicable because it was possible to regard a nerve-net as made up of switches. The work done in connecton with complexes of switches in the telephone industry was therefore very much in the same field, and it is not surprising that the usefulness of Boolean algebra was discovered in both connections, apparently independently. Claude Shannon published 'A Symbolic Analysis of Relay and Switching Circuits' (based on his MSc thesis, one of the most influential Master's theses ever) in 1938,[22] and McCulloch and Pitts 'A Logical Calculus of the Ideas Immanent in Nervous Activity' in 1943.[23]

The fruitfulness of studying the potential of randomly organized nerve-nets turned out to be limited. Marvin Minsky was, in the early fifties, a young research worker preparing for a PhD within the framework of nerve-net studies, under the influence of McCulloch and Pitts. By the time his thesis was finished, in 1954, he had come to the view that the real way forward in the development of learning machines was to allow much more elaborate structuring of the initial system (in the form of a digital computer simulation).[24] This suggestion marks one of the boundaries of the field that later became known as Artificial Intelligence. Before I turn in this direction myself, however, I shall describe what was at that point the main stream of cybernetics and whither it flowed.

Control in Organizations

Alongside the nerve-net work there were other research projects of some prominence within cybernetics. Wiener was not the first to see the relevance of psychology to the original cybernetics programme, which involved the study of 'control' in animals. He did, however, attempt to further its application, by including psychologists among those invited for the follow-up to the 1944 Princeton meeting. But psychology in the thirties was in the grip of a behaviourism which had more in common with the crude biological mechanism of the turn of the century than with the sophistication of Henderson, or Cannon, or Sherrington, and mainstream psychology was little affected directly by cybernetics; nor until later was it much touched by the AI work that displaced it. (On the other hand, it was a psychologist away from the mainstream, H. A. Simon, who seized hold of the new ideas and potential of the computer most enthusiastically: a psychologist who came to psychology through a primary concern with the practical problems of industrial management. His work is discussed below, on pp. 212ff.)

Wiener also welcomed the further widening of the network to bring in sociologists, anthropologists and students of economics. The social sciences were ready for cybernetic principles, which invoked concepts of function and the maintenance of steady states already in vogue (partly through the influence of Talcott Parsons, Crane Brinton and George Homans, who had attended Henderson's sociology lectures at Harvard in the thirties.)[25]

The implications of cybernetic ideas for the management of industrial concerns were as clear as they were for securing stability in the larger organization of the state itself. In place of the ideal of the legislature dictating decisions for the executive in a traditional hierarchical conception, there should be information flow in all directions; and decisions should emerge as a result of cyclical processes involving feedback. In terms intelligible to the old theory, an attempt to move towards the point would be to argue that the actual behaviour of workers (and not just what they ought theoretically to do, given the decisions that had been handed down to them), and their morale, were factors of vital importance to the decision-making process. That would be a justification of feedback mechanisms in the old central intelligence model: but what cybernetics was really proposing was a new model, whereby the decision making was a function not of a fully informed headquarters, but of the organization as a whole.[26]

Cybernetics Widened

The notion of 'system' as we are familiar with it today was much encouraged by cybernetics, though not invented by it. An early use of 'system' in an engineering context was in the title 'Systems Development' for a division of Bell Laboratories, set up in 1925, where telephone networks were the object of attention. But it was the wartime effort to apply mathematical techniques to military planning – the enterprise of 'operations research' (called 'operational research' in the UK) – that gave the notion of 'system' much of its modern cast.

Talk of 'system' was valuable to cybernetics because it helped focus attention on identities of function. Animal control systems are built of nerves and muscles, and electromechanical control systems of circuits and electromagnets; but for the purpose of understanding how they function (that is, how they exercise control) it can be illuminating to disregard many quite obvious features, like physical composition and physical structure, and ask instead how the different elements of each contribute functionally to the working of the whole. In place of chemicals or parts, *sub-systems* become the elements of analysis.

'Systems' became recognized as something of a discipline in its own right in the fifties, when the Systems Research Centre was set up at Case Institute of Technology, and other institutions in the USA and UK followed suit.[27] The Case Institute's centre involved a collaboration between control engineering, computation and operations research, and so represented a continuation of the cybernetic tradition. In other centres, the connection with traditional engineering was lost and the focus was exclusively on human systems as represented by industrial and other organizations.

By still others, notably Ludwig von Bertalanffy, the application of the concept of system was taken much further by what its promoters called 'general systems theory', which argued from the importance of the organization of the components of a thing, to the thesis that some immaterial organizing principle must be in play. General systems theory was effectively a twitch in the corpse of vitalism. Though it had superficial resemblances to cybernetics, it had none of its fecundity, and was in fact pointing in the opposite direction.[28]

The research techniques of modelling and simulation which are nowadays associated with 'systems' thinking sprang directly out of the functional perspective stimulated by both operations research and cybernetics. If what matters as regards the functioning of a system are the functional relationships between its elements, it will be legitimate to let abstract entities stand for the elements and write out the rules governing the elements which express those relationships. This gives an abstract representation of the system under study, and its properties can be explored. Mathematical modelling had long been a useful tool, but the advent of computers meant that the necessary calculations could be done quickly and repetitiously, allowing easy experimentation with different hypotheses. The most famous computer model is perhaps the 1970 World Model by Forrester, which explores the consequences for the future of the planet of the continuation of certain policies over resource usage, population growth and waste management.[29] The use of computers in simulation was in fact one of their early applications that went beyond the exclusively numerical – in the context of the design of guided-missile systems from 1954.[30] And Forrester's masterpiece WHIRLWIND was a simulation project, at the outset at any rate an attempt to build a flight-simulator.[31]

The Political Background

I have said that cybernetics began in effect as a joint research project between physiology and control engineering. But there was always more colour to it than that implies. It was launched and conducted within an explicit ideological framework, to which many of its exponents attached as much importance as to the purely scientific issues addressed. It was a political outlook that belonged very much to the 1940s, when economic circumstances were still defined in terms of the catastrophic collapse of the thirties. Wiener did his social thinking in this context, embodied in the USA in the New Deal, the response of Roosevelt's first administration (1933–7) to the great depression. It was the same context in which, on the other side of the Atlantic, there figured Keynes' *The General Theory of Employment, Interest and Money* (published in 1936). Politically, those ranged against Hitler defined themselves as essentially opposed to 'dictatorship', and the founders of cybernetics saw their ideas as developing a new, non-dictatorial conception of 'control'. In societies as in smaller organizations, their

One of Grey Walter's tortoises, the mascot of cybernetics

conception presented an alternative to the assumption that efficiency depended on a central intelligence responsible for decision making, and an army of agents ready only to carry the decisions through.

If Wiener was against dictatorship, he was also against its pretended opposite, the regime of the market or laissez-faire. He had no time for Adam Smith's idea that a 'hidden hand' in a free market would act like a governor on prices and wages, and preserve stability with mechanical precision. For stability, homeostasis, there needed to be the speedy and plentiful movement of information throughout a system's components, and this was just what failed to happen in the mass market society, where the ostensible means of spreading information – books, newspapers, radio – were corrupted by the profit imperative. Good communication and the stability this made possible, he believed, could be seen only in the simple societies described by anthropologists. (Margaret Mead was for a time an attender of Wiener's gatherings.)[32]

As we shall see in the next chapter, when the work on nerve-nets that cybernetics had sponsored stopped being productive, interest in learning was not abandoned. But a new approach to it was launched, and workers in the West at any rate marked the shift with a new name, 'Artificial Intelligence'. There were, on the other hand, problems where work continued without anything like a relaunch occurring: most importantly, work on robots. Robotics in fact became the main focus of AI effort during the sixties, and the pioneering thought of cyberneticists like Wiener, Ashby and Grey Walter (who had displayed his famous robot 'tortoises' at the Festival of Britain in 1952) had prepared foundations that were built on, not deserted.

In the Soviet Union and Eastern Bloc countries, such continuities were stressed at the expense of the reorientations. There, the label 'cybernetics' retained its currency – and does so still. But in the West, from the sixties on, it acquired an increasingly dated air.

Notes

1 This is the line reconstructed by Hodges: it is not drawn with absolute clarity in Turing's own papers. See Hodges, *Alan Turing*, p. 294.
2 Turing did address explicitly, and rejected, the objection that the nervous system is not a discrete-state machine. See Turing, 'Computing Machinery', *Mind*, 59 (1950), reprinted in Feigenbaum and Feldman, *Computers and Thought*, pp. 27, 28.
3 Redmond and Smith, *Project Whirlwind*.
4 Randell, *Origins*, p. 189.
5 See above, p. 162.
6 Details of the formation of cybernetics given here are based chiefly on Norbert Wiener, *Cybernetics* (MIT Press, Cambridge, Mass., 1947).
7 McColl, *Servo-mechanisms* (Van Nostrand, New York, 1945).
8 Wiener, *Cybernetics*, p. 11.
9 See below, p. 195.

10 This usage ignored the French 'cybernetique', coined by Ampère in 1834 to refer to the study of 'the means of government'; and Jacques Lafitte's 'mechanology', as the science of machines. See G. T. Guilbaud, *What is Cybernetics?* (Heinemann, London, 1959), pp. 2, 9.

11 W. B. Cannon, *The Wisdom of the Body* (Norton, New York, 1932), and C. S. Sherrington's Gifford Lectures, *Man on his Nature* (CUP, 1951), presented this synthesis to a non-specialist audience.

12 Allen, *Life Science*, ch. 4.

13 Claude Bernard, *An Introduction to the Study of Experimental Medicine* (Dover, New York, 1957).

14 Allen, *Life Science*, p. 101.

15 Wiener, *Cybernetics*, p. 19.

16 J. Y. Lettvin, H. R. Matturana, W. S. McCulloch and W. Pitts, 'What a Frog's Eye Tells the Frog's Brain', *Proceedings of the Institute of Radio Engineers*, Nov. 1959, pp. 1940–51.

17 See below, pp. 240–3.

18 Ramon y Cajal, *Recollections of My Life* (MIT Press, Cambridge, Mass., 1966); Allen, *Life Science*, ch. 4.

19 Frank Rosenblatt's 'perceptron' was one of the most thought-provoking devices to emerge. It is definitively discussed in Marvin Minsky and Seymour Papert, *Perceptrons* (MIT Press, Cambridge, Mass., 1968).

20 Later turned into a book; Ashby, *Design for a Brain*, (Chapman, London, 1960).

21 See, for example, Gordon Pask, *An Approach to Cybernetics* (Hutchinson, London, 1961), p. 82, note.

22 Shannon, 'A Symbolic Analysis of Relay and Switching Circuits', *Transactions of the American Institute of Electrical Engineers*, 57 (1938), pp. 713–23.

23 McCulloch and Pitts, 'A Logical Calculus of the Ideas Immanent in Nervous Activity', *Bulletin of Mathematical Biophysics*, 5 (1943), pp. 115–33. It was Pitts who brought mathematical logic to the McCulloch–Pitts partnership, having studied under Rudolph Carnap. See Wiener, *Cybernetics*, p. 13.

24 McCorduck, *Machines Who Think*, p. 84; and see below, p. 205ff.

25 Allen, *Life Science*, p. 110.

26 Stafford Beer, *Cybernetics and Management* (EUP, London, 1959).

27 D. P. Eckmann (ed.), *Systems: Research and Design* (Wiley, New York, 1961) is the Proceedings of the First Systems Symposium, which was held at the Case Institute.

28 Representative are von Bertalanffy, *General System Theory* (New York, 1968), and Ervin Laszlo. I have commented further myself: Vernon Pratt, 'Explaining the Properties of Organisms', *Studies in the History and Philosophy of Science*, 5 (1974), pp. 1–15.

29 The Club of Rome, *The Limits to Growth* (Pan, London, 1974).

30 G. Gordon, 'The Development of the General Purpose Simulation System' in R. L. Wexelblat (ed.), *History of Programming Languages* (Academic Press, New York, 1981), p. 404.

31 Redmond and Smith, *Project Whirlwind*.

32 Wiener, *Cybernetics*, ch. 8.

14 The Advent of Artificial Intelligence

As the study of nerve-nets ran into the sand, taking the heart of cybernetics with it, the potential of the computer was taken in a sharply different direction. A new network of workers developed, led by people who had for the most part completed their doctorates in the fifties (John McCarthy, 1951; Minsky, 1954; Allen Newell, 1957; but also Simon, 1943). They had links with the past, some with cybernetics, but they started something new. Their field simply came in with the rise of computers, since it had to do with the programming of these machines. (It had needed the genius of a Turing to devise 'programs' for machines that had yet to be built).[1] They found ways of enabling the machine to do things it had not been able to do before – solve geometry problems, play chess and draughts – and they tried to enable it to do other things, like recognize patterns and understand English. They thus created what McCarthy labelled (by using that phrase in the name of a conference at Dartmouth College, New Hampshire, in 1956) 'Artificial Intelligence'.[2]

AI thus slips in unobtrusively. There is no sudden innovation that marks its birth, only a steady growth in the virtuosity with which the new instrument of the computer was played, and a moment when a name that happened to stick was first proposed.

It is said that there was something distinctive about the programming projects that made this suggestion sound right, namely that they were attempts to get a machine to do what would otherwise require human intelligence:[3] and this has become a familiar 'definition' of the field. But arithmetic, for example, might easily be said to require human intelligence in the absence of any easier way of performing it, so that such a definition, taken too seriously, would make engines of AI out of the humble calculator or even the Pascal Box. There are also many examples of sophisticated computer applications, like the use of robots in industrial settings, which do take the place of intelligent human agency, but which are not now generally regarded as falling within the AI field. In fact a noticeable tendency within AI's short life has been for projects to be defined as belonging to it for just as long as it takes to solve their fundamentals, when some other field takes them over.

There are other ideas for delimiting the scope of AI, of course, but it is important first to review some of those early projects themselves, the projects that provide the context in which the idea of there being a new field made sense. And before that, the AI people and their network will be reviewed, for the field owes its identity as much to the human grouping that calls itself the 'AI community' as it does to any distinctive configuration of ideas.

The AI Network

The cohesion of the new network is certainly striking. Insiders stress a division, to begin with, between workers with Newell and Simon at Carnegie and those with Minsky and McCarthy at MIT and Stanford respectively, but outsiders see above all a single close circle of mutual citation and acknowledgement. Their apparent insularity is by no means unintelligible, since their instrument was very new and there was little relevant work by others to draw on. There were one or two exceptions, particularly, of course, in the parent field of cybernetics.

Selfridge's work was one. Working on heart flutter at MIT, he saw the importance very early of increasing the convenience with which data could be fed into the new machines. Well before the AI interest began to identify itself, therefore, he had tried to devise a sequence of machine instructions which would enable the machine to accept ordinary typescript as input.[4]

This involved getting the machine to accept slightly different versions of the same typed symbol as exactly that – different versions of the same symbol. In attacking this problem Selfridge launched a project that continues to absorb energy, the project of making machines recognize certain slightly different configurations of elements as constituting the same pattern (or, looking at it in another way, getting the machine to recognize the same identities as the human being). Visual pattern recognition was Selfridge's particular concern, but, in its general form, pattern recognition is a fundamental problem in almost all AI projects. Selfridge himself pursued his topic well into the AI era, and was perhaps one of only two major figures to have belonged centrally to both networks.

Shannon was the other. Wiener refers to him for the most part only to point out that someone else had arrived at his conclusions independently, but the relevance and importance of Shannon's work identifies him as belonging in the forties to the cybernetic movement, even if he was not a central member of the network.[5] At the close of the decade he gave AI another of its enduring preoccupations – the development of programs that play games, particularly chess[6] – and went on to influential work in the fifties in the AI field.[7]

Though he never joined the AI network himself, there was a third cybernetician the AI people reached out to: Frank Rosenblatt, whose perceptron had been one of the most discussed machines the movement had produced. He stayed and worked under the sagging banner of cybernetics into the fifties, and it was actually his work of this period, contemporaneous with their own, that the AI people were given to citing.

Otherwise, the new network looked outwards only to Turing, who had continued to explore the potential of 'intelligent machinery' through the forties,[8] and to Russell and Whitehead, for their work in setting out the propositional calculus. This work, as well as the seminal contributions of Turing in the thirties, had also, of course, been referred to by Wiener and his collaborators.

The first of the new projects that were later to be subsumed under AI took their inspiration from the disappointment of cybernetics' nerve-net studies. Minsky was, in 1954, a mathematician completing his PhD thesis on 'Neural nets and the brain model problem'. He had studied at Princeton under the influence of McCulloch and Pitts – as an apprentice cybernetician, as it were. But the experience served only to convince him that cybernetics was making neither the only nor the most fruitful use of the new machines. Cybernetics' nerve-net idea had been to use the machine to simulate randomly structured nerve-nets and see how these might become organized (that is, in a sense engage in learning) without central direction. But as Minsky pointed out, the only natural process we know of in which such self-organization had come about – evolution – had taken a very long time indeed. A better plan for a more limited schedule might be to eschew

Marvin Minsky

randomness and see what learning powers might be conferred upon the machine by designing a structure for it.[9]

Getting Machines to Learn

A founding project of AI was therefore to do with learning. From the first there was some ambiguity – a fruitful ambiguity – between an interest in learning as we already have it in animals and human beings, and a concern simply to provide the new machines with the capacity to 'learn'. Later, this ambiguity was developed, at least by commentators, into something of a contrast of approach within AI, when workers with a sophisticated psychological perspective (principally Newell and Simon) linked in with those who started from cybernetics (like Minsky). But this difference of focus never seemed to make much difference to the thrust of the programming effort that went on in what (it is nevertheless true) remained sub-camps of the AI community.

The learning project was launched in programming terms by A. L. Samuel, and he chose as his vehicle a computer programmed to play checkers (draughts). His idea was to find a way of getting the machine to 'remember' the moves and outcome of each and then to draw on that information to improve its decision making on subsequent occasions.[10]

In choosing to develop a game-playing program, Samuel was of course following an established tradition. Getting machines to play games had been a piece of fun long before the modern computer arrived, and many attempts had been made to design devices capable of rising, or at least appearing to rise, to the challenges of even intellectual games like chess.[11] In the

Figure 14.1 Eighteenth-century 'chess machine'

Source: Copyright *Scientific American*, 1950. Reproduced: J. R. Newman, p. 2125

eighteenth century people loved to be fooled by the device of Wolfgang von Kempelen, in which a small and capable chess player was secreted in a cupboard underneath the playing surface.[12] More recently, and more seriously, Torres y Quevedo had demonstrated a very impressive device in 1914, which played a king and a rook against an opponent's king. (Wiener played against a later version at the 1951 Cybernetic Conference in Paris.)[13] It was, moreover, a tradition taken up enthusiastically by the AI community in general, something that earned them a reputation in some quarters for frivolity.[14]

Chess playing programs were proposed the moment the modern computer became accessible, and indeed, in anticipation of this eventuality, Turing had devised such a program, which was capable of being worked through with paper and pencil.[15] At about the same time, Shannon published a discussion which was likewise drawn on heavily by those who produced the first programs actually to be run.[16]

The basics of representing chess playing on the machine are straightforward. There is no difficulty[17] in getting the machine to simulate a player of a game such as chess, if a 'player' is taken to mean someone who is able to move the pieces in accordance with the rules. In Shannon's scheme, for

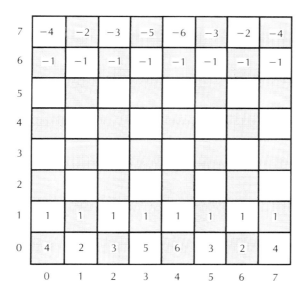

Figure 14.2 Coded chess board: a different number code for each type of piece, and squares are identified by number of row and column

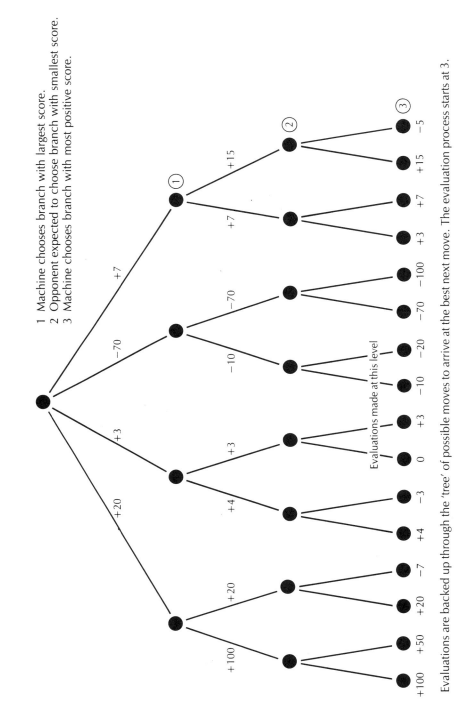

1 Machine chooses branch with largest score.
2 Opponent expected to choose branch with smallest score.
3 Machine chooses branch with most positive score.

Evaluations are backed up through the 'tree' of possible moves to arrive at the best next move. The evaluation process starts at 3.

Figure 14.3 Position evaluation in an early game program

example, the board was represented by a sequence of storage locations in memory, and the occupancy of each square was indicated by a code number placed in the appropriate location. For each piece there was a subroutine, capable of listing the destinations open to the piece from any of the positions it might occupy. A further subroutine enabled the machine to 'try' a move without altering permanently the codings of the actual position. Another was capable of listing all possible moves from a given position, and a final subroutine conducted an evaluation of any given position. A master program sequenced these subprograms into a single coherent operation.[18] The challenge comes in 'evaluation' – equipping the machine with the wherewithal to judge the merits of the different positions it 'tries'.

Games like chess or draughts are finite games in the sense that there is a fixed number of possible moves at any one point, and that any sequence of play is bound to lead in finite time to a conclusion – each player either wins, loses or draws.[19] This means that in theory the program could perform its 'evaluation' of any position simply by exploring the consequences of each continuation of play possible under the rules until, in each case, one of the three possible terminations is arrived at. It would not be enough, of course, to go on to choose on that basis any move that leads to a winning position, since this would be to neglect the choices open to the opponent. He or she cannot be relied on to make the best choice of move from the machine's point of view. On the contrary, the safest assumption is that the opponent will move so as to minimize the advantage to the machine. (This is the 'minimax' assumption articulated and explored by von Neumann in his work with Morgenstern, *The Theory of Games and Economic Behaviour*.[20]

If this is to be assumed, the machine has to work back from the terminal position possibilities through the points of possible choice that lead to them. At each such point (or 'node') one of the players will be choosing the move. On the minimax principle, if the machine is choosing, it will choose the path that leads to the position having the highest value of all the alternatives available from that node. If it is the opponent making the choice, the path leading to the position of least value will be chosen. In the light of these facts a derivative value can be attached to each node. This value will be equal to the highest value of the positions it makes available if it is the machine's turn (or 'ply', as it has been disarmingly termed), and to the least value of the subsequent position possibilities if it is the opponent who is to play. The same reasoning will allow the machine to follow ('back up') the terminal values right to the top of the 'tree' (see figure 14.3), and thus enable the best move to be identified.[21]

Unfortunately, in a game of the order of complexity of chess, the number of alternative continuations of play from the vast majority of positions is much too large for exhaustive exploration. For a game of 40 moves (on each side), Shannon works out that a machine calculating at the rate of one possible position per millionth of a second would require over 10^{95} years to decide on its first move.[22] The challenge, therefore, is to give the machine some means of evaluating a position without requiring it to explore all possible continuations to the point of termination.

Most straightforwardly, the machine can be made to attach appropriate scores to each piece retained on its own side, and to each piece lost by the opponent. Much more difficult are attempts to get it to identify the kind of piece configurations spoken of in chess books – for example, 'command of the centre of the board', 'mobility', 'degree of king protection', 'strength of pawn formation' – and to attach appropriate scores to positions where such characteristics are present. Guidance on the scoring can be found in chess books, where such matters are explicitly discussed; the books will offer guidance, too, on the question of devising an overall formula that combines the individual feature scores into an overall score for a position considered as a whole. Harder to transfer to programs are the identification skills the explicit discussions depend on, but which novices can only pick up by working through games and coming to see how concepts such as 'strength of pawn formation' apply; for of course quite different configurations of pawns can be covered by this description equally well. The chess programmer is involved here in the problem of pattern recognition – a sub-problem, in fact, of almost every AI project.

Michie records that experimentation by himself and Turing,[23] following wartime collaboration at Bletchley Park, must have been among the earliest efforts to program the new machines to play chess, but the first published

The MANIAC, one of the first machines to play chess in its spare time

report came from a group at Los Alamos in 1956. It was, as I mentioned earlier, the nuclear bomb program there at the Los Alamos Scientific Laboratory that created much of the immediate pressure for computer development (and continued to do so after the war).[24] Some of the workers there got their blackly-named machine MANIAC playing chess (a tremendous relief for it, presumably) in 1956, though to begin with it used a 6 × 6 rather than an 8 × 8 board.[25]

A second program was devised by Alex Bernstein, an experienced chess player who had access as a programmer to an IBM 704 machine, and published in 1958.[26] The vastly influential team of Newell, Shaw and Simon constructed a third, again first described in 1958.[27] (Others followed in the next decade.)[28]

I confess that I do not find it at all puzzling that games like chess should have been chosen as a focus for so much early programming effort, although I am much less confident of identifying the reasons correctly. Those involved offer a range of rationales: that the intellectual challenge of chess is so great that if we were able to program chess playing we would be able to program anything else; that the rules of chess offer a simplified version of life; that it gives us 'for the smallest initial structures, the greatest complexity'.[29] Samuel, who chose draughts rather than chess, speaks earnestly in his research papers of getting machines to learn as his objective,[30] but has made it clear through more informal channels that he got into the project as a money-raising gimmick: he wanted to build a big computer at his university (Illinois) and thought of running up a little draughts program as a way of attracting public interest and raising funds.[31] So Samuel for one tried to get a machine to play draughts because people generally were interested in it. Why people should be generally interested in games like chess, remains, as I say, though much speculated upon, unsettled.

Whatever the motivation behind it, Samuel's draughts program did make a clear contribution to machine 'learning'. Choosing draughts in place of chess because of its simpler rules, Samuel was able to draw on the pioneering work of C. S. Strachey, who had devised a basic draughts program in 1952.[32]

Samuel got the machine to 'learn' in two ways. First, it was programmed to 'remember' all the position evaluations it carried out. Whenever it had to evaluate a position it scanned this memory first. If the position had already been encountered, the evaluation was simply looked up and time saved which could be spent on a deeper search of the tree of alternative positions. Samuel likened this to rote learning in humans.

The second type of learning he tried to represent on the machine was a kind of 'learning by generalization'. Like the chess program, Samuel's draughts playing program was based on conducting evaluations of alternative positions. The program would analyse each position in an attempt to determine which 'features' it displayed (for example, 'strength in the centre'), apply a multiplier representing the presumed importance of this feature, if present, and arrive at a summary value for the position by adding up the values representing the identified features. By applying this evaluation function to each of the positions that could conceivably result from the presently considered one, in two or three moves' time, and by backing up these values to the current decision point, as in the chess case, what amounted to a prediction of the consequences of each preset option was arrived at. Samuel got his program to 'learn by generalization' by getting it to compare the evaluation of positions as actually encountered with the value predicted for them by the lookahead procedure. Thus the effectiveness of the formula used in the prediction was assessable, and could be improved by adjusting the weightings of its component elements.

The Second Tributary

In this early work on learning, one area of interest was the light it promised to throw on learning in animals and humans. This was the orientation of the cybernetic nerve-net studies, retained when structurelessness was abandoned. But there was also a less intellectual interest in making the new machines more useful, which it was argued they would undoubtedly be if they could be endowed with a capacity, however rudimentary, to 'learn' without having to have every last detail on every occasion spelt out to them. There was a similarly unfocused interest behind the pattern recognition work. Selfridge's project was to build into the machine a capacity to accept typescript as input, and so to improve ease and convenience of use, but there was also the thought that success would illuminate visual pattern recognition as a problem in psychology.

In the mid-fifties, a second tributary to AI joined the stream flowing from cybernetics, and this brought with it a different psychological perspective. It was one that drew a very much sharper line between equipping the machine with 'learning' powers and using the machine to study learning as it occurred in human beings. The new perspective – which went on to coexist with the concern with machine powers *per se* rather than ousting it – was rooted in a project of Simon's, at Carnegie, to develop a theory of decision making which would be useful in practical contexts of management and administration.

Simon, with a background in political science and economics, had published in 1947 an influential book called *Administrative Behaviour*, in which he began an attempt to answer some practical questions concerning decision making in organizations.[33] His investigations, however, revealed such great frailty in the existing basis for approaching these questions that he could only proceed by sinking new foundations. In the existing literature on administrative theory, all he could discover were statements so unspecific as to support with equal authority mutually contradictory recommendations; while psychology had had little to offer, in his estimation, since the death of the American psychologist and philosopher William James in 1910 – little, that is other than 'the nonsense syllable, and the rat'.[34] Neither field, in other words, had much that was relevant and helpful on the topic basic to Simon's interest, namely human decision making.

The discipline that on the face of it had been addresing this problem was economics, and also the field adjacent to economics that von Neumann and Morgenstern had delimited, namely the theory of games. But the account of rational decision making developed in economics could in no way be represented as an account of decision making as people actually conduct it, since it made a great swathe of unrealistic assumptions: complete knowledge by the decider of all available options, an ability to perform calculations of whatever complexity might be needed to determine which of these are best, and a complete and consistent system of preferences. To 'economic man' was thus attributed, Simon observes, 'a preposterously omniscient rationality'.[35]

Games theory, which attempted to calculate best strategies for parties in situations in which their interests at least partly conflict, extended this lack of realism. It was clear to Simon that any actual decision making, such as takes place in human organizations of one kind or another, can only happen in circumstances of relative ignorance. Only some of the options will be known about, only some of their consequences be explorable: and the question was, how does one go about maximizing rationality in circumstances such as these?

What we must accept in such circumstances, says Simon, is that to aim for the perfect solution is unrealistic. Our aim should be rather to arrive at a

Herbert Simon (left) and Allen Newell (right)

solution that is good enough for our purposes, in spite of the fact that it may be absolutely the best one possible.

It was a conclusion that was to converge with the work of Newell. Having specialized in physics as an undergraduate, and then in mathematics at the postgraduate level, he was working from 1950 on an air defence project directed at simulating an environment for a radar centre. In an air defence centre of that period, decisions had to be made on the basis of a flow of uninterpreted information generated by the radar sensors. Inefficiency in the decision making could be disastrous, and it was felt that there needed to be improvements made. The project which Newell joined, mounted by Rand, was to see whether improvements were obtainable by reforming the organizational structure of the decision-making process.

In 1954, stimulated, he tells us, by a report by Selfridge and G. P. Dinneen,[36] he decided that the way forward for his part of the radar centre project was to explore the potential of computers for handling 'ultra-complicated' problems.[37] As I have pointed out, others have already suggested that games such as chess might offer suitable challenges for this kind of exploration, and to begin with, Newell took chess playing as his vehicle.

A chess playing program is, of course, a program designed to make a series of well-founded decisions – which was exactly the focus of Herbert Simon's work. In particular, there was a clear parallel, for example, between the human decision maker (as conceived of by Simon) having to find sensible ways of restricting the number of options to consider, and the chess playing program (as designed by Newell) having to articulate ways of cutting down the vast number of possible moves from a given position, so as to establish a short list small enough to investigate in useful depth. If the parallel could be taken seriously, the decision-making behaviour of the machine could be compared with that of human beings and, so Simon thought, the correctness of any theory about sensible decision making evaluated. In the preface to the second edition of *Administrative Behaviour*, published in 1957, Simon is in fact claiming that the success of problem-solving programs yielded by the work initiated by Newell has already 'verified' the 'main features' of his theory.[38]

The potential convergence between Newell's interests and Simon's was realized when Simon, having helped launch a new graduate school at Carnegie Institute of Technology (the Graduate School of Industrial Administration), was appointed as a consultant to the Rand project in 1952. Two years later a firm association had taken shape. Cliff Shaw, who had been working on system development for the new computer just built at Rand, the JOHNNIAC,[39] made a third member of this enormously influential team.[40] Newell effectively joined Simon at Carnegie (later to become Carnegie-Mellon University) from 1955.[41]

One of the early decisions of the new team was to change vehicles, from chess playing programs to programs designed to solve problems in logic and geometry, on the grounds that more progress for effort expended was likely to come from the latter.[42] By the time of the first 'Artificial Intelligence' research seminar mounted at Dartmouth in June 1956, the Newell team had debugging runs of their logic theory machine to take with them, and by the end of the year it was working as they meant it to. It is this program that enjoys the reputation of being 'the first foray by artificial intelligence research into high-order intellectual processes'.[43]

Notes

1 B. V. Bowden (ed.), *Faster than Thought* (Pitman, London, 1953), ch. 25
2 'The Dartmouth Summer Research Project on Artificial Intelligence'; see McCorduck, *Machines Who Think*, pp. 96, 97.
3 Neilsson, quoted by Michie in N. V. Findler and B. Meltzer (eds), *Artificial Intelligence and Heuristic Programming* (Edinburgh UP, Edinburgh, 1971), p. 101.
4 Oliver Selfridge, 'Pattern Recognition and Modern Computers', *Proceedings of the 1955 Western Joint Computer Conference*, Session on Learning Machines, pp. 85–111.
5 See above, p. 197.
6 Shannon, 'Programming a Digital Computer for Playing Chess', *Philosophy Magazine*, 41 (1950), pp. 356–75; 'Automatic Chess Player', *Scientific American*, 182 (1950), p. 48; reprinted in J. R. Newman (ed.), *The World of Mathematics* (Simon & Schuster, New York, 1956), pp. 2124–33.
7 Newell and Simon, *Human Problem Solving* (Prentice-Hall, Englewood Cliffs, NJ, 1972), p. 667.
8 See, for example, Turing, "Intelligent Machinery", *NPL Report* (1948), reprinted in C. R. Evans and A. D. J. Robertson (eds), *Cybernetics* (Butterworths, London, 1968); and Turing, 'Computing Machinery', *Mind*, 59 (1950), reprinted in Feigenbaum and Feldman, *Computers and Thought*, Section 1.
9 See the account in McCorduck, *Machines Who Think*, pp. 85–7.
10 Samuel, 'Some Studies in Machine Learning Using the Game of Checkers', *IBM Journal of Research and Development*, 3 (1959), pp. 211–29, reprinted in Feigenbaum and Feldman, *Computers and Thought*, Section 2.
11 E. Lasker, *The Adventure of Chess* (Dover, New York, 1959), ch. 10.
12 Shannon, 'Automatic Chess Player', in Newman (ed.), *World of Mathematics*, p. 2125.
13 H. Zemanek, 'Central European Prehistory of Computing', in Metropolis et al. *History of Computing*, pp. 587–610; H. Vigneron, 'Les Automates: Le Jouer d'Echec Automatique de M. Torres y Quevedo', *La Nature*, 13, June 1914, pp. 56–61.
14 See, for example, Bowden, Preface to Melzer and Michie, *Machine Intelligence 7*, p. ix.; and the President of IBM, reported in McCorduck, *Machines Who Think*, p. 159.
15 Bowden, *Faster than Thought*, ch. 25. Michie had apparently been involved in this; see his *On Machine Intelligence* (Edinburgh UP, Edinburgh, 1974), p. 51.
16 Shannon, 'Programming a Digital Computer for Playing Chess'.
17 Though there is some tedium if restricted to machine code, as were the pioneering Los Alamos chess team, Bernstein and Samuel. See notes 21, 25 and 26.
18 Shannon, 'Programming a Digital Computer for Playing Chess'.
19 See discussion by Allen Newell, J. C. Shaw and H. A. Simon, 'Chess-Playing Programs and the Problem of Complexity', in Feigenbaum and Feldman, *Computers and Thought*, p. 42.

20 Von Neumann and D. Morgenstern, *The Theory of Games and Economic Behaviour* (Princeton UP, Princeton, 1947).

21 Samuel, 'Machine Learning', in Feigenbaum and Feldman, *Computers and Thought*, Section 2.

22 Shannon, 'Automatic Chess Player', in Newman, *World of Mathematics*, p. 2127.

23 Michie, *On Machine Intelligence*, p. 51.

24 N. Metropolis, in Metropolis et al., *History of Computing*, pp. 457–64.

25 J. Kister et al., 'Experiments in Chess', *Journal of Computing Machinery*, 4 (1957), pp. 174–7.

26 Bernstein et al. 'A Chess-Playing Program for the IBM 704 Computer', *Proceedings of the Western Joint Computer Conference*, 1958, pp. 157–9.

27 Newell et al, 'Chess-Playing Programs', in Feigenbaum and Feldman, *Computers and Thought*, pp. 39–70.

28 For reviews, see Newell and Simon, *Human Problem Solving*, pp. 698, 699; McCorduck, *Machines Who Think*, pp. 160ff.

29 Minsky (ed.), *Semantic Information Processing* (MIT Press, Cambridge, Mass., 1968), p. 12.

30 Samuel, 'Machine Learning', in Feigenbaum and Feldman, *Computers and Thought*, Section 2.

31 McCorduck, *Machines Who Think*, pp. 148, 149.

32 C. S. Strachey, 'Logical or Non-mathematical Programmes', *Proceedings of the Association for Computing Machinery*, 1952.

33 Simon, *Administrative Behaviour* (The Free Press, New York, 1957), p. xiii.

34 Newell and Simon, *Human Problem Solving*, p. 874.

35 Simon, *Administrative Behaviour*, p. xxiii.

36 Selfridge, 'Pattern Recognition', pp. 91–3; Newell and Simon, *Human Problem Solving*, p. 882.

37 Newell and Simon, *Human Problem Solving*, p. 882

38 Simon, *Administrative Behaviour*, p. xxvii.

39 See note 29, p. 173.

40 Newell and Simon, *Human Problem Solving*, p. 883.

41 McCorduck, *Machines Who Think*, pp. 132–5.

42 Newell and Simon, *Human Problem Solving*, p. 883.

43 Feigenbaum, in Feigenbaum and Feldman, *Computers and Thought*, p. 108. The alternative idea for a geometry problem program also figured centrally at the 1956 Dartmouth seminar, with Minsky making significant contributions. A working program was completed shortly afterwards. See H. Gelernter and N. Rochester, 'Intelligent Behaviour in Problem-Solving Machines', *IBM Journal of Research and Development*, 2 (1958) pp. 336–45.

15 Mechanizing Logic

A 'problem' in logic is, generally speaking, a requirement that a proof of a stated proposition be given. This was the kind of problem-solving the Newell team's logic theory machine program (hereafter, the 'logic theorist' or 'LT') carried out. As with the chess player, it is straightforward to represent the principles of the proof-generation 'game' on the machine. The elements of propositions can be given numerical codes, and the proposition as a whole represented as a sequence of memory locations holding these codes. Rules of inference can be seen as allowing certain transformations of these propositions. The rule of detachment means, for example, that if we have the theorem

If both p and q are true, then at least p is true

and also the theorem

Both p and q are true

we can detach 'at least p is true' from the first proposition as an independent theorem. In other words, the rule of detachment allows us to 'transform' the theorem

If (both p and q) implies p

into

p

so long as we also have

Both p and q

These rules can therefore be represented as subroutines which perform specified transformations on stored propositions when the appropriate conditions are met.

A program might be written, then, with both a set of axioms and a set of inference rules represented in it. It is also clear that a further proposition – one for which a proof is sought – might be represented in it too. And since a proof is essentially a sequence of propositions, each one derivable from one or more of its predecessors by one or more of the rules of inference, there is no difficulty in the idea of proofs being represented in the machine. The question is only how we get such proofs produced.

Nor is this a difficult question. Every time any of the rules of inference achieves a new proposition by transforming in a legitimate way one of the axioms, we have a proof – a proof of the proposition so generated. And each of these derived propositions, since it has been proved, may be added to the stock of propositions held – that is, each becomes a theorem. One way of generating a proof for a given proposition is therefore to apply the rules systematically to the axioms, and then to the set of axioms and theorems this produces, and then to the larger set of axioms and theorems this produces, and so on, until a theorem is proved which is identical with the proposition for which a proof is sought. Newell's team calls the procedure suggested here the 'British Museum algorithm', 'in recognition of the supposed originators of procedures of this type'.[1]

The disadvantage is that it takes too long. The Newell team's rough estimate in 1957 is that to generate in this way proofs for the 86 theorems developed under Chapter 2 of Russell and Whitehead's *Principia Mathematica*, using the axioms and rules of that work, would have taken the

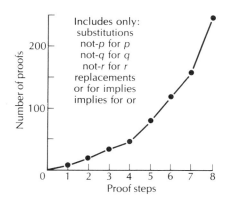

Figure 15.1 Number of proofs generated by the first few steps of the British Museum algorithm

Source: Feigenbaum & Feldman, *Computers & Thought* (see note 27, p. 173 above) p. 116

JOHNNIAC hundreds of thousands of years.[2] One route towards a practical proof-finder was, therefore, to find ways of cutting down the number of candidate proofs thrown up by the machine – or at least, ways of enriching the candidate proofs thrown up in the early stages of a run with ones which had an improved likelihood of being the proof sought.

Theorem Provers for Propositional Logic – LT and GPS

The Newell team's idea was to use the structure of the proposition to be proved as a guide for focusing the program's attention on a relatively small number of possible proofs. They thus replaced the British Museum algorithm, which started with the axioms and attempted to work forward to the proposition to be proved, with a procedure that started with the proposition and attempted to work backwards to one of the things that had already been proved. As a problem-solving strategy this of course felt much more familiar, much closer to what seems intuitively to be the human approach to problems, which regards working blindly through all the logical possibilities as the antithesis of 'intelligent'.

The first step of the Logic Theory program is to work through the axioms and any further propositions already listed as proved by the system (i.e. theorems), matching each up in turn against the target proposition. The question it asks is: could the first of each pairing of propositions be transformed into the second by making a legitimate substitution (i.e. one that is sanctioned by the axioms or propositions already proved)?

To adapt the example in the Newell team paper of 1957, suppose the proposition to be proved is

    p implies that q implies p   1.1

and one of the axioms is

    p implies either q or p.   1.2

In the course of comparing its stock of axioms and theorems against the target, this particular pairing will be encountered. The program will note that the main operator is the same in the two cases ('implies'); and then that to the left of the main operator the variable is the same ('p'), but that the operands to the right are different. It then asks whether this difference can be reconciled by applying substitutions.

Does it have among its axioms or theorems a proposition which says that

    q implies p

can be replaced by something else? Let us suppose that it does indeed have listed the definition

LT(problem, theorems):
1   Substution-submethod(problem),
        if succeed stop and report immediate proof.
2   insert problem on untried-problems at end;
3   generate untried-problems(=> current-problem):
4   Detachment-submethod(current-problem);
5   Chaining-forward-submethod(current-problem);
6   Chaining-backward-submethod(current-problem).,
        stop and report no proof and nothing more to do.

Substitution-submethod(problem):
1   generate theorems:
2   apply SB(theorem, problem),
                if fail continue generation;
3   reconstruct-proof from problem,
                stop LT and report result..

Detachment-submethod(problem):
1   generate theorems:
2   test if theorem of form A ⊃ B,
                if false continue generation;
3   apply DT[theorem](problem) (=> new-problem),
                if fail continue generation;
4   apply Substitution-submethod(new-problem),
                if succeed stop process;
5   insert new-problem on untried-problems at end..

Chaining-forward-submethod(problem):
1   test if problem of form A ⊃ B,
        if false stop;
2   generate theorems:
3   test if theorem of form A ⊃ B,
                if false continue generation;
4   apply CF[theorem](problem) (=> new-problem),
                if fail continue generation;
5   apply Substitution-submethod(new-problem),
                if succeed stop process;
6   insert new-problem on untried-problems at end..

Chaining-backward-submethod(problem):
1   test if problem of form A ⊃ B,
        if false stop;
2   generate theorems:
3   test if theorem of form A ⊃ B,
                if false continue generation;
4   apply CB[theorem](problem) (=> new-problem),
                if fail continue generation;
5   apply Substitution-submethod(new-problem),
                if succeed stop process;
6   insert new-problem on untried-problems at end..

Figure 15.2 Flow diagram of the Logic Theorist

Source: Feigenbaum & Feldman, *Computers & Thought* (see note 27, p. 173 above) p. 119

q implies p = either not-q or p   1.3

This allows it to add to its list of theorems:

p implies either not-q or p   1.4

It then notes that the only difference between this and the target proposition is that one has q where the other has not-q.

Suppose finally that the program has also been given the following rule:

> Any propositional formula can be substituted for any propositional variable within an expression provided only that the same substitution is made throughout the expression.

(This is one of the rules of inference, the rule of substitution, that is treated as basic in the logical system set out in *Principia Mathematica*.)

In the proposition labelled 1.4 above, now among the program's theorems, the rule of substitution allows not-q to be replaced by q, without any other change (since q occurs in it just the once). By applying the rule of substitution to 1.4 the program thus generates

p implies either q or p   1.5

which it can then recognize as identical with the axiom 1.2. Thus a proof of 1.1 is arrived at.

A proof of the target proposition is reached easily, in this case, by the application of what the Newell group called the 'method of substitution'. For other propositions, other resources may have to be invoked. The 'detachment method' sought to discover a proposition which the axioms (together with any theorems) show would prove the target proposition if only it could be proved itself. For example, if the target proposition is B and one of the axioms is 'A implies B', then the detachment method notes A is something to try and prove, since success would also prove B.

Two other methods – forward and backward 'chaining' – likewise tried to identify propositions which if provable would prove the target, in their case by exploiting the 'transitivity' implication ('if p implies q and q implies r, then if p is true, so is r').

These resources – substitution providing proofs, and detachment and chaining passing useful propositions forward to see if substitution could prove them – enabled the Logic Theory program to produce proofs for most of the provable propositions put to it in humanly reasonable times. Of the 52 theorems from Chapter 2 of *Principia Mathematica* which were put to the program, it produced proofs for all but 14.[5]

The battery of methods used by the Logic Theorist are in a sense much weaker than the British Museum algorithm. We know that given time, the latter will produce a proof of any provable proposition put to it. But this is not true of the Logic Theorist. Its methods cut down (enormously) on the number of possibilities checked out as the sought-for proof, but at the risk of cutting out successful candidates. This is the point of calling them 'heuristic', a term the Newell team took from the work of George Polya (who had once taught Newell)[6] on methods of proof in mathematics. 'A process that may solve a given problem, but offers no guarantees of doing so, is called a heuristic for that problem,' say Newell et al.[7] – though the point of a heuristic method is, of course, not that it opens up the possibility of failure, but that it enhances the likelihood of success.

The Newell team rather misleadingly contrast a heuristic method with an 'algorithmic' one, which suggests that there is something non-deterministic about heuristics.[8] No such suggestion is appropriate. The program Newell et al., and many successors, devised to carry out heurisitc methods are perfectly deterministic. Their distinction is just that they do not work systematically through all possible solution candidates, but apply short cuts instead, rules that eliminate less likely candidates and allow concentration on those that are more likely. Heuristic programs may be seen as *ipso facto* intelligent ones: but if so, the intelligence is all directly contributed by the programmer.

The fact that the Logic Theorist generated these early *Principia Mathematica* proofs so promptly was almost a mark of failure in the context of the Newell team's particular project. Their object was not so much to get a machine to generate proofs as to design a computer simulation of human problem solving, and human beings generally have to spend a good deal of time familiarizing themselves with symbols and symbol manipulation before they are able to suggest proofs. Mathematicians and logicians interested in the foundations of mathematics had none of this psychological concern, and they pointed out, correctly but unnecessarily, that proofs could be generated more efficiently and more reliably using different algorithms.[9] The interest of Newell and his team was to explore the way in which human beings did it.

Their method was to set alongside the printed 'trace' of the steps executed by their program the records of students asked to think aloud as they tried to grapple with the type of problem treated by the machine. Feedback of this kind led to the development of a new program, the General Problem Solver, or GPS.

Already, in the Logic Theorist, there was the beginning of a strategy devised in terms of goals and 'sub-goals': if the proof of the target expression could not be generated directly, the Logic Theorist tried to find another proposition, which, if proved, would allow by detachment the derivation of the target. Proving this intermediate proposition thus became a sub-goal.

This approach was taken further by the GPS. When given a problem, the GPS attempted to identify a series of lesser problems which if solved would amount to the solution of the problem as presented. A first operation was the comparison of likely axiom with target, to identify the differences between them. The type of differences affected by a given operator were listed in the machine, which, having identified a difference, worked its way through the relevant operators, looking for one which would eliminate it. If such an operator was found, and it could be applied to the axiom, it was applied, and the difference eliminated – and one step towards the final goal was achieved.

The appropriate operator, however, might not be applicable to the axiom as it stood: some transformation might be necessary. The program then sought to establish whether such a transformation would be permissible, by seeing whether the transformation was legitimized by the rules. That is, the program set up a new sub-goal, that of generating a proof for the required expression. This was, of course, exactly the same type of problem it was presented with in the first place, so that it could again bring all its resources to bear on it. If successful, a selected operator could be applied on the newly proved expression and the difference between axiom and target that was being worked on could be eliminated – and another step towards the overall goal was made. 'These methods,' explain Newell and Simon, 'form a recursive system that generates a tree of sub-goals in attempting to attain a given goal. For every new difficulty that is encountered a new sub-goal is created to overcome this difficulty.'[10]

List Processing

In developng the Logic Theorist, the Newell team sought ways of making the task of coding instructions for the computer easier. Ultimately, in any application, the machine needed to have its memory cells loaded with binary numbers, some of which coded for instructions.[11] An early invention was a program called a translator, which converted numbers input in decimal form into the mandatory binary, and which allowed mnemonics to be used to specify instructions instead of number codes (again by translating them into binary).

The development of other programs called assemblers made the management of the computer's memory very much easier. With an assembler program in place, an operator could type in a convenient symbol and leave it to the machine to translate it into an actual address. Similarly, an operator could refer symbolically to a location by specifying simply how far away it was from another (i.e., relative, then called 'regional', addressing), and the machine would work out for itself what actual address was meant.

To save the chore of repeating often-used sequences of machine instructions – such as would be involved in adding two numbers, for example – the concept of a subroutine was introduced, first as a programming innovation, but subsequently reflected in special instructions recognized by the hardware. Just as it was possible to provide the machine with a program that would translate mnemonics into binary, so, once the idea of a subroutine existed, it was possible to create a program that would translate any arbitrarily defined input into code calling sequences of subroutines. Each symbol input would thus stand for whatever operation the subroutine complex carried out.

Facilities for getting the machine to accept algebraic expressions directly and to work them out were devised in this way, the translation program accepting the algebraic formulas and producing the binary numbers which constituted instructions to the machine to carry out the appropriate computation. One of the earliest translators was FORTRAN (FORmula TRANslation) which, because of the enormous library of procedures now written in it, still flourishes.[12]

Translators, assemblers, and the idea of the high level language – of which FORTRAN was an early example – were all conceived before the pioneering AI workers began to articulate any special programming-aid needs. For their part, they were interested in manipulating not numbers but symbols of a less restricted kind, and soon a new way of organizing the storage of data in the machine was devised with their particular purposes in mind.

The most straightforward way of keeping track of where coded data is located within the memory of a computer is to store it sequentially, and note the start of the sequence and the serial number of each item within the sequence. A given datum can then be retrieved by adding the serial number to the address of the start location. For most numerical applications, this approach works well, since what is usually required in such contexts is for a number to be taken from one location and have some operation performed upon it, and for the result to be stored. But non-numerical manipulations often require something different. Here the manipulation is typically not on a single datum but on a sequence of data: elements of the sequence are to be deleted, or moved, or extra elements added. Serial storage is inconvenient for these operations, because much shuffling backwards and forwards of data essentially unconnected with any particular operation is necessitated.

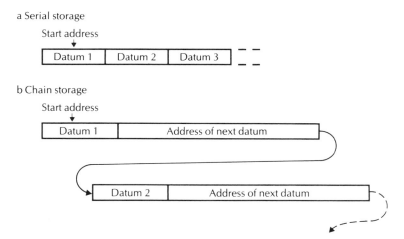

Figure 15.3 Serial and chain storage

For example, to insert a new datum near the beginning of a serial sequence means that all the data stored after the insert have to be moved one location on to make room.

Programming is made easier in these contexts if data is stored in chains. The first datum of a sequence to be stored is placed in a location: and the next one or two locations are used to store an address, namely the address of the location in which the second datum of the sequence is to be stored. This location in its turn is followed by the address of the third datum, and so on. Amending sequences is then much easier, involving the alteration of just a few addresses.

The data structure that results was called by the early programmers a 'list': 'A list is a set of words tied together by having the address of each word in the list recorded in the word that occurs just prior to it in the list.'[13]

It is also desirable for symbol manipulation purposes to be able to treat as units lists that are combined in various ways: not just end-to-end (which would produce a bigger list) but with branching. These were called list structures, and Newell gives us a simple example (see figure 15.5).

The development of a 'list processing' language with these features was pursued by the Newell team in parallel with their work on the Logic

a Serial storage insertion

1 Move all these data on

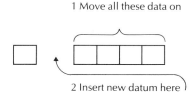

2 Insert new datum here

b Chain storage insertion

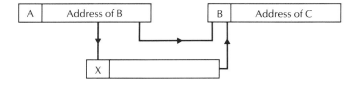

1 Put X in spare location.
2 Put address of B in location following X.
3 Put address of X in place of address of B in location following A.

Figure 15.4 Serial and Chain storage: insertion

Theorist. Their first attempts in this general direction led to languages oriented to the specific programming task in hand – first chess playing, and then logic theorem generation. Collectively known as Information Processing Language I (IPL–I), and first described by Newell and his associates at the influential Dartmouth conference of 1956, they were put aside in favour of a fresh start, making more of the list idea. This yielded IPL–II, the language in which the Logic Theorist was coded. IPL–III was revised into IPL–IV before becoming operational, and this was the language in which the two very influential programs by Newell et al. (the General Problem Solver and a chess playing program),[14] as well as F. M. Tonge's assembly line balancing program, were written.[15]

Other attempts to exploit the list idea were also made. In 1960, Gelernter added a list processing facility to FORTRAN and called it the FORTRAN List Processing Language, or FLPL. This he used for his program for proving theorems in plane geometry. Victor Yngve's COMIT, developed in 1958 to help program would-be language translators, used list ideas. Most influential, however, indeed so much so that it eclipsed all other attempts in the same direction and gave the AI community its *lingua franca*, was the development by McCarthy at MIT of LISP (LISt Procesor) from 1955.

Though LISP was devised in the first place to provide a convenient means of programming a computer to manipulate strings of symbols (as distinct from numbers), this is not the only, or even the most important, contribution this type of language has to make. The crucial point is rather that computer programs themselves are represented in the machine as a sequence of codes, and that a list processing language like LISP makes it easy to treat programs themselves as manipulable data. Since the programs that are thus manipulable include the program that is doing the manipulation, we have here the facility to program recursively: to instruct a progam to do things to itself. One application of this potential is in theorem-proving, for it means that logical form can be treated as manipulable. Turing showed that the class of computable functions was coextensive with the class of functions that could be calculated if recursive techniques were part of the repertoire.[16] The power to program recursively means that all computable functions fall within the computer's scope.[17]

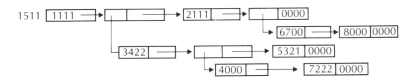

Figure 15.5 Example of a list structure given for an early list programming language

Source: Newell, IPL–V Manual, (see note 12) p. 9

LISP had another contribution to make. Although it was not a design objective at the outset, it was proved in 1976 that, with some amendments to the original definition, each syntactically correct statement in LISP amounted to a symbolization of a well-formed formula in the propositional logic.[18]

Mechanizing the Predicate Logic

I have explained how, under the genius of Frege, a calculus was devised that made possible the systematization of arguments in which degrees of generality, working within propositions, played a key role.[19] The innovation was to treat a proposition on the model of a mathematical function applied to an argument, and then to construe degrees of generality in terms of second-order functions. I have also described how it was this predicate logic that enabled logicians to explore the foundations of mathematics during the first decades of the present century, yielding several attempts at axiomatization, a sustained and rigorous study of the relationship between mathematics and logic itself, and Hilbert's program of proving mathematics to be nothing other than a purely formal system.

In exploring a logical system – discovering what theorems follow from any given axiom-set – logicians may proceed intuitively: positing a proposition, because the implications of its being provable would be interesting for some reason or another, and then casting about for a proof. But in some circumstances, casting about is unnecessary. For it may be that in a given logical system, following a definite set procedure in relation to any putative theorem can be guaranteed to yield a verdict on the question of whether it is indeed a theorem or not. The exploration of systems of this kind can be taken over by computer. All that is needed is to devise a program that will carry out the checking procedure. Then, given some kind of automatic generator of candidate-theorems, the machine can list genuine theorems of the system by applying the checking procedure to each one in turn.

For the propositional calculus (that is, the elementary part of the predicate calculus which does not involve quantification), such a mechanical checking procedure is indeed available – in fact, there are several. I shall explain what is known as the 'truth-table' method.

Truth Tables

As I have indicated, the propositional logic analyses statements into propositions and operators. An operator (for example, '... and ...') links two propositions to make a new one: the two propositions 'p' and 'q' are linked to form the single proposition 'p and q'.

Rules of argumentation may then be expressed in terms of the 'implication' operator, 'if ... then ...'. Supposing it is argued that a certain conclusion, 'C', is true because it is implied by 'B', and 'B' is implied by 'A', which we know to be true. How might the rule that is being appealed to here be expressed?

Using 'p', 'q' and 'r' to hold places for any particular propositions, the following formula would seem to serve:

If p is true, then, if p implies q and q implies r, r must be true

As a statement of a rule that sets out that a certain conclusion follows from premises of a specified kind, this expression is itself a proposition: a proposition whose truth will be a matter of whether the rule is a valid one or not. If the rule is valid, the proposition expressing it will be true; and if invalid, false.

Is there a way of telling whether a compound proposition is true or not? Ordinarily, it might seem that if a composite proposition is constructed by linking together simpler ones, the truth of the product will depend on the truth of the components, and on what effect the linking 'operators' have upon that truth. For example, suppose I link 'Hegel was a great logician' with 'Frege was a great logician' by means of the operator '... and ...', thus constructing the compound proposition 'Hegel was a great logician and Frege was a great logician'. The effect of the operator ('conjunction') is such as to make the compound true if and only if each of the conjoints is true, so it would seem that we can only know whether the conjunction is true once we know the truth of the two components.

For a proposition that expresses a rule, however, we cannot just look to the truth of the component propositions, because these are not definite assertions about things but, ultimately, just propositional variables – 'p', 'q', etc: symbols that hold places indeterminately for any definite assertion. Nevertheless, whatever the definite assertion we may think of as substituting or a propositional variable, it will be either true or false. This is enough to allow us to work out whether the rule expression is true or not.

What we can do is to work through the possible combinations of substitutions of propositions that were true and propositions that were false for the propositional variables that occur, and determine in each case whether this would produce overall truth or falsity. That is, we can ask these questions: supposing each component proposition were true, would the resulting compound be true? And then: would the compound be true if the components were all false? And then: what if the first component were true but the others false – would the compound be true? What we would have to do would be to work our way through all the possible combinations of truth and falsity of component propositions, which might be a long job: but when complete we would be able to say whether or not the compound propositions that would be produced by the hypothesized substitutions were true or not. And if they were all true, this would show that the compound expression was true for all possible substitutions and therefore true as it stood.

Suppose, for example, we use the symbol 'p' to hold a place for

Tables 8a, b. Truth tables

a Truth table for 'if p then not-not-p'

Proposition:	p	Not-p	Not-not-p	If p then not-not-p
	T	F	T	T
	F	T	F	T

b Truth table for 'if both p and q then at least p'

Proposition:	p	q	Both p and q	If both p and q then p
	T	T	T	T
	T	F	F	T
	F	T	F	T
	F	F	F	T

propositions and that our candidate for an expression of a valid rule (that is, candidate theorem) is:

If p is true then it is not the case that p is not the case

Could this proposition under any substitutions bear the truth-value 'false'? There are only two possibilities to be considered, one where 'p' is true and the other where 'p' is false. When 'p' is true, 'not-p' is false, 'not-not-p' is true, and the whole proposition 'p entails not-not-p' would as a result have the truth-value 'true'. But when 'p' is false, 'not-p' is true, 'not-not-p' is false and 'p entails not-not-p' is again true. Thus the proposition under test is shown to yield a true proposition, whether what is substituted for 'p' is a true proposition or a false one. It is shown, therefore, to be true as it stands, a theorem of the system. These calculations of truth-values can be set out in the form of a 'truth table' (see table 8a).

When more than one propositional variable is involved, the truth table associated with a complex proposition naturally becomes larger. The truth table for the formula 'If both p and q then at least p' is shown in table 8b. Once again, whatever combination of truth-values of 'p' and 'q' is substituted, the truth-value for the resulting proposition as a whole is always 'true': the general formulation is therefore a theorem.

Though Frege used truth-tables in 1879, we owe to Charles Peirce the consolidation of this idea into a method for testing for validity.[20] Its widespread use, however, is due to the use made of it by Post, Lucasiewicz and Wittgenstein in the 1920s.[21]

Working out the truth table of a given proposition is clearly a straightforward task for the type of machine I have been describing, and theorems in the propositional logic can be proved in this way. The time required, however, should not be underestimated, since the number of lines in a truth table rises exponentially with the number of propositional variables involved (the number of lines being 2^n where n is the number of variables). It has been calculated that a computer operating as fast as conceivably possible, set to work at the beginning of the universe as we know it (3×10^{10} years ago?), would have yet to complete a truth table for a proposition with 110 component variables.[22]

Alternatives to the truth-table method of proving theorems in the propositional calculus have been explored (because of the calculus's application to, among other things, switching circuit design) with some success, but developments along those lines are overshadowed by advances in the mechanization of the much more potent predicate logic.[23]

Nevertheless, possessing mechanical proof-procedures for the propositional logic has been of interest not to logicians alone. Propositional logic has its practical uses, because it catches the kind of argument we use in some cases to draw implied information from a body of facts, and this has meant the beginnings of general utility for non-mathematical mechanical reasoning. To this I shall return shortly.

Proof-procedures in the Predicate Logic
But what of the predicate logic? Is there a definite or mechanical procedure in this more powerful logic for testing the provability of any well-formed formula that might be constructed? This is a version of a question alluded to already: the question of the completeness of a formal system, investigated for arithmetic under Hilbert's influence by Gödel and others in the thirties.[24] What was shown then was that for arithmetic and systems of equivalent complexity there was no such procedure.[25]

In the course of these investigations, however, it emerged that procedures that went half the required distance could be devised: that is to say, it proved possible to devise a procedure that would return an affirmative answer whenever fed with a proposition that was valid. Confronted with an invalid proposition, though, the procedure might never terminate. Uncertainty therefore arose, because once the procedure had been initiated in connection with a given candidate-theorem, no-one could tell until and unless it reached a conclusion whether its non-termination was due to the proposition's being invalid (in which case the procedure might never terminate), or to the fact that it had not quite finished yet (which was quite consistent with the proposition's being valid).

This fundamental limitation on devising definite procedures for, and thus on the mechanization of, predicate logic has not been circumvented in the decades following its discovery, and this has left logicians and mathematicians with their jobs. In formal systems of the complexity of arithmetic anyway, there are theorems that cannot be proved by machine.

Nevertheless, the procedures devised by Gödel and others in the thirties for picking up (some) valid candidate-theorems were of great interest to logicians, and have since yielded techniques of considerable significance in the practical application of logic. They were first devised, obviously, not as programs for the universal machine, which had at that time still to take any kind of concrete form, but as mathematical formulae. It was not until the early fifties, when the new machines were demobbed, that there was opportunity to try their capabilities for pure logic (as it appeared at that stage). P. C. Gilmour was among the first to run actual programs,[26] using an IBM 704; Hao Wang and a team led by D. Prawitz were others.[27] Later, a variety of proof procedures were published.[28]

Expert Systems

The interest of mechanizing logic, either in part or in whole, is not restricted to those with an esoteric concern with the development of formal systems, namely mathematicians and logicians themselves. It carries a much more utilitarian potential than that, because the type of logic we can now mechanize catches a good deal of the reasoning we use in our practical affairs. The most sustained attempt to realize some of this potential so far has been the project of mechanizing the use we make of reason to draw implied information from a body of facts. An example I have already used makes clear the principle: if I know the connection between illness and temperature, and I know that Tom has a temperature, I can infer that he is ill.

More sophisticated medical judgements can follow the same pattern, where the doctor puts together the rules expressing the links between symptoms and particular diseases, other rules expressing the implications of various tests, and the facts he or she obtains from examining the patient, to arrive at a diagnosis. When the attempt is made to mechanize such a process it produces what is known as an 'expert system'. I shall outline one of the most celebrated representatives of the genre, although its venerable vintage means that it involves a mechanization of the propositional logic only.

In the 1974 MYCIN program, the expertise that is available in the field is represented as a 'data-base' in the form of conditional statements or rules of the general type 'if p then q', where 'q' is the conclusion to be drawn if symptoms or other circumstances comprising 'p' obtain. For example, 'q' might be 'The patient is suffering from menigitis', and 'p' a list of symptoms that, when present together, indicate this illness.

The system is asked to evaluate a function called REGIMEN, whose value is the recommended treatment. To carry out this evaluation it turns to any rule in its data-base that carries an implication for REGIMEN in its consequence clause. There is in fact only one such rule, Rule 092, which says, briefly, that if a pathogen or pathogens have been identified, REGIMEN should receive the value of the most appropriate treatment in the light of the micro-organisms present. The treatment is actually taken from a look-up table, so the rub of the program lies in the correct identification of the micro-organisms.

The system, then, seeks to apply Rule 092. It will therefore seek to establish the antecedent, that is, that some pathogens are present. It does this by investigating any rule in its data-base which has the presence of pathogens as a conclusion. Again, this will be a matter of checking on the truth of the antecedents of such rules, each of which may call for the investigation of other rules, and so on. Sometimes the user is asked to supply required information. Sometimes the system obtains it from its own data-base. In the end (if some pathogens have been succesfully identified) the antecedent of the goal rule, Rule 092, is established as true, and the action stipulated in the consequent takes place. REGIMEN is given the appropriate value from the look-up table, in the light of the organisms identified as present, and this value – a course of treatment – is output.

The heart of the system is, therefore, an ability to carry out the operations of propositional logic: to carry out some action (perhaps note something as a conclusion) on condition that some specified other things are established.

Looked at slightly differently, a program like MYCIN can be seen as a theorem-prover. It establishes that a certain proposition, stipulating in effect a certain treatment, follows from the facts – the facts stored in the data-base, supplemented by any facts fed in by the user. The simplest kind of interrogation of a data-base is a search, as when one looks up an address by looking for a match between a name one presents and the same name stored in code in the machine. More sophisticated programs like MYCIN allow not just the straightforward recall of facts already put into the machine, but the drawing out, by the application of propositional logic, of some of the implications of such facts. Its task in effect is to prove that such-and-such a proposition *follows from* any combination of other propositions that the system has been given.[29]

I have explained that though Godel and others had demonstrated that there is no way of mechanically checking candidate-theorems for validity in the predicate logic, programs were devised in the fifties which exploited the known formulae for identifiying validity. Despite the theoretical limitations, these techniques have proved the basis for the development of practically effective data-base interrogation systems using the predicate logic, the so-called 'expert systems' of today. Because the predicate logic catches so much of our ordinary reasoning processes (almost all of our reasoning, in fact, that goes with certainty from premise to conclusion) these systems seem to have very far-reaching potential. Wherever we have at present a person whose services are valuable because they have knowledge – the knowledge of symptoms and cures that a doctor has, the knowledge of the tax system that a tax consultant has, the knowledge of law that a solicitor has – there we have a potential redundancy. These various expertises, insofar as they depend on drawing from accumulated facts and principles conclusions that apply to the particular case in hand, can be mechanized.

Possibly even more general in impact and potential in recent years has been the devising of programming languages and programming environments that rest on this same capacity of the machine to perform according to the rules of the predicate logic – 'logic programming' as it was first called,[30] the Programming in Logic that became the language PROLOG.[31] Programming in PROLOG is a matter of building up a 'knowledge-base', of putting into the system all the things you can think of that are true about the 'problem domain' that concerns you. The program runs in response to the problem you then put to it: and its running takes the form of an attempt to prove that hypotheses that would solve your problem follow from what the system has been told.

Besides the development of systems capable of (predicate) logical reasoning, there has also been, since 1963, real and promising progress in AI research with a number of other fundamental problems: how to get a machine to communicate using natural language (for example, English, as contrasted with computer codes such as FORTRAN or LISP), how to get a machine to generate a useful map of its environment from visual information (machine vision), how to get a machine to control complex sequences of actions in realistic environments (robotics). In addition, it must be remembered that the value of many ideas floated and brought to maturity under the auspices of AI has already been seized on and applied in all kinds of mundanely successful projects of the wider computer science community. Nevertheless, from the viewpoint of 1987 it is perhaps the potential of the expert system and 'logic programming' that appears as AI's most fundamental contribution to the brain project so far.

Notes

1 Allen Newell, J. C. Shaw and H. A. Simon, 'Empirical Explorations with the Logic Theory Machine: A Case Study in Heuristics', *Proceedings of the Western Joint Computer Conference*, 15 (1957), in Feigenbaum and Feldman, *Computers and Thought*, p. 115.

2 Allen Newell, J. C. Shaw and H. A. Simon, 'The Logic Theory Machine', in Feigenbaum and Feldman, *Computers and Thought*, p. 115.

3 For an introduction to the propositional calculus see, for example, Prior, *Formal Logic*, ch. 2.

4 Newell et al., 'Logic Theory Machine', in Feigenbaum and Feldman, *Computers and Thought*, p. 121.

5 Memory limitations of the JOHNNIAC ruled out the others.

6 And von Neumann: see McCorduck, *Machines Who Think*, p. 211.

7 Newell et al., 'Logic Theory Machine', in Feigenbaum and Feldman, *Computers and Thought*, p. 114.

8 Hunt, *Artificial Intelligence*, p. 6.

9 Hao Wang, 'Toward Mechanical Mathematics', *IBM Journal for Research and Development*, 4(1960), pp. 2–22.

10 Newell and Simon, 'GPS, A Program that Simulates Human Thought', *Lernende Automaten* (R. Oldenbourg KG, 1961), reprinted in Feigenbaum and Feldman, *Computers and Thought*, p. 286.

11 It is salutary to return periodically to the sober truth that 'physically, a program is simply the contents of an ordered set of locations in the primary memory of a computer' (Hunt, *Artificial Intelligence*, p. 21).

12 Newell, Shaw and Simon, *Information Processing Language–V Manual* (1st edition: Rand Corporation, Santa Monica, California, 1960; 2nd edition: Prentice-Hall, Englewood Cliffs, 1964), p. 7.

13 Newell et al., *IPL–V Manual*, p. 8.

14 Newell et al., 'GPS', in Feigenbaum and Feldman, *Computers and Thought*; Newell, Shaw and Simon, 'Chess-Playing Programs', *IBM Journal of Research and Development*, 2 (1958) pp. 320–35.

15 Tonge, 'Summary of a Heuristic Line Balancing Procedure', *Management Science*, 7 (1960), reprinted in Feigenbaum and Feldman, *Computers and Thought*, pp. 168–90; Newell et al., *IPL–V Manual*; John McCarthy, 'History of LISP', in Wexelblat, *Programming Languages* Section IV.

16 Alonzo Church, following a suggestion of Gödel, argued in 1936 that every calculable function is recursive. See 'An unsolvable problem of elementary number theory', reprinted in Davis, *The Undecidable*, pp. 89–107. In the same year, Turing showed that this was equivalent to his own demonstration that calculability could be interpreted as Turing-machine-computable. See 'On computable numbers, with an application to the Entscheidungsproblem', reprinted in Davis, *The Undecidable*, pp. 116–51.

17 McCarthy, 'A Basis for a Mathematical Theory of Computation', in P. Braffort and D. Hirschberg (eds), *Computer Programming and Formal Systems* (Amsterdam, North Holland, 1963), pp. 33–70.

18 R. Cartwright, 'A Practical Formal Semantic Definition and Verification System for Typed LISP', *Stanford AI Lab. Technical Report AIM–296*, Stanford, California. See McCarthy, 'History of LISP', in Wexelbat, *Programming Languages*, Section IV.

19 See above, pp. 182–5.

20 C. Hartshorne and P. Weiss (eds), *Collected Papers of Charles Sanders Peirce* (Harvard UP, 1960), iii, paragraph 387.

21 Prior, *Formal Logic*, p. 16; W. and M. Kneale, *Development of Logic*, p. 420; Church, *Mathematical Logic*, p. 162.

22 J. C. Shepherdson, 'The Calculus of Reasoning', in J. E. Hayes and D. Michie (eds), *Intelligent Systems* (Ellis Horwood, Chichester, 1983), p. 14.

23 Shepherdson, 'Calculus of Reasoning', in Hayes and Michie, *Intelligent Systems*, ch. 1.

24 See above pp. 185–8.

25 Shepherdson, 'Calculus of Reasoning', in Hayes and Michie, *Intelligent Systems*, ch. 1.

26 J. A. Robinson says the very first. See Robinson, 'Logical Reasoning in Machines', in Hayes and Michie, *Intelligent Systems*, p. 19.

27 Gilmour, 'A Proof Method for Quantification Theory'; Wang, 'Toward Mechanical Mathematics'; Prawitz et al., 'A Mechanical Proof Procedure'.

28 Prawitz et al., 'A Mechanical Proof Procedure', p. 102.

29 E. Shortliffe, *Computer-Based Medical Consultations* (Elsevier, New York, 1976).

30 By Robert Kowalski – see Robinson, 'Logical Reasoning in Machines', in Hayes and Michie, *Intelligent Systems*, p. 33.

31 Robert Kowalski, 'Predicate Logic as a Programming Language', *Proceedings of the IFIP–74*, pp. 556–74. PROLOG was first developed by A. Colmerauer and colleagues at the University of Marseilles: see Colmerauer, H. Kanoui, R. Pasero and P. Roussel, 'Une Système de Communication Homme-Machine en Français', *Rapport Groupe d'Intelligence Artificielle*, Université Aix-Marseille, Luminy.

Conclusion

The year 1960 did not mark the end of AI, but we can take it as marking the end of its emergence. Effort in the the field has expanded very considerably, but to a striking extent the pioneers of the fifties launched the projects that have continued to provide the challenges, and, even more notably, laid out the fundamentals of techniques whose potential continues to be the main focus of effort.

By the end of the fifties there was a network of researchers, mostly either at MIT or Carnegie-Mellon, and a name for what the network was engaged in, the study of 'Artificial Intelligence'. There was also the beginnings of a literature, appearing ultimately in formal computer journals but often circulating for months and even years beforehand in mimeographed form. 1963 picks itself out as a milestone in virtue of being the year in which the first effective move to map this literature and thus the emergent field was made. Two leading members of the network made a selection of papers which, in their judgement, would serve collectively to articulate achievements to date and to define the lines along which further progress promised. This was *Computers and Thought*, edited by Edward A. Feigenbaum and Julian Feldman.

Work on chess and draughts players and on the Logic Theorist figured centrally, and so did programs that applied the LT approach in other problem areas: one by James R. Slagle that solved calculus problems of the kind that might be set sixth-form or junior university students, and Tonge's program to work out the best organization for an assembly line production system. Gelernter's early geometry-proving machine, which also had the benefit of the Logic Theorist behind it, is there too.

To these unequivocal success stories were added representative work on pattern recognition (which had made a measure of useful progress) by Selfridge and Ulric Neisser, and by Leonard Uhr and Charles Vossler, and papers addressing the natural language handling problem and serving at least to expose something of its magnitude (especially the piece by Robert K. Lindsay). A further section included a description of the General Problem Solver under the heading 'simulation of cognitive processes'. Minsky's

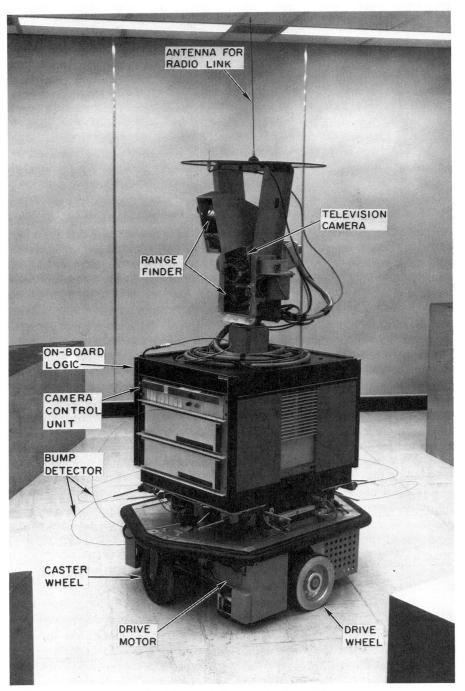

ANTENNA FOR
RADIO LINK

TELEVISION
CAMERA

RANGE
FINDER

ON-BOARD
LOGIC

CAMERA
CONTROL
UNIT

BUMP
DETECTOR

CASTER
WHEEL

DRIVE
MOTOR

DRIVE
WHEEL

Shakey, developed at Stanford Research Institute in the 1960s

reflective 'Steps Towards Artifical Intelligence', together with a considered bibliography, rounded the collection off.

These judgements to a remarkable extent have stood the test of time – confirming the thesis that foundations were laid in the fifties which have been since not superceded but built upon. Strikingly, however, no paper is included to represent the project of mechanizing the predicate calculus. Here the editors' close perspective leads them to miss something quite seminal, for it is the project of mechanizing the prodicate calculus that has yielded the expert system, and it is the expert system that dominates the horizon current AI workers look towards.

What principles do these programming acheivements rest on? Not many. There are the formulae of the predicate calculus, devised prior to the arrival of the machines, but converted into programs by Wang, Gilmore, Prawitz and others from 1957 on. There are also the formulae of the propositional logic, as developed by Russell and Whitehead, programmed by Newell and Simon first of all in the Logic Theorist, and then exploited by a number of others.

There is the idea of economizing on searching for things, of finding practical alternatives to the usually impractical strategy of working through all the theoretical possibilities in simple sequence. This had already yielded in the Newell team's early work the 'search tree'. The general idea of a heuristic procedure, of which this was an example – of an uncertain but practical short cut in place of impractical certainty – proved seminal.

Then there is the idea, taking firm shape in the General Problem Solver, and again very influential, of analysing a complex problem into a series of simpler sub-problems, the solutions of which constitute so many means to the end represented by the solution of the problem set.

Finally, the principle of treating concepts and propositions as lists of symbols, the components of which could be easily got at and moved about, had been developed in the most influential of the list processing languages, LISP. The use of LISP served, and still serves, almost to define the field.

Minsky himself highlights the concrete achievements of that first decade that might strike the alien interplanetary tourist:

> Some machines would be seen proving mathematical theorems of rather undistinguished character. A few machines might be playing certain games, occasionally defeating their designers. Some might be distinguishing between hand-printed letters.[1]

This is an (uncharacteristically) low-key resumé of the achievements of AI in its first few years, and it catches nicely the two ways in which those achievements may be viewed. They are at once spectacular and disappointing. They are spectacular if one retains a sense of their issuing from machines, with all the limitations people had got used to thinking matter was heir to: but disappointing in the light of the vaulting ambition of those early years – 'General Problem Solver' indeed!

Freddy, developed at Edinburgh University

Though it is foolhardy to attempt a judgement on work since 1963, when the trees are all too close for the wood to be seen, my own view is that the ambiguity present in AI work up to that point remains in the record of the two-and-a-half decades since. Perhaps it would be agreed at any rate that for the brain project over these years there has been neither disaster nor final success; and what this means, I think, is that if we are to arrive at a view of that still exciting enterprise, we must do so without knowing whether it will succeed or not.

The Historical Placing of AI

I have said baldly that there is no story to AI, just a number of projects with aims and strategies that we can with hindsight see to be interestingly related. I have dwelt on three, Gottfried Leibniz', Charles Babbage's and Alan Turing's.

Leibniz thought in terms of a foolproof means of resolving disputes. Reasoning, he thought, was a matter of recognizing relationships of inclusion between concepts, relationships that depended on identities. Once science had been completed and its results incorporated in a reformation of our concepts, so that each one was an accurate map of the thing it represented, it should be possible to draw up rules of thumb that would enable such identities to be picked out and related appropriately to the proposition under contention. Such procedures might be left to be conducted with pen and paper, or, as the feasibility of the mechanical calculator suggested, they could be engineered into a machine.

Babbage's great plan was first and foremost for a machine capable of every mathematical calculation. But beyond that there was also the idea that the machine would possess the capacity to perform algebra, with algebra now thought of as a language – the language without which the laws governing the phenomena studied by science could not be properly expressed. The Analytical Engine would thus have had the capacity to manipulate symbols according to the rules of a symbol-system that is more general than the mathematical, the symbol-system which caught in its rules the form of the principles according to which the physical universe operated.

Turing's project was to build not a mechanical reasoner nor a machine capable of understanding the universal language of algebra, but a machine that would have powers coextensive with those of a human brain. It had been shown, in 1936, that as far as 'definite procedures' went, the powers of a very simple machine, like those of the glorified typewriter described by Turing in that year, equalled those of a machine of any degree of greater complexity. Though the brain might appear to be highly sophisticated, therefore, so long as it could be regarded as a discrete-state machine, the project of building an electronic equivalent could be regarded as feasible.

Three conceptual contexts, three aims, three projects, having perhaps just one thing in common – their failure so far to achieve (in their own terms at least) entirely satisfactory realization. Three separate stories, then. And yet of, course, there is something more.

It is not that recent achievements represent dreams come true after all. Leibniz and Babbage and Turing each had the conceptions of his age, and it was these that gave sense to their dreams as surely as they did to their waking thoughts. Some kind of overarching plot, however, there certainly appears to be – a story of dramatically wider scope than any of the particular ones I have told. Who its author is I find it hard to say.[2] But the plot itself is the evolution of formalism, and it extends from one end of the Modern age to the other.

Formalism and the Mind

The Modern rise of formalism is rooted in the explosion in mathematics and its applications at the dawn of the Modern age, an explosion set off by increases in economic activities, especially international trade.[3] Mathematical thinking at that point becomes the model of thinking of other kinds, which comes therefore to be conceived of as *representational*.

In this representational conception of thinking, there is already an advance for the idea that analysis must proceed by distinguishing form from content, rules of grammar from meaning conveyed, structure from substance structured. It registers the assumption that a concrete thing can be substituted for by something else – a thought, a sound, a mark – in virtue not of anything shared but of a convention. And formalism is already on the advance, too, at that launching of the Modern period, within mathematics itself, where numbers have already been distinguished from numbers of things. Vieta's invention of the algebraic symbol takes it further: a letter used to stand not for *a* number, but indifferently for *any* number. This allowed the recognition of the general form of equations previously used merely as individual recipes for computations, and it launched algebra as their study.

Leibniz' project reflected these gains. It invoked the idea that thinking, in particular reasoning, was representational, and proposed to use symbols written on paper or relations between parts in a machine to take the place of concepts in the mind. Nevertheless, as we see from our present perspective, the formalist conceptions Leibniz was drawing on were subject to limitations. The idea of an 'uninterpreted' symbol had not yet arrived. Vieta had perhaps hinted at it, and Leibniz himself glimpsed the possibility, but it played no role in his developed thoughts. The symbols in his mechanical reasoner would have stood for things and for things' features. He was not in a position to think of them as in themselves meaningless place-holders. This is why half of his project was the reformation of our concepts. He had to make sure that the content of these was right – that is reflected the true constitution of the things they were concepts of – since any reasoner would be working on these directly.

His conception of reason corresponded to his representational view of thinking. Its function was to recognize identities: to determine whether a relation of inclusion held between two concepts by determining whether the one was identical with a component of the other. Reasoning was thus the working through of a definite procedure of the same general kind as had already been mechanized in the calculator, which made the construction of a mechanical reasoner seem feasible. In this sense his conception of reason was a formalistic one. But it relied on concepts being meaningful.

The clear notion of an uninterpreted symbol became fully established only in the nineteenth century, when formalism resumed its progress with a vengeance.[4] The new period was ushered in by the revolution wrought, or at any rate registered, by Kant in our conception of the way in which we interact with the world and the nature of our knowledge of it. In place of the seventeenth century idea of our thoughts and our expression of those thoughts as providing a map of reality in symbols, the Kantian conviction was that whatever intelligibility reality seemed to have, including its apparent structure, came not from reality itself but from the apparatus of the understanding that we brought to our commerce with it. Thoughts were from this point on not simple mappings but artefacts, the result of what our senses provided us with 'synthesised' by the application of concepts provided by our understanding.

This represented a tremendous leap forward for formalism, for the form/content distinction is now seen as applicable not simply to every thought, as it had been before, but to what had previously been regarded as the very content of what Leibniz used to call 'concepts'. Put another way, 'concepts' before Kant are lists of features belonging to a thing. They are thought of as maps of little bits of reality. But after Kant, they are processors, brought by us to our experience to mince and mould what our senses deliver into digestible pieces. They provide the means of our grasping what bears in upon us, of making our experience intelligible.

A whole new realm of formal enquiry thus opens up: what is the structure of our concepts? The old enquiry, moreover – identifying the essential features of things and laying out the facts in an authoritative compendium or encyclopaedia: the project, science's project, that Leibniz thought might take as much as a few decades to complete – took on an utterly new order of complication, and its realization was seen to recede into the more or less indefinite future.

It was the English reformers of algebra, again at the beginning of the nineteenth century resurgence, who took the lead in extending formalism along a different front. For it was they who finally established a clear distinction between an uninterpreted symbol-system on the one hand, and a possible interpretation of such a symbol-system on the other.

This is not yet the idea that there might be a multiplicity of symbol-systems, each in its own terms as satisfactory as any other, which is the new thought that takes shape with William Hamilton and yields alternative algebras, alternative geometries, and in the end alternative logics. Babbage, Peacock and the others may have established the idea of an uninterpreted symbol-system, but they entertained no thought of there being more than one of these. The rules that governed manipulations of symbols in algebra were, they thought, reflections of the form of the principles according to which the universe ran.

Hamilton arrived at his new idea, that it might be legitimate to devise an *alternative* symbol-system, in the course of his search for a way of treating algebraically the effect of forces acting on a body in three dimensions. His solution (published in 1844) was to devise a new kind of number, the 'quaternion', which was defined in terms of a set of symbolic rules differing from those of the established algebra. (The commutative law of multiplication, a × b = b × a, is abandoned.)[5] Other algebras followed: from Grassman in 1844, from Cayley in 1857, and subsequently something of the order of a couple of hundred more.[6] The notion of 'algebra' gets replaced by that of 'algebras', each system of symbols defined by its own rules. Within such systems, as explored by the mathematician, the symbols do not stand for anything. They are meaningless, or uninterpreted. But there may be systems of things whose relationships mirror those of the abstract formal system: in which case they constitute a possible 'interpretation' of the algebra, and it can be applied to that field.

William Hamilton, 1805–65

On yet another front, and at the same time, Boole was devising the first calculus of logic, perfecting the distinction in that field between syntax and content. The fact that he was able to devise a calculus isomorphic with the calculus that had just been clarified in the domain of magnitudes – mathematics – gave formalism wonderful encouragement; though that was as nothing compared with the effect of Frege's subsequent triumph, towards the end of the century, in finding an articulation of the form of logical relationships across (almost) the whole spectrum of rigorous argument.

Formalism, therefore, if we define it as a determination to insist on the distinction between form and content wherever possible, and to urge the importance of the former over the latter, is present in the work of Vieta, Descartes and Leibniz in the seventeenth century. It finds, however, an entirely new vigour with Kant, and marches forward with the English algebraists, with Boole, and with Frege, who, taking his cue from mathematics, pursued what he saw as the articulation of the formal structure of thought.

When we come to the contemporary project, the building of a brain, the advance of formalism continues. The idea is that a discrete-state machine will do all that a brain does, and this is tantamount to explaining the logical functioning of the brain exclusively in terms of rule-governed manipulation of uninterpreted symbols. Since the functioning of the brain is assumed to yield whatever is ascribed to the mind, what we have here as a presupposition of the brain project is a formal theory of the mind. Thoughts dissolve into nested sets of subroutines.[7]

If this is the historical placement of the brain project, then, riding the crest of formalism as it sweeps in from the seventeenth century, what are we to say of its prospects?

Prospects for the Brain Project

There are three rather different questions, of different orders of sophistication, to address when we ask what happens next.

The first asks what progress is likely to be made with problems currently regarded as central. What, for example, of getting machines to handle natural language? In one of the most breathtaking 'etceteras' to issue from a responsible pen, Turing wrote in his 1950 paper that in order to teach a computer English, 'things would be pointed out and named, etc.'.[8] There has since been much toil and something less than success. One project has been the coding in the computer of an unprecedentedly large corpus of English language text, in the conviction that it is only by the sustained and close analysis of substantial texts that progress is to be made. The task of allocating each word of the corpus to an appropriate grammatical category has recently been completed, and now the team is tackling the problem that has emerged as central over the last decades, namely the fact that human natural language handlers appear to interpret ambiguous utterances clearly by drawing on quantities of contextual information about the world that are in computer terms enormous. It is suggested that we must look to statistical techniques to substitute for the dauntingly large data-bases that the human approach implies.[9]

It is now thought that other peculiarly resistant problems that AI work has identified may be rooted in this same problem of natural language. For example, recognition of objects in the visual field may depend on the use of natural language, a possibility explored by R. F. Simmons' work on teaching the machine to recognize features of line drawings. This makes the machine analyse the structures first of all in terms of verbal descriptions.[10] More generally, there is the possibility that it is our language that gives us our human way of representing knowledge. McCarthy, for one, has recorded that the key unsolved problem in AI 'is how to express formally that information that is normally expressed in ordinary language.'[11]

There is also important progress to be made in the systematization of types of reasoning that have yet to yield to the standard predicate logic – arguments hanging on tense differences, for example, and those trading on notions of obligation and on degrees of necessity. And there is a great swathe of ordinary reasoning to be mastered which does not pretend to be logically rigorous, but which deals in degrees of plausibility or reasonableness.

At a second level, we can ask about the aspects of human mentality that present techniques show little sign of coming to grips with. The most striking feature of human life as it is appreciated by the person living it is, of course, consciousness – the fact that we see the world from a point of view. There are those who think that consciousness will somehow 'emerge' in a machine once the sophistication of its organization exceeds a certain point; but even they cannot suggest what specific features consciousness demands.

There is also the problem, at this level, of the representation in the machine of goals, recognized as a key issue in sophisticated AI projects. In human beings, goals are often given in conscious experience as feelings of one kind or another, and it may be that for progress to be made along fronts such as these, the role of the phenomena of consciousness in the government of human behaviour cannot be left out of consideration.

The representation of goals is bound up with another challenging problem, and one that absorbed much attention in the robot projects of the sixties. This is the integration of the exercise of different machine competences into a system that mimics 'intelligence' in a plurality of dimensions – which is, of course, actually a mark of real intellingence, 'the ability to make a plausible shot at almost anything.'[12] Though one exercise of intelligence may be mimicked successfully in isolation, which may superficially support the idea of a lack of distinction between mimicking and the real thing, the difference may come out when several exercises are synthesized.[13]

A difficulty that is felt in some quarters to undermine the whole brain project is the problem of 'intentionality', the way in which our thoughts point to things beyond themselves. It is said that an irreparable weakness of the formalist theory of the mind, which the brain project is wedded to, is exactly that a thought characteristically refers to something beyond itself – is 'about' something – in a way that an uninterpreted symbol cannot refer, and cannot be 'about' anything. The point made is that our thoughts possess *meaning*, whereas the representations manipulated in machines do not and cannot. So here we have (it is argued) a dimension of human mentality, and an utterly pervasive one, that cannot be caught by programming, intrinsically limited as programming is to laying down rules for the manipulation of formal (that is, meaningless) symbols.[14]

But the third question, at the deepest and most difficult level, is about our concept of mentality itself.

We currently set great store by the very aspects of our mentality that lend themselves to replacement by machine. Often, for example, the powers of the quiz champion, or else those of the lightning reasoner, are taken to be the acme of human intelligence. But data-retrieval and formal reasoning are, of course, among the things the machine now does extremely well – and will do better and better. There are, on the other hand, aspects of our mentality that we currently push out to the periphery: notably, what the psychologists call 'affect'. In spite of some whistling in the wind, we have not got a clue about how to get a machine to feel for example, sad. 'It is hard to see what it could mean to say that a computer hopes,' says Weizenbaum.[15] Feeling angry, miserable, guilty, tired, or hopeful – these do not seem to be construable in terms of the manipulation of uninterpreted symbols.

What we must try to imagine are alternatives to the concept of mentality which sets our agenda today, but which belongs to a framework of ideas that will surely, like its predecessors, pass. From this point of view the 'problems' faced by the formalist theory of the mind may be seen to amount to anomalies, which, when other factors align with them, will be counted as reasons for a conceptual reorientation.

What I myself envisage is less the computer reaching some kind of limit in its emulation of thinking as we currently picture it to ourselves, than our taking a fresh look at the picture, partly in the light of those things that the machine becomes able to do for us, and then changing our ideas about which aspects of thinking or mentality are truly important – that is, about what thinking is. Calculating has already, perhaps, been demoted as not at all distinctive of human thought. Logical reasoning from known facts and principles could easily go the same way, as the expert system becomes a familiar desktop aid. But it is only insofar as we regard calculation and reasoning as central to human thinking that machines will seem capable of thought in general. Recall from the periphery those aspects of mentality that resist the representational construal, and success for the brain project seems more doubtful than distant.

Notes

1 Feigenbaum and Feldman, *Computers and Thought*, p. 406.
2 O'Neill links the nineteenth century resurgence, at any rate, with professionalization (O'Neill, *Against Formalism*, ch. 17, Section 2), just as Rorty associates the growth of formalism in philosophy with professionalization (*Mirror of Nature*, ch. III, Sections 3, 4).
3 See above, Ch. 3; cf. Klein, *Greek Mathematical Thought*.
4 'The most distant consequences – and the most difficult ones for us to evade – of the fundamental event that occurred in the Western *épistème* towards the end of the eighteenth century may be summed up as follows: negatively, the domain of the pure forms of knowledge becomes isolated, attaining both autonomy and sovereignty in relation to all empirical knowledge, causing the endless birth and rebirth of a project to formalize the concrete and to constitute, in spite of everythng, pure sciences; positively, the empirical domains become linked with reflections on subjectivity, the human being, and finitude, assuming the value and function of philosophy, as well as the reduction of philosophy or counter-philosophy.' (Foucault, *Order of Things*, pp. 248, 249.
5 Hamilton, *On Quarternions, or a New System of Imaginaries in Algebra* (1844), reprinted in H. Halberstam and R. E. Ingram (eds), *The Mathematical Papers of Sir William Rowan Hamilton*, Vol. III, *Algebra* (CUP, Cambridge, 1967), pp. 355–62.
6 See, for example, H. Eves, *An Introduction to the History of Mathematics* (Holt, Rinehart & Winston, New York, 1976), p. 393.
7 'Programmers [...] know that there is never any "heart" in a program. There are high-level routines in each program, but all they do is dictate that "if such and such, then transfer to such and such a subroutine". And when we look at the low-level subroutines, which " actually do the work", we find senseless loops and sequences of trivial operations, merely carrying out the dictates of their superiors. The intelligence in such a system seems to be as intangible as becomes the meaning of a single word when it is thoughtfully pronounced over and over again.' (Minsky, in Feigenbaum and Feldman, *Computers and Thought*, p. 447).
8 Turing, 'Computing Machinery', in Feigenbaum and Feldman, *Computers and Thought*, p. 35.
9 E. S. Atwell, 'Constituent-likelihood Grammar', Newsletter of the International Computer Archive of Modern English, 7, May 1983, pp. 34–67.
10 Simmons, 'Natural Language Question Answering Systems', *Communications of the Association for Computing Machinery*, 13 (1970), pp. 15–30.
11 Quoted in McCorduck, *Machines Who Think*, p. 218.
12 Michie, *On Machine Intelligence*, pp. 51, 52.
13 Michie, *On Machine Intelligence*, pp. 105, 106.
14 See, for example, John Searle's 1984 Reith Lectures, *Minds, Brains and Science* (BBC, 1984).
15 Joseph Weizenbaum, *Computer Power and Human Reason* (W. H. Freeman, San Francisco, 1976), p. 209.

Index

Index by Geoffrey C. Jones